NATIVE
AMERICAN
NATIONALISM
AND
NATION
RE-BUILDING

SUNY series, Tribal Worlds: Critical Studies
in American Indian Nation Building
———————
Brian Hosmer and Larry Nesper, editors

Native American Nationalism and Nation Re-building

PAST AND PRESENT CASES

EDITED BY

Simone Poliandri

Published by State University of New York Press, Albany

© 2016 State University of New York

All rights reserved

Printed in the United States of America

No part of this book may be used or reproduced in any manner whatsoever without written permission. No part of this book may be stored in a retrieval system or transmitted in any form or by any means including electronic, electrostatic, magnetic tape, mechanical, photocopying, recording, or otherwise without the prior permission in writing of the publisher.

For information, contact State University of New York Press, Albany, NY
www.sunypress.edu

Production, Jenn Bennett
Marketing, Fran Keneston

Library of Congress Cataloging-in-Publication Data

Native American nationalism and nation re-building : past and present cases / edited by Simone Poliandri.
    pages cm. — (SUNY series, tribal worlds: critical studies in American Indian nation building)
Includes bibliographical references and index.
ISBN 978-1-4384-6069-7 (hc : alk. paper)—978-1-4384-6068-0 (pb : alk. paper)
ISBN 978-1-4384-6070-3 (e-book)
    1. Indians of North America—Government relations.   2. Indians of North America—Land tenure.   3. Indians of North America—Politics and government.   4. Indians of North America—Ethnic identity.   5. Nationalism—North America—Case studies.   6. Nation-building—North America—Case studies.   I. Poliandri, Simone, editor.

E93.N284 2016
323.1197—dc23   2015022256

10 9 8 7 6 5 4 3 2 1

Contents

Foreword   ix
   Larry Nesper and Brian Hosmer

Acknowledgments   xi

Introduction: Nationalism and Nation *Re*-building in
Native North America   1
   Simone Poliandri

1. Building on Native Sovereignty: From Ethnic Membership
   to National Citizenship   29
   Sebastian Felix Braun

2. The Antics of Anticipation in an Odyssey of Self-Rule   61
   Jackie Grey

3. The Mi'kmaw Path to First Nationhood: A Roadmap,
   Some Strategies, and a Few Effective Shortcuts   93
   Simone Poliandri

4. The Boundaries of Indigenous Nationalism: Space, Memory,
   and Narrative in Hualapai Political Discourse   123
   Jeffrey P. Shepherd

5. Courting the Nation: Articulating Potawatomi Nationhood
   at the Indian Claims Commission   155
   Christopher Wetzel

Conclusion: The Push for Change Continues 183
    Wanda Wuttunee

Contributors 195

Index 199

Illustrations

Figure 3.1　Indian Brook (now Sipekne'katik) First Nation's band council former official letterhead.　107

Figure 3.2　Eskasoni First Nation's sign at the northern entrance of the reserve along Shore Road (Route 216) on Cape Breton Island, NS.　107

Figure 3.3　Until very recently, this street sign was located on Willow Street, one of the main arteries of Truro, at the intersection with the McClure's Mills Connector Road, which provides access to and from Provincial Highway 102.　109

Figure 4.1　"Original Yuman Territories" from *Spirit Mountain: An Anthology of Yuman Story and Song* ©1984 The Arizona Board of Regents.　128

Figure 5.1　Potawatomi Indian Claims Commission Dockets. This table provides a synopsis of the various treaties and lands for which parts of the Potawatomi Nation filed claims.　159

Foreword

Larry Nesper and Brian Hosmer
Series Editors

Tribal Worlds: Critical Studies in American Indian Nation Building

We are delighted to share this latest contribution to the SUNY series *Tribal Worlds: Critical Studies in American Indian Nation Building*. Over the past several years, we have had the opportunity to share several pathbreaking studies exploring historic roots and contemporary expressions of Indigenous self-determination, sovereignty, and nation building. From the outset, our goal was straightforward—and challenging. From its inception, we envisioned a series showcasing emerging research on how Indigenous peoples have forged and are forging modern communities amidst national and international pressures and the ongoing effects of settler colonialism. We have sought studies that blend ethnography with archival research and that situate current expressions of tribal governance and reservation political economy within comparative and historical contexts.

Native American Nationalism and Nation Re-building, edited by Simone Poliandri, extends this conversation. Through a series of interlocked case studies produced by anthropologists and historians, this volume offers additional insights into processes of indigenous nation building. The studies assembled by Poliandri tell us a great deal about how tribal communities are constructing nationhoods through the development of institutions in the present by drawing upon historical frameworks. More than simply resuscitating older national identities or building novel structures, these cases remind us that enacting indigenous sovereignties are creative acts, pursued and conducted within particular historical and cultural frameworks. This is the essence of rebuilding, a phenomenon we understand as fundamental to encountering and overcoming the conditions of settler colonialism in the United States and Canada.

Decades ago, Vine Deloria Jr. challenged Indigenous academics to resist the obvious attractions of the ivory tower to apply their talents to meeting the great challenges, on the ground and in the field. We think Poliandri's volume is a step in the direction of embracing that charge in that the essays detail the ways in which aspirations are and have been operationalized. As such, they suggest models for practical action in analogous contexts.

Acknowledgments

Many people contributed to make this book a finished product and deserve recognition. To begin, I am deeply grateful to Brian Hosmer and Larry Nesper, the co-editors of SUNY's *Tribal Worlds* series, for encouraging and full-heartedly supporting my efforts in putting this volume together. Since the inception of this project in the context of one Native American/Indigenous Studies Association (NAISA) meeting a few years ago, Brian and Larry have been instrumental in offering both invaluable suggestions on the broad intellectual architecture of the volume and careful advice all the way down to the small details of style. A labor of love, indeed.

I wish to extend my gratitude to NAISA for providing the intellectual and collegial context within which this project took shape and developed, as well as the many participants in its annual meetings since 2009 who have offered direct comments to early versions of some of the essays during panels or engaged me and the other authors in fruitful, multi-topic discussions that eventually found their way into this volume. I also acknowledge and thank indirectly the tribal nations that hosted each of those NAISA meetings.

I am grateful to the authors contributing to this volume for accepting this challenge with enthusiasm, producing outstanding essays, and displaying remarkable patience while waiting for this volume to take shape and proceed through the many editorial stages. I also thank them for the many intellectual exchanges we have had over the course of a few years while working on this volume. I have developed friendships that I cherish.

I extend my deepest gratitude to the anonymous reviewers, whose suggestions and critiques resulted in making this a stronger and better collection than what we started with, as well as the copyeditor and the indexer for their thorough work.

I extend my gratitude to Amanda Lanne-Camilli, acquisitions editor at SUNY Press, for her kind assistance. I commend Amanda, particularly, for addressing one potentially disrupting editorial "situation" with remarkable promptness, efficiency, and professionalism, reducing the issue to a mere bump in the road. I also wish to acknowledge the project editor, Jenn Bennett; the editorial assistant, Jessica Kirschner; the marketing director, Fran Keneston; and the production personnel for their dedication and outstanding work.

As far as my individual contribution to this volume goes, I wish to thank the many Mi'kmaw people who offered their help, ideas, support, and friendship since the onset of the research process that informs my essay. I cannot list you all for lack of sufficient space and confidentiality purposes, but you know who you are. Wela'lioq! (Thank you!)

I wish to thank Framingham State University for supporting my travelling to NAISA conferences between 2010 and 2014, and the Center for the Advancement of Research and Scholarship at Bridgewater State University, my current academic home, for a course release and a small grant that allowed me to finalize the manuscript.

Finally, I offer my gratitude and immense love to my wife Meredith and my wonderful daughter Olivia, who have offered unconditional support throughout the process. They have certainly built a sizable time credit that is overdue for settling.

Despite the help we have received, the authors and I are responsible for the content of this book. As the volume editor, responsibility falls ultimately on my shoulders, and I apologize for any inaccuracies this book may contain.

Introduction

Nationalism and Nation Re-building in Native North America

Simone Poliandri

Nationhood and nationalism have recently emerged as some of the leading expressions of tribal belonging and community self-determination among Native North American peoples.[1] They have become increasingly connected with issues of political and economic sovereignty, sense of peoplehood, identity, territoriality, citizenship, and the development and maintenance of cultural capital. This collection of essays offers a broad range of perspectives on the role of Indigenous nation building in the lives of Native American peoples and communities. The contributors argue for the centrality of nationhood and nationalism in molding and, concurrently, blending the recent political, social, economic, and cultural strategies that Native American peoples have adopted toward self-definitions and self-determination.

Concurrently, Native American nationalism and nation building have been the topic of several academic and nonacademic studies that have addressed these issues from a multitude of angles, including (but not limited to) political, legal, geographic, epistemological, ethical, historical, and cultural.[2] Thomas Biolsi (2005) discussed the Native peoples' recasting of Indigenous geographies stating that in the United States "Native nationhood is a critical site of identity and political struggle for Indian peoples" (254). Asserting sovereignty over reservation territories as only one of the many perceptions of geopolitical space that Native Americans possess and employ in social and political struggles, Biolsi observed that a "national indigenous space" extending beyond reservation boundaries represents a further context where American Indians can "assert and exercise their Indianness" (249). Pushing the argument forward, Larry Nesper (2007) illustrated the creation of tribal codes and tribal courts among the Lac-du-Flambeau Ojibwe of Wisconsin as a testimony to the recent appearance of "tribal states" among Native Americans in the United States. Centering his analysis on several court cases dealt with by an Ojibwe Tribal Court, Nesper observed, "Especially with the emergence and development of courts in reservation societies, it seems appropriate to speak of 'tribal states'" (675; quotes in original), and "Reservation governments . . . are becoming statelike. . . . The process entails the codification of law and the development of courts" (676).

Mohawk scholar Taiaiake Alfred (2009) offered an opposite perspective regarding the ongoing formation of an Indigenous national sentiment. In discussing the current formation of Indigenous political identity in Canada, Alfred underscored the relations of Indigenous nationhood with traditional Indigenous philosophies and values as the appropriate archetype, on the one hand, and the Euro-Canadian concepts of citizenship and state institutions as the inappropriate colonially based models, on the other. Building on the works of Holm et al. (2003) and Corntassel (2003) that offer "peoplehood" as the basis of Indigenous nationalism in place of tribe or band, Alfred addressed the impasse between the Indigenous people's need to (re)define and implement their own forms of governance and the unfitting political terminology (including citizenship, state, courts, and so forth) available to First Nations leaders as a result of a long history of institutional colonialism. He discussed the issue in these terms:

> The concept of Indigenous nations conceptualized along the state formation spectrum is itself a European derived concept and a reframing of traditional Indigenous nationhood and identities. . . . It promotes a governing principle that replicates the state in categorizing and organizing of people by government institutions on the basis of rights that are generated by legal and judicial processes. This form of nationhood and citizenship is an assimilative approach to Indigenous identity. (2009, 12)

More than a decade earlier, Alfred (1995) had already underscored the importance of Native North American communities' reassertion of their tribal nationhood, thus defying the collective or pan-Indian efforts that characterized Native political action in the 1960s and 1970s. In this, he laid the ground for other scholars who gave preferred treatment to the tribal sovereignty over the Indian sovereignty discourse. Wilkinson (2005), for instance, was among the most successful authors tackling the issue of nationhood from a tribal perspective; yet, departing somewhat from Alfred's position, Wilkinson attributed the rise of sovereignty as a political goal to the concurrent and coordinated tribal responses to the common challenge posed by the Termination policy of the 1950s and the subsequent successful pan-Indian quest for self-determination of the late 1960s and 1970s.

Attention to tribal claims to nationhood has continued to characterize more recent analyses. While discussing Navajo cultural identity and self-rule, Diné scholar Lloyd Lee observed that "American Indian identity is interwoven with nation building and access to resources," and as a consequence, "American Indian identity studies are advancing the discussion on how each Native nation should develop and maintain self-rule" (2006, 79). In a follow-up essay titled "The Future of Navajo Nationalism," Lee reiterated the concept of tribally unique nation building and called for the development of a "serious discussion" about Navajo nationalism or national independence among Navajo people. To this goal, Lee highlighted that Navajo people "need to set objectives that reflect their cultural identity" (2007, 54). Lee defined nationalism as "the devotion to the interests or culture of one's nation [and] to have aspirations for national independence in a country under foreign domination" (2007, 54). Already in 1991, sociologist Anthony Smith wrote in his work titled *National Identity* that "today national identity is the main form of collective identification" (170); furthermore, Smith argued that "nationalism is an ideological movement for attaining and maintaining the autonomy, unity, and identity of a nation" (74; italics in original); finally, and most important, Smith underscored that "nationalism is about 'land,' both in terms of possession and (literally) rebuilding, and of belonging where forefathers lived and where history demarcates a 'homeland' " (70; quotes and parentheses in original). Most recently, Brian Hosmer and Larry Nesper engaged a group of scholars from different disciplines in a conversation on both historical and contemporary "definitions and manifestations of Native nationhoods" (2013, 4). This work aimed at (and successfully managed) sampling the eclectic evolution of tribal nationhood in North America as well as shedding light on how nationhood matters differently to different Native actors, as a result of processes of colonization, decolonization, and the evolution of Native cultural practices of belonging. Finally, Mohawk anthropologist Audra Simpson (2014) has recently offered an alternative and refreshing perspective on the recent developments of tribal nationhood and sovereignty, focusing on the case of the Mohawk people of Kahnawà:ke. While calling out and exposing the still-active colonial agenda of the U.S. and Canadian settler states, disguised under the conciliatory politics of multiculturalism and juridical recognition, Simpson illustrated the alternative "politics of refusal" that the Mohawk are in the process of exercising to define and actualize their own notion of nationhood—a notion, she claims, to be "driven by their refusal of recognition, their refusal to be enfolded into state logics, and their refusal, simply, to disappear" (2014, 185). Refusing then becomes, in the context of nation building, a strategy toward exercising sovereignty—precisely, "nested sovereignty," which Simpson identifies as indigenous sovereignty existing within the larger state sovereignty—to design and implement an alternative idea of nation, one that has yet to overcome the challenges of the settler states' historical territorial expropriations and their imposition of the legal terms of tribal-nation belonging.

All these perspectives highlight several key motifs that have characterized the development of Native nationalism and nationhood in the twentieth and twenty-first centuries. Although not exhaustive (and it could not be otherwise given the wide breadth and ever-evolving makeup of nationalism and nationhood), the array of themes that these authors highlight is noteworthy because it includes the connection of tribal nationhood with tribal identity, the resiliency of tribal nation-building efforts in the face of centennial colonial pressure, the link between historical and contemporary nation-building efforts, and the importance of tribal cultures in the definition of tribal nationalism and shaping of nation-building paths.

These themes, and others linked to them, sparked a discussion that I started with Hosmer and Nesper during the 2009 Native American/Indigenous Studies Association (NAISA) meeting in Minneapolis and, eventually, led to the publication of this volume in their co-edited *Tribal Worlds* series. This conversation was extended to a wider group of scholars, some of whom participated in a themed session at the 2010 NAISA conference in Tucson and ended up contributing to this volume. The purpose of this collection is to present some of the ideas on indigenous nationalism and nationhood that emerged from those exchanges, as well as ground them in case studies that link our scholarship with the tangible nation-building efforts of indigenous communities in North America. The contributing authors echo and, at the same time, build on these themes in order to move the discussion of Indigenous nationhood further and offer additional evidence of the variety of their manifestations. This volume provides a variety of perspectives on Native American/First Nations nationalism and nation-building from different disciplinary backgrounds and sample cases throughout North America. A common theme interlacing all contributions is the broad consideration of nationalism and nationhood, not just as political and institution-building issues, but as processes including social, cultural, legal, economic, and historical factors.

Nation Building as Nation *Re*-building

Although the phrase "nation building" identifies one of the key aspects of recent and contemporary life of most Native American tribes and First Nations, it is more accurate to talk about nation *re*-building (hence the title of this volume), as many, if not most, tribal nations in the United States and Canada already went through a nation-building (or, actually, *re*-building) process in the 1800s and early 1900s, when colonial imposition forced them to recast their role in the history of the continent. It can be argued, in fact, that the European and American nation-building era of the nineteenth century was characterized by and partially grounded in the concurrent colonial process of destruction and subsequent reconstruction (albeit in crippled or profoundly changed forms in many cases) of Indigenous nations (Hobsbawm 1992). Therefore, I agree with Oren Lyons, Haudenosaunee Faithkeeper of the Onondaga and Seneca Nations, that we should really be talking about nation *re*-building rather than nation building, because Native peoples have always been here and are not newly built (2007, viii).

Several Indigenous and non-Indigenous scholars share this vision. Taiaiake Alfred (2005) spoke of resurgence and regeneration of Indigenous peoples, where the prefix *re-* clearly refers to an Indigenous-driven process of change or inversion from the long history of dominance and dispossession in the North American and, more broadly, global contexts. Along these lines, Jeff Corntassel highlighted the importance for Indigenous peoples to achieve *sustainable self-determination*, namely a process guaranteeing creating permanent self-determination opportunities that are culturally, economically, and environmentally viable besides the recognition of the necessary, but not sufficient, political and legal rights. This, Corntassel maintained, will lead toward "a more holistic and dynamic approach to *regenerating* indigenous nations" (2008, 105; emphasis added). Indigenous sustainable self-determination, Corntassel and Songhees

First Nation member Cheryl Bryce added (2012), must be asserted rather than negotiated with the governments, as in the case of Bryce's efforts to stir up community action toward reclaiming ancestral homelands in order to revitalize distinct cultural practices, such as traditional food systems, in Lekwungen (Victoria and the greater Victoria area in contemporary British Columbia).

Native American nationalism and nation *re*-building at the beginning of the twenty-first century are necessarily different from what tribal nationhood and nation *re*-building were in the past, albeit many of the similarities relate to the challenges posed by Euroamerican colonialism and postcolonialism.[3] Tribal nations such as the Choctaw and the Cherokee were targets of the U.S. relocation (and subsequent misappropriation) policy of the 1830s and undertook a rebuilding of their nations in Oklahoma that was all but a smooth process. The nation rebuilding that has taken place since the late twentieth century has many aspects in common, as well as many differences with the process that developed one hundred and fifty years earlier (Lambert 2007; Sturm 2002).

What certainly changed are the social, economic, and political idiosyncratic goals that tribal nations have identified as best for the reconstruction, maintenance, or flourishing of their own communities. Among the major improvements in such a process is the fact that, over the last four decades, North American tribal nations have acquired (for the most part) the right and capacity to select their own nation-building paths rather than being bestowed one, as, for instance, during the mildly successful U.S. Indian Reorganization Act era of the 1930s and 1940s. In the United States, such a leap toward self-determination was made possible by a shift in federal Indian policy and the implementation of game-changing federal legislation. The reference is, of course, to the 1975 Indian Self-Determination and Education Assistance Act (Public Law 95-698), which propelled a series of policies and subsequent regulations aiming at increasing indigenous communities' control over tribal affairs in several areas, spanning from education to economic development (Cornell and Kalt 2010).

Today, the establishment of tribal citizenship, economic success in several fields of enterprise, territorial reconstitution or expansion, institutional development (including the restoring of traditional values and practices), and, often, a combination thereof characterize the nation *re*-building efforts of tribes and First Nations all over Turtle Island/North America. Whether debating tribal membership—as among the Anishinabek of Ontario, Nova Scotia Mi'kmaq, and Oklahoma Cherokee[4]—or pursuing financial success—like the Seminole, Lakota, Mississippi Choctaw, and Mashantucket Pequot have done[5]—or applying traditional principles to the creation of tribal courts—like the Navajo and the Lac-du-Flambeau Ojibwe, among hundreds, have done[6]—or focusing on the restoration of traditional clan systems, as well as the access to traditional lands and natural resources—as among the Haudenosaunee, the Confederated Salish and Kootenai Tribes, the Apsáalooke, and the Mi'kmaq[7]—it is undoubted that such efforts have recently soared at the forefront of tribes' and First Nations' nation *re*-building agendas.

This neither implies that Native nation-building efforts have appeared only recently nor that such efforts must be purely considered a response to colonial invasions and impositions. Native American nation building is a process that started in precontact times—albeit based on premises and ideas of nation different from the Euro-American ones—and continued during the early period of European colonialism. In fact, it made no sense to talk about "Native Americans" before Euro-Americans achieved military and political dominance on the continent, as pan-Indianism developed as both a reaction to colonial aggression and a Euro-American intellectual construction, another of those "fantasies of the master race" that contested author Ward Churchill (1998) contributed to expose.

The links to the precontact and postcontact pasts are evident and, at the same time, necessary to understand today's tribal expressions of nationhood and nationalism. In a seminal work discussing Native American sovereignty, Vine Deloria and Clifford Lytle stated, "[Since pre-contact times] Indians had a good idea of nationhood" (1984, 9), which embodied the concern for the preservation of people and land, a key concept to understand the current Native American perceptions of the world. Lakota scholar Hilary Weaver, also known as Ga no was'het, might very well hint at this idea of people-based nationhood in saying that Indigenous identity is "connected to a sense of Peoplehood" (2001, 245). A decade later, such a statement is ever more true, as Native American identity, in so far as it is constructed and managed in relation to governments and other peoples, relies on nationhood as one of its pillars. Deloria and Lytle pushed their political analysis forward underscoring that Native movements toward self-determination have recast their goal from the achievement of *self-government*—which implies that the people are ready to assume decision-making responsibilities, yet under the recognition and monitoring by a superior political power (i.e., the U.S. and Canadian federal governments), and thus inadequate— to the establishment of *nationhood*—which implies free and unrestricted decision making within the tribal community (1984,

13–15; emphasis in original). The pivotal differences in this transition are, on the one hand, the change in the level and scope of Native peoples' aspirations—which are limited in the case of self-government and much broader in the case of nationhood—and, on the other hand, the nature of the status to be achieved—where self-government is not a Native idea (although a useful one to set up the base from which to undertake negotiations) while Indigenous nationhood can be when grounded on traditional Indigenous philosophies (to paraphrase Taiaiake Alfred, 2009).

Yet it is undoubtedly true that recent developments of Indigenous nationhood have more often than not implied the adoption of Western models of nationhood as well as the identification and pursuit of institutional goals that stem from such dominant models. This point surfaces in scholarly perspectives such as Paul Treanor's (1997).[8] Treanor presents nationalism as a "world order" that allows different expressions and number of states and nations as variants of one world order, but does not allow other entities (other than nations, that is) from achieving state status. In other words, he contends, "nationalism is a blocking world order [that] excludes other worlds" (6.1). In fact, this structural model is not threatened by either global or local forces: on the one hand, as a "world order," nationalism cannot be eroded by extra-national or global forces, as it is already "100% global [and, thus, it] cannot logically be further globalized" (4.1). On the other hand, the emergence of alternative nations and states to the existing ones does not imply the deterioration or dissolution of the "world order," but rather the conformation of the new entities to the existing model and their transformation into new expressions of the force they once opposed. This particular perspective compels minorities, including Indigenous and Native American peoples, to conform to the national model in order to achieve self-determination. Such a model, in Treanor's words, is based on a strong resistance to change and it is "past-based," where "the purpose of the nation [is] to project the past (as collectively remembered) into the future, as little changed as possible" (6.4). This resonates well with many Native American peoples' attempts to maintain unspoiled perspectives of their pasts as guide for the present and future. In this sense, Native peoples are well equipped to recast themselves into "modern" national entities within the existing "world order."

Still, this also implies that they have to play another people's game—that is, the necessity to adopt Western concepts of nation and nation building in full or in part—albeit adding their own idiosyncratic elements and values in order to assert their sovereignty. Coulthard (2007) drew on Fanon in analyzing the reproduction of colonial structures to warn against such a pitfall in the Canadian Indigenous peoples' contemporary quest for political recognition of rights to self-government, treaty rights and, more broadly, cultural distinctiveness. Rather than liberating, Coulthard maintained, contemporary Indigenous politics of recognition:

> . . . promises to reproduce the very configurations of colonial power that Indigenous peoples' demands for recognition have historically sought to transcend. More specifically, . . . the reproduction of a colonial structure of dominance like Canada's rests on its ability to entice Indigenous peoples to come to identify, either implicitly or explicitly, with the profoundly asymmetrical and non-reciprocal forms of recognition either imposed on or granted to them by the colonial-state and society. (2007, 439)

Pushing forward this analysis—or, better, exposure—of the fallacies of state recognition and reconciliation as misguided mechanisms that promise (but do not intend) to actualize Indigenous peoples' claims of sovereignty, Coulthard (2014) recently called for a *resurgent politics of recognition*, allowing Indigenous peoples to empower themselves through revived cultural practices as radical alternatives to the structural dimensions of colonial power. In Canada, Coulthard maintains, the means by which the colonial relations of power are negotiated and reproduced are no longer violence and coercion, but rather accommodation (of sanitized, or acceptable, Indigenous claims) and reconciliation (which ideologically places the abuses of settler colonialism in the past).

This view resonates and aligns with the painstaking work of exposing discursive domination—that is, the subtle maintenance of colonial state hegemony through the constraining of Indigenous sovereign efforts and paths toward empowerment within the limits of Euroamerican legal terminology and institutional procedures—that Alfred (2005) and Nadasdy (2005, 2012), among others, have undertaken in the service of unmasking false decolonization processes. Presented in these terms, the road toward nationhood appears as a corralled path that tribal communities and leaders must follow inescapably in an alleged ever-losing (or compromising) battle with the dominant culture. A rather discouraging perspective, indeed.

Yet I think otherwise. First, speaking of nation *re*-building implies that Native peoples exercised self-government as nations since precontact times. Three decades ago, Boldt and Long offered this picture when they wrote of "*nations* of people [that] regulated their internal and external relations" (1984, 545; emphasis in original). Second, I believe that tribal nations' selective adoption of nation-building traits and strategies entails agency and creativity, something akin to the process that James Clifford called "Indigenous articulation" (2001), rather than forced compromise to greater forces and foreign models. In fact, the actual practice of sovereignty, rather than the unexpressed and unpracticed potential of it, requires Native peoples to develop their own governing institutions that are stable, effective, and matching tribal cultural ideas (traditional or not) of governance. Cultural match also does and will guarantee a higher degree of community support (Cornell and Kalt 1998). This necessarily means that there must be different paths and strategies, with different degrees of similarities and differences, toward pursuing and achieving tribally customized expressions of nationhood. Conceived as such, an idiosyncratic statement of tribal cultural values based on traditional philosophy, nationhood can be considered a synonym of peoplehood without running the risk of representing the transformation into a new idea "derived primarily from the old European heritage, and with a singular focus distinct from the old Indian culture and traditions" (Deloria and Lytle 1984, 12).

Cherokee/Creek scholar Tom Holm, Diane Pearson, and Ben Chavis presented the analogy between the concepts of nationhood and peoplehood when discussing Native American group identity and its connection to sovereignty, which is "inherent in being a distinct people" (2003, 17). Building on the earlier thoughts on Indigenous group identity by Edward H. Spicer (who introduced the concept of "enduring people") and Cherokee anthropologist Robert K. Thomas,[9] Holm, Pearson, and Chavis presented a model of peoplehood in which four equally important pillars interlock to provide a group's sense of identity and place in the natural and spiritual environments: language, sacred history (which includes oral traditions, kinship structures, and customs), territory, and ceremonial cycle. These elements make peoplehood a holistic reality that embodies nationhood more accurately than band or tribe. The inclusion of language, territory, ceremonies, and sacred stories in the peoplehood model elevate nationhood from a mere expression of sociopolitical organization to a denominator of indigenous and, specifically, tribal identity.

In this sense, peoplehood is a different kind of nationhood than that included in the common Western academic hierarchical definitions of forms of political organization which identify bands and tribes as the lowest and the nation-state as the most developed. Such definitions rely on criteria that highlight the distinction between pre-state or unsophisticated political units with relatively small-size populations where relations are mainly determined by ancestry and clanship versus the "modern" expression of political aggregation where centralized governments regulate the individual and group lives of large populations, whose main aggregative principle is bureaucratic citizenship rather than common ancestry. Yet gauging Native nationhood based on such a hierarchical model runs the risk of repeating the Darwinian perspectives employed in colonial times that placed Native peoples in a pre-state or nonstate stage, which were consequently utilized to justify assimilation in the name of Western superior institutions. These ideas also gave sense to expressions such as "domestic dependent nations," which Supreme Court Justice John Marshall used in his landmark ruling in the *Cherokee Nations v. Georgia* case of 1831, thus creating both a standard and a precedent that would be instrumental in the erosion of tribal nationhood in times to come (Holm, Pearson, and Chavis 2003).

Corntassel (2003) recognized the four-pillar model of peoplehood as a promising solution to overcome the host states' monopolies on the policies of identification of Indigenous peoples and, concurrently, to refocus on the Indigenous peoples' goals of political, social, economic, and cultural autonomy. At the same time, Native nations' rebuilding of nationhood reflects a rebuilding of tribal identities that have also taken forms often departing from models featuring the much-expected "traditional" elements—this being a stereotype in itself: Native peoples always/only look backward to walk forward. For instance, although only a minority of Native North American communities own or run casinos and gambling facilities, this is one of the many available roads that some tribal nations have chosen to achieve economic self-sufficiency. The way that the so-called "casino tribes" have chosen to do so—for instance, by employing pan-Indian symbols, such as the statue of an unidentified Indian archer shooting into the sky at a central meeting point in the Mashantucket Pequot's Foxwoods complex, to highlight tribalism—can also be considered an expression of sovereignty (Cattelino 2008). Choosing how to be and how to self-represent are privileges of sovereign people. "Perhaps the preponderance at Foxwoods of stereotypical signs of Indianness embodies the constructedness of modern Pequot identity—or, rather, the modernity of the Pequots' reconstructed identity" (Anthes 2008, 208). Pequot identity and nationhood are not reducible to a core of essential elements preserved (or survived) from a turbulent colonial past and strategically selected in the last forty years. Rather, they embody a national core that has been shaped through processes of displacement, diaspora, and rebuilding that are still in the making and challenge claims of cultural continuity as the foundation of tribal nation building. As traditional symbols of nationhood have been all but obliterated, Pequot cultural identity and nationhood have necessarily departed from a process of continuity (Anthes 2008, 215).[10]

In this process, several Native North American tribal nations have acquired elements of the Western concept of nation-state, albeit utilized in different degrees and forms. One recent example of such adoption is the creation of tribal passports by the Haudenosaunee people in an effort to assert their sovereign right to define their citizenship and nationhood. In July 2010, this national right was put to test when the Iroquois national lacrosse team attempted to use them for international travelling to the World Lacrosse Championships in the United Kingdom. The United Kingdom refused to grant entry to the team under such documents, which Britain, Canada, the United States, and the international community do not recognize as valid travel documents issued by a country, meeting the strict security requirements in a post–September 11 world. The team refused to relinquish their documents in exchange for U.S. and Canadian equivalent passports. The incident sparked a political dispute on the extent of tribal nation sovereignty.[11]

It is evident that many, if not most, of these adoptions have occurred as response mechanisms to the encroachments onto tribal and First Nations' political sovereignty by the U.S. and Canadian federal, state, and provincial governments. Nevertheless, it is important to keep in mind that although "[t]ribes now commonly refer to themselves as 'nations,' [t]his does not signify status as nation-states" (Cornell and Kalt 2010, 5; quotes in original). On the one hand, such a notion highlights the power deficiencies of tribal nations, which lack the prerogatives (such as maintaining a standing army, printing currency, and so forth) of their hosting nation-states, the United States and Canada. On the other hand, the very concept of tribal nationhood possesses an idiosyncratic cultural history and nature, thus transcending the sole administrative and bureaucratic nature of Western statehood. As Mohawk anthropologist Audra Simpson insightfully contended, the notion of Indigenous nationhood expresses a political reality "inextricably joined to culture" and, therefore, "demarcates identity and seizes tradition in ways that may be antagonistic to the encompassing frame of the state" (2000, 114). Simpson (2014) developed this argument further in her ethnographic-based discussion of the Mohawk's politics of refusal to let go of the notion that they are a nation other than the United State and Canada. In this sense, the Haudenosaunee passport incident as well as the quests for tribal citizenship of the Kahnawà:ke Mohawk (Simpson 2000, 2014) and the Nova Scotia Mi'kmaq (Poliandri 2011, as well as Chapter 3 in this volume), for instance, embody the actualization of cultural difference in a leveled political arena rather than attempts to close (or reduce) the bureaucratic gap between Indigenous and dominant expressions of governance and sovereignty. This reflects the convergence of new, "modern" aspirations—be they financial success and self-sufficiency or an increase in education (more and more toward secondary and postsecondary) (Brayboy et al. 2012)—and the proper, culturally determined form of nationhood necessary to achieve such goals. The palatable aspect of this shift, one that offers Native peoples a much greater chance to attain actual success, is the fact that tribal nations are now more and more in control over their choice of nation form, once a responsibility (or imposition) of the Euroamerican governments.

In this regard, Duane Champagne (2002) discussed the political, cultural, and economic challenges that twenty-first century globalization poses to the Native American nations. Champagne called for a strategy of survival and thriving based on traditionally oriented values and cultural ideas. Yet, as Champagne reminded us, this process need not strive to rebuild or replicate the social and political tribal structures of the past, which are unfit to the contemporary world. Rather, values and cultural orientations—such as a holistic perception of life (one that does not compartmentalize social, political, religious, economic, and family life) and a political approach based on negotiation, accommodation, and respect for autonomy of individual and groups (thus different from the Western and U.S. self-maximizing and individualistic experience)—must serve as guidelines for sustainable structures that can meet the challenges of a globalizing world. *Tribal capitalism*—the economic model that aims at collective tribal accumulation rather than individual accumulation and makes reinvestment of profit into the tribal community its cornerstone—embodies this structural solution and has been recognized as such by most contemporary tribal nations (Miller 2013).

Stephen Cornell and Joseph Kalt, co-directors of the Harvard Project on American Indian Economic Development, illustrated in clear terms the shift in tribal economic success since the 1975 change in U.S. federal Indian policy aimed at granting self-determination to tribal nations. Despite a rocky start due to a lack of business experience, education capital, and governmental decision-making capacity, U.S.-based tribes shifted gear rapidly in the following decade and many attained economic success, albeit most tribal communities still face enduring social problems.

> By the second half of the 1980s, however, self-determination had become a widespread and systematic restructuring of tribal governments and their relations with the federal government. This restructuring has acquired a name as the "nation building" movement. It is being manifested by wholesale changes in tribal institutions and policies as the Indian nations themselves rewrite their constitutions, generate increasing shares of their revenues through their own taxes and business enterprises, establish their own courts and law enforcement systems, remake school curricula, and so on, across the panoply of functions commonly associated in the United States with state governments. (Cornell and Kalt 2010, 12; quotes in original)

Cornell and Kalt (1998) had already laid down the foundation of this perspective in the previous decade when they published the results of the Harvard Project in many papers, all pointing at the combination of sovereignty and nation building as the formula for the success of Native economic development. "Sovereignty, nation-building, and economic development go hand in hand," they wrote. "Without sovereignty and nation-building, economic development is likely to remain a frustratingly elusive dream" (1998, 188–189). According to this perspective, which the authors of this volume share, nation building and the implementation of sovereignty have been instrumental in turning things around for tribal nations and continue to fuel the political and economic renaissance of many tribes.

In the United States, economic development has gained momentum in Indian Country since the late 1980s, partially as a result of policies of self-determination that allowed tribal nations to acquire greater control over their own affairs. However, although economic growth is promising, results are still tenuous. Social indicators, such as levels of poverty, health, substance abuse, and education rates, to name a few, still offer a grim or negative picture (HPAIED 2008). Corntassel and Witmer (2008) have attributed the curtailing of the economic and political development of U.S.-based American Indian tribal nations, as well as their capacity to self-represent on their own terms, to the increased encroachment of state governments in tribal affairs since the passage of the Indian Gaming Regulatory Act (IGRA) in 1988. The introduction of IGRA, Corntassel and Witmer maintain, marked the beginning of the current "forced federalism" Indigenous policy era in which the transfer of federal powers to state governments compelled tribal nations into "dangerous political and legal relationships with state governments that challenge their cultures and nationhood status" (2008, 5). Such a shift has implied the necessity of Indigenous nations to enter compacts on taxation, gaming, harvesting rights, and other areas of tribal enterprise with state governments that have historically been hostile to them. These relationships have become particularly antagonistic "when economic development issues such as gaming are being negotiated" (2008, 23). Yet Corntassel and Witmer are keen to remark that the sole focus on economic and political issues runs the risk of addressing challenges to the development of Native nationhood that require also cultural and spiritual solutions, in line with the four-pillar model offered by Holm, Pearson, and Chavis (2003).

A Multifaceted Approach to the Understanding of Native Nationalism and Nation Re-building

Contemporary Indigenous nation *re*-building must be understood and discussed for what it is: a multifaceted dynamic process that includes cultural resurgence, social development, regaining control over historical representation, economic development and self-sufficiency, political self-determination, and legal autonomy. This volume strives to survey this eclectic reality—or, more accurately, realities, as every tribal/First Nation has been walking an idiosyncratic path made up of a unique, localized combination of the aforementioned elements—by presenting cases that speak to the economic facet of Native American nation building (Braun), the cultural and political aspects of nation building (Poliandri), the historical representation of nationhood (Shepherd), and the historical and legal affirmation of nationhood (Wetzel and Grey).

In his provocative and visionary Chapter 1, Sebastian Braun argues that the nation represents the most appropriate context in which American Indian peoples can attain successful economic development in the United States. In particular, economic and political participation are key stepping stones toward the exercise of "true sovereignty" which, Braun contends, American Indians are being prevented from regaining in the present system. Thus the central question that Braun asks and attempts to answer is, "How can existent sovereignty (based on membership) be enhanced to achieve and practice true sovereignty (based on citizenship)?" The question then becomes one of structure rather than one of efficacy under the current conditions. "To achieve true sovereignty the system needs to be broken," Braun states. In this perspective, empowering the communities entails a holistic solution granting political control, the legitimacy of a cultural interpretation of the world, and economic self-sufficiency that will allow American Indian communities to define their own relationships with their social, natural, and spiritual environments. By pointing to a solution that addresses the nation as a whole rather than any of its parts and by approaching the problem from an economic and political angle, Braun builds on the work of scholars such as Mohawk economist Dean Howard Smith, who discussed the compatibility of economic development with cultural integrity and, in fact, argued for the centrality of the former to guarantee the maintenance of the latter (1994; 2000).

Reservation lands are necessary but not sufficient to the exercise of sovereignty by Native nations, because such territories are located at the economic and social periphery of the United States. In fact, Braun contends, these are usually linked to or, more often, even economically dependent on the rural areas they are adjacent to, which in turn are peripheral to the social, political, and economic centers of the country, located in the cities. Thus, Native lands can be seen as "the periphery of the periphery," a reality that has been known and, unfortunately, has not changed much over the last one hundred and more years.

Braun argues that failed solutions to the problem have included ethnification (the strategy aimed at making American Indians simply another ethnic group in the American mosaic, thus ignoring their legal diversity, while "allowing" the retention of their cultural diversity, thus celebrating the politically "harmless" components of such diversity), de-nationalization (which implied stripping Native Americans of their tribal nationhood and re-nationalizing them as Americans under the overt goal of integration and participation in a progressive society yet pursued through the, more or less, covert strategies of forced assimilation and sociocultural debilitation), and de-territorialization (which since the establishment of the reservation system and the allotment policy has meant dispossession, on the one hand, and making the remaining Native-controlled territories "the periphery of the periphery").

The alternative, or real, solution that Braun explores lies in the context of tribal citizenship, whose control the American Indian nations have legally and politically enjoyed already for several decades. This, Braun envisions and discusses in detail, is where true sovereign efforts must be invested in order to break the system of control and dependency. Although aware of the high degree of improbability that such a vision will come true in the short term as well as the myriad of challenges to such a development, Braun nevertheless invites the reader to seriously engage in the exercise of "re-imagining realities outside of the boxes we are delivered by hegemonic forces and practices." After all, colonialism can be portrayed as a series of enduring boxes—in the form of social and cultural values, economic and political systems, military dominance, and legal and administrative control—that were built around once-sovereign peoples and have prevented (or hindered) their full development as autonomous nations. Given that much has been unsuccessfully attempted to break such constraints, it might be very well worth to consider alternative approaches.

In Chapter 2, Jackie Grey traces the political assertions of the Aquinnah Wampanoag nation of Noëpe (today's Martha's Vineyard) by looking at how anticipation of dispossession, resistance, and territorial struggles developed in juridical documents and Indigenous political discourse over the last three hundred years of colonial history. Specifically, anticipation has been mostly expressed in legal form and lies at the core of the Aquinnah Wampanoags' claims to self-government in the critical period of Aquinnah history stretching between the early 1970s and today. At the same time, Grey contends, anticipation has worked as a force fueling, diverting, and often opposing tribal and nontribal efforts to secure and maintain power over land on Noëpe, the ancestral land for the Wampanoag Indigenous population, or Martha's Vineyard, a territorial symbol of wealth and prestige for the non-Native population for the last two centuries.

Looking at the nation-building process undergone by the Wampanoag of Noëpe, Grey examines the development of the struggle for land control as a series of moves and responses on the part of two factions of the Aquinnah Wampanoags and the non-Native residents of the island based on anticipating events and consequences as well as on anticipating the opponents' responses and subsequent moves. It was in the midst of legislative threats to declare indigenous coastal lands "forever wild" (an enduring colonial fantasy, some might say) that the Aquinnah Wampanoag revamped their nation-building efforts by chartering the Wampanoag Tribal Council of Gay Head in 1972. Adding the status of legal entity to their nationhood allowed the Wampanoag to gain leverage to defend their collective interests, most notably the control over their "common lands" symbolized by their annual harvesting ceremony locale, the cranberry bogs.

In her analysis, Grey highlights a three-hundred-year trajectory connecting a seventeenth-century written declaration with which an Aquinnah Wampanoag sachem reaffirmed the Indigenous people's perennial link with and right to the territory; a lawsuit initiated in 1974 in which the

Aquinnah Wampanoag searched for the return of unoccupied, communal lands; the resulting controversial 1983 settlement agreement between part of the Wampanoags (led by the tribal council) and the town of Gay Head, the state of Massachusetts, and a non-Native citizens' group; the subsequent U.S. Senate hearings to discuss the opportunity of the settlement's Congressional ratification into law; and the still unfolding developments of the Noëpe Wampanoags' struggle for sovereignty and nation building in the twenty-first century. The litigation ended with the ratification of a settlement whose settler-law language aimed at anticipating future conflict but, at the same time, troubled the Aquinnah Wampanoag self-rule. The close reading of the testimonies before the U.S. Senate Committee on Indian Affairs at a 1986 hearing attended by several Aquinnah tribal members, retrieved from written and oral accounts, reveals a complex web of anticipated moves and consequences, unanticipated developments, and contrasting visions that pitted tribal members against tribal members and tribal members against non-Native residents of Noëpe in trying to secure control over the representation of historical reality and present opportunities.

In the end, Grey's chapter highlights once again how Indigenous nationhood is rooted in territory as well as the social, cultural, and emotional ties to these tribal lands. "What will endure," Grey states, "is Aquinnah land." Yet such ties are not crystallized in time but, rather, remain fluid and changing. The deep connections to tribal land allow the tribal nation's past to remain anchored to its present and the future as both assets of developing identities and tangible resources for decolonized survival and success.

In Chapter 3, Simone Poliandri discusses the recent nation-building process in the First Nations of Eastern Canada and highlights some of the ways in which nationhood and nationalism have developed in the social and political arenas among the Mi'kmaw people of Nova Scotia. Poliandri introduces the phrases "First Nationhood" and "First Nationalism" to indicate the idiosyncratic character of Native North American peoples' expressions of nationhood and nationalism.

As in the other cases discussed in this volume, Poliandri underscores that Mi'kmaw nation building and national sentiments also possess a strong territorial component, which for the Mi'kmaw people entails connections to their entire traditional territory, Mi'kma'ki (which includes the Maritime provinces of Canada, part of Quebec, part of Newfoundland, and part of northern Maine), to the space of the reserves, and to the areas under land claims. Grounding his arguments on ethnographic, administrative, juridical, and secondary evidence, Poliandri identifies three dimensions of Mi'kmaw nation building and the contexts in which they have developed in recent years: First Nationhood as tribal sentiment, thus expressed by people from the entire Mi'kma'ki; First Nationhood expressed by single Mi'kmaw bands (or communities); and First Nationhood and nationalism expressed by Mi'kmaw people from single Canadian provinces (Poliandri 2011).

Analyses of the highly controversial Marshall case, which culminated in the landmark 1999 Supreme Court case ruling on First Nations resource access in the Maritimes, the experiences of several generation of Mi'kmaw children in the infamous Shubenacadie Indian Residential School, and sociocultural events such as the Mi'kmaw powwow trail and the summer celebration of the Mi'kmaw patron saint, St. Anne, elucidate how the Mi'kmaw nation-building process takes place at the tribal dimension. Concurrently, the recent phenomenon of single Mi'kmaw bands introducing themselves and acting as national entities highlights a newly developed form of nation building and national sentiment played at the local level. Furthermore, Mi'kmaw nationhood and nationalism have most recently emerged in the provincial dimension, where bands from single provinces act as units in dealing more effectively with the provincial and federal governments. Both the analysis of the Made in Nova Scotia Process, the umbrella agreement placing the Nova Scotia Mi'kmaw bands and the provincial and federal governments at the table of negotiations, and the 2008 *Mi'kmaq of Nova Scotia Nationhood Proclamation* by the Assembly of Nova Scotia Mi'kmaq Chiefs are evidence of this new context in which Mi'kmaw nation building has recently been developed. Finally, the essay contemplates the formulation and implementation of a viable definition of "Mi'kmaw citizenship," which represent the most recent challenges in the nation-building efforts of the Mi'kmaw people. In sum, the multicontext development of First Nationhood and nationalism among the Mi'kmaq highlights a complex and multifarious process that speaks volumes about dynamic concepts of nation and nationhood that are concurrently tied to traditional visions, historical developments, and current social, political, and economic strategies.

In Chapter 4, Jeffrey Shepherd discusses the historical forces and events that led to the formation of modern Hualapai nation and national sentiment. Shepherd situates the formative core of modern Hualapai nationhood and nationalism at the intersection of a precolonial sense of peoplehood, ties to ancestral land, and a shared set of family, band, and tribal memories with the process of development that these underwent in facing and dealing with the unfolding of the U.S. colonial enterprise. Conquest, dispossession, and confinement met processes of resistance, recasting, and creation of the modern Hualapai political discourse. Survival entailed challenging the dominant historical vision with collective memories and alternative ideas of territorial belonging.

Shepherd discusses the effects that a changed cultural geography and spatial distribution of peoples had on Pai bands' redefined identities as "bands negotiated new relationships with each other as they faced a common set of experiences" and as Pai headmen demanded the establishment of a common reservation in the early 1880s, which Shepherd deems "a turning point in the Hualapai history because it signaled the preservation of a piece of their homelands," despite the immense problems associated with the image and reality of reservation life, and set the basis for their modern sovereignty. He argues that this spatially meaningful event, the bureaucratization and racialization of independent Pai bands into a single group (the Hualapai), and the common experiences of internment and escape that marked the history of non-native colonial settlement of northwestern Arizona in the second half of the nineteenth century forged a new collective identity and became focal points for the development of the Hualapai national identity.

Shepherd identifies the creation of centralized Hualapai political institutions representing the rights of all Pai bands as evidence of the development of a nationalist sentiment (or, at the very least, a collective political strategy) among the Pai band members, who progressively absorbed the Hualapai group identity. Hualapai nationalism became grounded in land claims and resource access struggles that united Pai bands in the challenge against common threats and, in the process, saw the emergence of a Hualapai nationalist rhetoric based on a mixture of tradition, history, and progress discourse, which was amply used in U.S. courts.

Shepherd highlights how the fight against the railroad development through their territory (a common experience by many western tribes over many decades since the 1850s), the return migration to the reservation by many off-reservation Hualapai residents, the creation of a highly contested Indian Reorganization Act government in the 1930s, and the contentions sparked by the U.S. termination policy spearheaded by the Indian Claims Commission in the 1950s were key elements in shaping the Hualapai nation-building process in one way or the other in the twentieth century. This is when Hualapai nationhood established itself unequivocally as a further identity layer alongside family and band identities.

Shepherd brings attention to the complex process that gave life to a Hualapai historical narrative tying distinct Pai bands into a unified body politic, the Hualapai Nation, which was then projected onto the timeless past as it eclipsed the bands' unique histories. Such was the result of U.S. colonialism and Indian policies onto the Pai cultural, political, territorial, and institutional histories, which remain a definitive legacy for how Hualapai people conceive of themselves in today's northern Arizona.

In Chapter 5, Chris Wetzel discusses the processes of contemporary Native nationhood and revitalization through the analysis of treaty negotiations as critical loci of national narratives and national identity formation (or reconstitution). The case of the Potawatomi Nation as it faced the Indian Claims Commission (ICC), the institution that worked under the U.S. Congress between 1946 and 1978 to address tribal outstanding land claims, is enlightening. Wetzel sheds light on the process that led nine Potawatomi bands, the major by-product of the aggressive removal campaigns by the U.S. colonial government in the early 1800s that forced the scattering of a once-whole nation, to recast their nationhood into a unified imagery as they proceeded through several litigation cases before the ICC. Potawatomi Nation is presented here as a "continuous, flowing thing," rooted in the connections of places, families, and culture, as well as in the "Potawatomi experiences of larger and persistent relationships." The keyword here is "relationships," the existence of which, unbroken and persistent, albeit challenged and changed, provides an enduring foundation to Potawatomi nationhood.

Wetzel embarks on an important and careful, not to mention fascinating, analysis of the Potawatomi people's testimonies before the ICC, which brings to light the underlying presence of such relationships in Potawatomi lives. On the one hand, the extensive citation of the direct testimonies makes sure this important component of the Potawatomi communal memory is kept front and center in the recent history of the self-determination efforts by the communities. It also assures that the core of Potawatomi national discourse, which these testimonies embody, is kept within the pulsing realm of flesh-and-blood community members, rather than being relegated to stale administrative records. On the other hand, Wetzel's excursion into the ICC sessions somewhat highlights the paradox of finding some of the traces of the reconstruction of Potawatomi nationhood and the Potawatomi national discourse in the very context, the U.S. body politic which the ICC represented, where these had been usually challenged, if not opposed—the latter a demonstration of the resiliency of the Potawatomi's (and, by extent, Native American tribal nations') sense of peoplehood and desire for self-determination. In the end, Wetzel signifies that despite a three-decade-long intricate process that resulted in substantial monetary compensation for the Potawatomi and "a complex national future," the archival record nonetheless reveals "recurring narratives of the Nation expressed by the Potawatomi," which ultimately bridge the past, present, and future of the Potawatomi Nation.

Taken together, the chapters featured in this volume offer a heterogeneous portrait of the historical and current developments of Native nationhood and nationalism. At the same time, they provide evidence of common challenges and strategies in the nation *re*-building paths of different tribal/First Nations. These include making the link between nation building and unique tribal identities and cultures an asset of contemporary nation *re*-building; bridging past and present in the service of providing groundwork and legitimacy to the current nation *re*-building attempts; and the resiliency and continuity of tribal nation-building efforts despite the centennial colonial attacks to sovereignty and self-determination. Among the common themes across this volume's contributions is also the significance of space (conceived both as traditional territory and colonial reservation) in the current construction of Native national identity. Whether related to historical memory and the narrativization of peoplehood, as in the case of the Hualapai, the temporality of Indigenous claims to sovereignty, as in a recent court case regarding Aquinnah Wampanoag tribal land, or the demarcation of successful financial assets as cultural and social emblems of Indigenous space, as in the case of the Mi'kmaq, territory constitutes an inalienable and necessary element connecting Native American peoplehood and nationhood. Concurrently, the creation and maintenance of Native American national identity have also overcome structural territorial impediments, as in the case of the Potawatomi, and might benefit from the inclusivity of citizenship rather than the exclusivity of ethnicity. In all cases, the political effectiveness of nationhood in promoting and sustaining sovereignty presupposes Native full participation in and control over economic development, the formation of historical narrative and memory, the definition of legality, and the exercise of governance.

On the one hand, all Native nations face similar challenges which include (1) the building of institutions capable of tackling current social, cultural, economic, legal, administrative, and political issues and the acquisition of sufficient jurisdiction to effectively and actually self-govern; (2) the building of viable economies; (3) the retaining of tribal culture (including language); and (4) the retaining of both unique tribal citizenship (thus separate from U.S. or Canadian citizen status) and, at the same time, the possibility to be part of the U.S. and Canadian states. On the other hand, each tribal nation and First Nation has developed from a unique history and faces unique challenges. The significance of this volume lies in acknowledging the idiosyncratic nature of Native nations and their nation *re*-building processes, and sampling such a diverse pool of experiences. Finally, the authors of this book share the belief that Native American/First Nations nationhood is a work-in-progress in which, as Wanda Wuttunee reminds us in her concluding piece, the push for change is unstopped.

In fact, one disclaimer is in order. The following chapters discuss a few cases exemplifying the nation *re*-building paths of First Nations/Native American tribal nations. By no means does this volume claim to offer a complete and definitive perspective on the recent developments of nationalism and nation *re*-building in the experiences of Native North Americans. Rather, the authors offer a series of considerations and perspectives that wish to open a virtual forum for discussion in which scholars, nonacademic tribal members, policymakers, and general readers can meet to address these poignant issues for the Native North American peoples in the twenty-first century.

Notes

1. I acknowledge that the tribal nation's or First Nation's name is the most accurate and respectful term when referring to specific peoples, institutions, and things. However, it would be unfeasible to spell out the individual names of each tribe and First Nation when referring to the Aboriginal groups of the United States and Canada in a general way. To this purpose, and due to the lack of an agreed-on universal term among Native peoples, the terms Native, Native American, Native North American, First Nations people, Aboriginal people, Indigenous people, American Indian, and Indian are used interchangeably in this volume. For a detailed discussion of the politics of naming, see, among others, Bowd and Brady 1998; Yellow Bird 1999.

2. See, for instance, Jorgensen 2007 and the "Nation Building Series," ten 30-minute segments produced in 2006 by the University of Arizona's Native Nations Institute, available in audio and video formats at http://nni.arizona.edu/nnitvradio (accessed September 2015).

3. There are open discussions among Native American Studies scholars as well as tribal members on whether we have entered a postcolonial period or we are still in the colonial era.

4. See the Union of Ontario Indians' website at http://anishinabek.ca/anishinabek-nation-citizenship.asp (accessed September 2015), Poliandri 2011, and Chapter 3 in this volume; Jodi A. Byrd, "'Been to the Nation, Lord, but I Couldn't Stay There': American Indian Sovereignty, Cherokee Freedmen and the Incommensurability of the Internal," *Interventions*, 13(1) (2011): 31–52; Jessica Jones, "Cherokee by Blood and the Freedmen Debate: The Conflict of Minority Group Rights in a Liberal State," *National Black Law Journal*, 22 (2009): 1–55; S. Alan Ray, "A Race or a Nation? Cherokee National Identity and the Status of Freedmen's Descendants," *Michigan Journal of Race and Law*, 12 (2007): 387–463; Sturm 2002; and the official website of the Descendants of Freedmen of the Five Civilized Tribes at http://www.freedmen5tribes.com (accessed September 2015).

5. See, for instance, Cattelino 2008; Sebastian Felix Braun, *Buffalo Inc.: American Indians and Economic Development* (Norman: University of Oklahoma Press, 2008); Cornell and Kalt 1998; Stephen Cornell and Joseph P. Kalt, "Two Approaches to the Development of Native Nations: One Works, the Other Doesn't," in Jorgensen 2007, 3–33; Sandra Faiman-Silva, *Choctaws at the Crossroads: The Political Economy of Class and Culture in the Oklahoma Timber Region* (University of Nebraska Press, 2000); Anthes 2008; John J. Bodinger de Uriarte, *Casino and Museum: Representing Mashantucket Pequot Identity* (University of Arizona Press, 2007); and Laurence M. Hauptman, James D. Wherry, and William T. Hagan, eds., *The Pequots in Southern New England: The Fall and Rise of an American Indian Nation* (University of Oklahoma Press, 1993).

6. See, for instance, Sandra Day O'Connor, "Lessons from the Third Sovereign: Indian Tribal Courts," *Tulsa Law Journal* 33(1) (1997): 1–6; Gloria Valencia-Weber, "Tribal Courts: Custom and Innovative Law," *New Mexico Law Review*, 24 (1994): 225–263; the official website of the Navajo Judicial Branch at www.navajocourts.org (accessed September 2015); Larry Nesper, "Tribal Courts and Tribal States in the Era of Self-Determination: An Ojibwe Case Study," in *Beyond Red Blood: American Indian Politics and Activism since 1900*, ed. Daniel M. Cobb and Loretta Fowler (Santa Fe, NM: School for Advanced Research Press, 2007), 243–261; and Nesper 2007.

7. See, for instance, Theresa McCarthy, "Dęni: s nisa'sgao'dę?: Haudenosaunee Clans and the Reconstruction of Traditional Haudenosaunee Identity, Citizenship, and Nationhood," *American Indian Culture and Research Journal*, 34(2) (2010): 81–101; Simpson 2000; Jacqueline R. Papez, "Native (Hydro) power: Alternate Avenues for Achieving Native Control of Natural Resources on Tribal Lands, with Focus on Hydropower Dams," *Idaho Law Review*, 46 (2010): 671–733; Ken Coates, *The Marshall Decision and Native Rights* (Montreal & Kingston: McGill-Queen's University Press, 2000); and Poliandri 2003.

8. As I find it unnecessary to indulge in yet another detailed literary review of the general theories of nationalism, I invite the reader to refer to this and other academic sources for this purpose.

9. See Edward H. Spicer, *Cycles of Conquest: The Impact of Spain, Mexico and the United States on the Indians of the Southwest, 1533-1960* (Tucson: Uni-

versity of Arizona Press, 1962); *Yaquis: A Cultural* History (Tucson: University of Arizona Press, 1980); Robert K. Thomas, "Colonialism: Classic and Internal," *New University Thought*, 4 (1966–67): 44–53.

10. The Pequot nation offers an example of the tribal capitalism model, which other tribal nations, such as the Seminole (Cattelino 2008), Millbrook Mi'kmaq (Poliandri 2011), White Mountain Apache, and the Mississippi Choctaw, have adopted successfully. The Pequot case is also an example of deterritorialization and subsequent reterritorialization (Appadurai 1996) in their own territory, which is a process peculiar to Native North American peoples that differs from the processes of relinquishing territorial ties and reforming them somewhere else in the geocultural imaginary of global migrant peoples. As the global migrants' reterritorialized locality is generally a product of imagination, Native peoples' one is not, as it is usually based on the recuperation of previously occupied (thus, historically owned) land.

11. See, for instance, Thomas Kaplan, "Iroquois Defeated by Passport Dispute," *New York Times*, 16 July 2010, available at https://www.nytimes.com/2010/07/17/sports/17lacrosse.html?_r=0; John Wetenhall, "Iroquois Lacrosse Team Prevented From Traveling to Championships," *ABC News*, 13 July 2010, available at http://abcnews.go.com/US/passport-snafu-leaves-iroquois-lacrosse-team-stranded/story?id=11152661; Gale Courey Toensing, "UK denies travel visas for Iroquois Nationals," *IndianCountryTodayMediaNetwork.com*, 20 July 2010, available at http://indiancountrytodaymedianetwork.com/node/81058; Felicia Fonseca, "Iroquois passport dispute raises sovereignty issues: Team forfeited games and headed home," *News from Indian Country*, 17 July 2010, available at http://www.indiancountrynews.com/index.php/sports-sections-menu-76/9646-iroquois-passport-dispute-raises-sovereignty-issues-team-forfeited-games-and-headed-home; "Iroquois Nationals Lacrosse team delayed for World Games by Homeland Security passport fiasco," *News from Indian Country*, 12 July 2010, available at http://www.indiancountrynews.com/index.php/crimejusticecourts-a-lawsuits-sections-menu-109/9565-iroquois-nationals-lacrosse-team-delayed-for-world-games-by-homeland-security-passport-fiasco; and the Iroquois Nationals Lacrosse official website at http://iroquoisnationals.org. All accessed in September 2015. For a more extensive list of media articles about this issue, see the "News: Iroquois Nationals Passports/Visa Issue" section of the American Indian Law Alliance website at http://www.ailanyc.org/news-3 (accessed September 2015).

References

Alfred, Gerald R. (Taiaiake). 1995. *Heeding the Voices of Our Ancestors: Kahnawake Mohawk Politics and the Rise of Native Nationalism*. Toronto: Oxford University Press Canada.

———. 2005. *Wasáse: Indigenous Pathways of Action and Freedom*. Peterborough, ON: Broadview Press.

———. 2009. *First Nation Perspectives on Political Identity.* First Nation Citizenship Research and Policy Series, Building Towards Change. Ottawa, ON: Assembly of First Nations.

Anthes, Bill. 2008. Learning from Foxwoods: Visualizing the Mashantucket Pequot Tribal Nation. *American Indian Quarterly* 32(2): 204–218.

Appadurai, Arjun. 1996. *Modernity at Large: Cultural Dimensions in Globalization.* Minneapolis: University of Minnesota Press.

Biolsi, Thomas. 2005. Imagined Geographies: Sovereignty, Indigenous space, and American Indian struggle. *American Ethnologist* 32(2): 239–259.

Boldt, Menno, and J. Anthony Long. 1984. Tribal Traditions and European-Western Political Ideologies: The Dilemma of Canada's Native Indians. *Canadian Journal of Political Science* 17(3): 537–553.

Bowd, Alan, and Patrick Brady. 1998. Note on Preferred Use of Ethnic Identity Labels by Aboriginal and Non-Aboriginal Canadians. *Psychological Reports* 82: 1153–1154.

Brayboy, Bryan McKinley Jones, Amy J. Fann, Angelina E. Castagno, and Jessica A. Solyom. 2012. Postsecondary Education for American Indian and Alaska Natives: Higher Education for Nation Building and Self-Determination. *Association for the Study of Higher Education (ASHE) Higher Education Report* 37(5).

Cattelino, Jessica R. 2008. *High Stakes: Florida Seminole Gaming and Sovereignty.* Durham, NC: Duke University Press.

Champagne, Duane. 2002. Challenges to Native Nation Building in the 21st Century. *Arizona State Law Journal* 34(1): 46–54.

Churchill, Ward. 1998. *Fantasies of the Master Race: Literature, Cinema, and the Colonization of American Indians.* San Francisco: City Light Books.

Clifford, James. 2001. Indigenous Articulations. *The Contemporary Pacific* 13(2): 468–490.

Cornell, Stephen, and Joseph P. Kalt. 1998. Sovereignty and Nation-Building: The Development Challenge in Indian Country Today. *American Indian Culture and Research Journal* 22(3): 187–214.

———. 2010. *American Indian Self-Determination: The Political Economy of a Policy that Works.* HKS Faculty Research Working Paper Series RWP10-043, John F. Kennedy School of Government, Harvard University. http://dash.harvard.edu/handle/1/4553307 (accessed September 2015).

Corntassel, Jeff. 2003. Who is Indigenous? 'Peoplehood' and Ethnonationalist Approaches to Rearticulating Indigenous Identity. *Nationalism and Ethnic Politics* 9(1): 75–100.

———. 2008. Toward Sustainable Self-Determination: Rethinking the Contemporary Indigenous-Rights Discourse. *Alternatives* 33: 105–132.

Corntassel, Jeff, and Cheryl Bryce. 2012. Practicing Sustainable Self-Determination: Indigenous Approaches to Cultural Restoration and Revitalization. *Brown Journal of World Affairs* 18(2): 151–162.

Corntassel, Jeff, and Richard C. Witmer II. 2008. *Forced Federalism: Contemporary Challenges to Indigenous Nationhood*. Norman: University of Oklahoma Press.
Coulthard, Glen S. 2007. Subjects of Empire: Indigenous Peoples and the 'Politics of Recognition' in Canada. *Contemporary Political Theory* 6: 437–460.
———. 2014. *Red Skin, White Masks: Rejecting the Colonial Politics of Recognition*. Minneapolis: University of Minnesota Press.
Deloria, Vine Jr., and Clifford Lytle. 1984. *The Nations Within: The Past and Future of American Indian Sovereignty*. New York: Pantheon.
Harvard Project on American Indian Economic Development (HPAIED). 2008. *The State of Native Nations: Conditions under U.S. policies of Self-determination*. New York: Oxford University Press.
Hobsbawm, Eric J. 1992. *Nations and Nationalism since 1870: Programme, Myth, Reality*. Second Edition. Cambridge: Cambridge University Press.
Holm, Tom, J. Diane Pearson, and Ben Chavis. 2003. Peoplehood: A Model for the Extension of Sovereignty in American Indian Studies. *Wicazo Sa Review* 18(1): 7–24.
Hosmer, Brian, and Larry Nesper, eds. 2013. *Tribal Worlds: Critical Studies in American Indian Nation Building*. Albany, NY: State University of New York Press.
Jorgensen, Miriam, ed. 2007. *Rebuilding Native Nations: Strategies for Governance and Development*. Tucson: University of Arizona Press.
Lambert, Valerie. 2007. *Choctaw Nation: A story of American Indian Resurgence*. Lincoln: University of Nebraska Press.
Lee, Lloyd L. 2006. Navajo Cultural Identity: What Can the Navajo Nation Bring to the American Indian Identity Discussion Table? *Wicazo Sa Review* 21(2): 79–103.
———. 2007. The Future of Navajo Nationalism. *Wicazo Sa Review* 22(1): 53–68.
Lyons, Oren. 2007. Foreword. In *Rebuilding Native Nations: Strategies for Government and Development*. Edited by Miriam Jorgensen, pp. vii–ix. Tucson: University of Arizona Press.
Miller, Robert J. 2013. *Reservation "Capitalism": Economic Development in Indian Country*. Lincoln: University of Nebraska Press.
Nadasdy, Paul. 2005. *Hunters and Bureaucrats: Power, Knowledge, and Aboriginal-State Relations in the Southwest Yukon*. Vancouver: University of British Columbia Press.
———. 2012. Boundaries among Kin: Sovereignty, the Modern Treaty Process, and the Rise of Ethno-Territorial Nationalism among Yukon First Nations. *Comparative Studies in Society and History* 54(3): 499–532.
Nesper, Larry. 2007. Negotiating Jurisprudence in Tribal Court and the Emergence of a Tribal State. *Current Anthropology* 48(5): 675–699.
Poliandri, Simone. 2003. Mi'kmaw People and Tradition: Indian Brook Lobster Fishing in St. Mary's Bay, Nova Scotia. In *Papers of the Thirty-Fourth*

Algonquian Conference, ed. H.C. Wolfart, pp. 303–310. Winnipeg: University of Manitoba.

———. 2011. *First Nations, Identity, and Reserve Life: The Mi'kmaq of Nova Scotia*. Lincoln: University of Nebraska Press.

Simpson, Audra. 2000. Paths toward a Mohawk Nation: Narratives of Citizenship and Nationhood in Kahnawake. In *Political Theory and the Rights of Indigenous Peoples*. Edited by Duncan Ivison, Paul Patton, and Will Sanders, pp. 113–136. Cambridge: Cambridge University Press.

———. 2014. *Mohawk Interruptus: Political Life across the Borders of Settler States*. Durham, NC: Duke University Press.

Smith, Anthony D. 1993 [1991]. *National Identity*. Reno: University of Nevada Press.

Smith, Dean Howard. 1994. The Issue of Compatibility between Cultural Integrity and Economic Development among Native American Tribes. *American Indian Culture and Research Journal* 18(2): 177–205.

———. 2000. *Modern Tribal Development: Paths to Self-Sufficiency and Cultural Integrity in Indian Country*. Walnut Creek, CA: Altamira Press.

Sturm, Circe. 2002. *Blood Politics: Race, Culture, and Identity in the Cherokee Nation of Oklahoma*. Berkeley: University of California Press.

Treanor, Paul. 1997. Structures of Nationalism. *Sociological Research Online* 2(1). http://www.socresonline.org.uk/2/1/8.html (accessed September 2015).

Weaver, Hilary N. 2001. Indigenous Identity: What Is It, and Who Really Has It? *American Indian Quarterly* 25(2): 240–255.

Wilkinson, Charles. 2005. *Blood Struggle: The Rise of Modern Indian Nations*. New York: Norton.

Yellow Bird, Michael. 1999. What We Want to Be Called: Indigenous Peoples' Perspectives on Racial and Ethnic Identity Labels. *American Indian Quarterly* 23(2): 1–21.

CHAPTER 1

Building on Native Sovereignty

From Ethnic Membership to National Citizenship

Sebastian Felix Braun

> Membership has its "privileges," but citizenship has its "duties" and "rights." No one is ever called an "enrolled member of France." I say not enough Indians are "citizens."
>
> —Scott Richard Lyons 2010, 171

In April 2014, thousands of people protested against the planned Keystone XL pipeline in Washington, D.C. Much about the protest was not unusual. What stood out, however, at least to the media, was the name of the organization behind the protests: the Cowboy and Indian Alliance. In many people's eyes, cowboys and Indians are still supposed to be opposites. But in the West, and on the Great Plains, it has long been the case that Indians are cowboys, and that cowboys feel marginalized, as Indians do (e.g., Braun 2008; Iverson 1997; Wagoner 2002). As Zoltan Grossman has shown, cowboy and Indian alliances are nothing new (2003, 2005; see also Freedman 2007). Especially in the face of environmental threats, local people in the West and elsewhere have built bridges across cultural and ethnic differences to protect landscapes that are significant to all: "beginning in the 1970s, members of Native and rural white communities unexpectedly came together to protect the same natural resources from a perceived outside threat" (Grossman 2005, 21). Even forty years ago, however, I would argue that such alliances between local people were not absolutely unexpected from a local perspective, as local communities had been living with each other for a long time (Braun 2013b). The success of such alliances, Grossman argues, can be measured beyond their immediate success against these threats: "The alliance can be successful if it sustains the relationships after its immediate environmental cause fades away. It can also be successful if it broadens relationships beyond environmental issues, to build more equal and stable political, economic, and cultural links between the communities" (2005, 24). I would like to take this one step further: we should not be surprised if communities, after coexisting for over a hundred years, find more commonalities between them than with other, nonlocal, communities, even if those are supposedly ethnically connected. Grossman is right when he writes that "Native/non-Native environmental alliances exemplify an interethnic movement constructed not around a common state citizenship but around a common 'place membership.' The symbolic frame of place membership is based on people living in a particular naturally or culturally significant place rather than within a particular political boundary" (2005, 25). This is undeniably true, but I would take it further. Living in a common place means to assign similar meanings to this location, and when people share meanings, they form a community—at least in relation to the domains in which they share meanings. As a general argument, theories of nationalism and ethnic genesis suggest that people who have built such symbolic frameworks around common places might develop a perception of social and political commonalities. What I would like to explore here is the possibility for a common political society, building on this, and whether it would be a positive development for American Indian nations and their sovereignty.

Sovereignty

Communities are sovereign when they control different aspects of their lives: cultural expression and meaning, ecological relations, political and economic decisions, their own histories, their organization, and so on. Sovereignty, more than simply a political state, is also a cultural, economic, and mental state of being.[1] All of these aspects are interrelated; that is, a politically subjected nation is also economically and culturally dependent, and one that is culturally or economically subjected is equally politically dependent. These situations influence how people relate to the natural, social, and spiritual worlds.

Sovereignty has been a point of contention for Indigenous peoples in North America for as long as political groups existed on the continent, just as it has been elsewhere. Societies merged, split, traded, built alliances, sought help, and engaged in many other relations that defined and redefined the nature of their sovereignties. The arrival of Europeans, who progressively attempted to impose their political and cultural powers over those nations that were already established on the continent, did not initially change these dynamics, albeit introducing new variables in the form of new values and institutions. Each European power brought with it different notions of how to establish and maintain relationships with other nations, and each Native nation had its own ideas and practices, as well. Here, I am interested not so much in revisiting the histories of interaction—some of cooperation, some of genocide—that developed from the contacts among all of these cultures. Rather, I want to provide an analysis of the problem of true sovereignty for American Indian nations in the United States.

Native nations are still "domestic dependent nations," as defined in the 1831 Supreme Court decision, *Cherokee Nation v. Georgia*, which means that they are inherently sovereign yet the federal government imposes its own sovereignty over theirs by assuming guardianship over its wards. In practice (if not in theory), ever since the last truly sovereign Native nations were forced to live on federally controlled reservations in the last decades of the nineteenth century, the situation of all American Indian societies is that of colonized nations. In a sense, one may contend that they are in part colonized by themselves, as they are also citizens of the United States. Exerting colonial and in general hegemonic power over others often puts them in such a double bind. Yet here I am interested in the relationship of American Indians as citizens of their own, separate nations.

To see American Indians as "citizens" of their own societies is obviously a viewpoint modeled on the concept of the liberal state. The idea of citizens, that is, interested members of a political unit, invested with categorical, not personal rights, is a hallmark of modernity, the relatively new idea—for Europeans, too—that legal and political rights should be depersonalized, independent of kinship relation, status, profession, or religion. Matthew Fletcher rightly points out that "American intervention into traditional indigenous communities had the effect of importing a form of the notion of the 'consent of the governed' into tribal governance. As a result, like people who are or can become American 'citizens,' individual Indians are or can become tribal 'citizens' or 'members'" (2007, 104–105; quotes in original). In other words, this historical intervention has shaped Native American contemporary practices of citizenship or membership. That historical fact is clear. What is less clear, however, is that a citizen and a member are not the same, and that there are consequences following from the categorization as a "tribal member" or a "tribal citizen."

As Simone Poliandri points out in the Introduction to this volume, some indigenous thinkers, like Alfred, have argued that Native government should rest on "traditional indigenous philosophies" (see also Lyons 2010, 170). The argumentations by Alfred and other "new traditionalists" (Lyons 2010, 132–146) build tightly controlled ethnic memberships that manage "links between legal legitimacy and cultural authenticity by suggesting that those who are not members are excluded naturally and inevitably because they are not authentic in the specific criteria of knowledge, practice, and identity on which specific criteria are based" (Barker 2011, 83). Such arguments might be antimodern if they also refute the concept of national sovereignty;[2] it is impossible to speak of nations in the modern sense, however, without allowing that concept to intervene in traditional forms of belonging. If American Indian nations are sovereign and want to be recognized as sovereign nations, they need to exercise sovereignty as nations, and nations have citizens. Thus, the question I ask and attempt to answer here is: how can existent sovereignty (based on membership) be enhanced to achieve and practice true sovereignty (based on citizenship)?

A truly sovereign nation needs to have enough cultural, political, and economic power to take independent decisions on critical issues, as well as to define its own path in this interrelated world. It decides on the state of emergency (Schmitt 1993, 13). Liberal systems, such as the so-called free markets, often replace political control (obvious public control) with economic control (hidden, indirect control over discourses that in turn dominate political choices). Economic control is not a less invasive, less consequential, or more benevolent form of power, however; ultimately, as a form of power, it too is political. The 1976 Report on Reservation and Resource Development and Protection by the American Indian Policy Review Committee affirmed this: "It is impossible to attain economic self-sufficiency and political self-determination in a system which perpetuates economic dependence" (2). This was a revolutionary statement, and as such was largely ignored in the discussions over reforms of American Indian policy. It showed clearly that regaining true political or economic sovereignty is impossible for American Indian nations within the present system. On a broader level, all aspects of Native sovereignty are made impossible to achieve. To achieve true sovereignty, and this is what makes the statement revolutionary, the system needs to be broken.

Projects to address self-sufficiency and self-determination on American Indian reservations have ultimately failed because they either cannot work outside the existing system or because they approach singular issues, such as economics, politics, or what passes for culture, as independent variables instead of as an interrelated whole. To regain sovereignty in the sense of empowering communities to define their own relationships with their social, natural, and spiritual environments, a holistic solution is needed, one that addresses the state of the nation as a whole: political control, a cultural (that is, symbolic) interpretation of the world, and economic self-sufficiency. Here, I focus mostly on political and economic factors, with the clear understanding that both politics and economics are cultural expressions: they cannot exist outside cultural meaning. While I assume that politics and economics are interrelated, thus using a Marxist perspective to approach the problem, such a perspective makes sense only when discussed within a cultural framework of holistic liberation (see Wuttunee 2004). This means that I am arguing, as I have done elsewhere (Braun 2008), for the centrality of culture as the foundation of any community development project. Poor communities have a poor likelihood of maintaining "cultural integrity," as Smith writes (2000, 15); they also have a poor likelihood of maintaining sovereignty. The poor, however, as Leonardo Boff writes, "are not simply those who do not have: they *do* have. They have culture, ability to work, to work together, to get organized, and to struggle. Only when the poor trust in their own potential, and when the poor opt for others who are poor, are conditions created for genuine liberation" (1997, 108; italics in original).

I start this chapter by laying out the problem in the broadest terms. I define the fundamental problem to be overcome as a system of interconnected economic, cultural, political, and geographic peripheries. This system of marginalization extends beyond Indian Country and renders rural people and places in general marginal, but it has its largest impact on rural Indian reservations. Economic marginality might be the most visible consequence, but poverty is connected to a devalorization of culture, history, and sovereignty. I then briefly provide a sketch of historical "solutions," attempts that focused on the integration of American Indians into the American mainstream. These attempts at erasing cultural, political, and economic sovereignty resulted in experiences of deeper alienation by Native communities and made the rebuilding of sovereign nations that much more difficult. Finally, I propose a potential alternative solution for the building of communities, the resurrection of sovereignty, and the improvement of community well-being. I emphasize potential: I see this proposal as the opening of a discourse, not as a definitive blueprint. However, open dialogue and the weighing of alternative ideas seem to me necessary parts of any creative solution to poverty, oppression, and marginalization, as well as critical strategies to challenge the existing economic-political systems.

The Problem: Land, Economics, and Sovereignty

Economic and political situations and interests vary greatly among Indigenous groups across North America and, specifically, within the United States. It is fair to say that all Native nations' sovereignty has been heavily affected by the alienation of lands. Land not only affects political territory and economic production, but also cultural interpretation, as it is a direct expression of the history of the nation. This is so for indigenous and nonindigenous societies (Thornton 2008, 7). After all, strip malls and exurbia also are an expression and a consequence of relations to land. However, there are currently, and there have always been, large differences between Native societies in their economic and political interests. On the one hand, some American Indian nations have created an economic and political base as capitalist controllers over wealth transactions that are not tied to land but take place in the collective imagination of what used to be called bourgeois parlors. These are, for example, those who have built thriving economies on on- and off-reservation tribal gaming operations. The top five percent of tribal casinos generate around forty percent of all revenues created by Native casino operations, and the top seventeen percent generate around seventy percent (National Indian Gaming Commission 2011). This economic wealth does not automatically translate into political or cultural sovereignty, but these nations are trying to achieve at least the latter to some degree (Lawlor 2006), and many have successfully converted economic influence into considerable political power, at least regionally. On the other hand, there are nations that are still directly dependent on the land for both sovereignty and economy, so that the historic and current alienation of land remains among the most pressing intellectual, cultural, political, and economical issues they are facing. In this, they are not too different from their non-Native neighbors; in fact, it is the need to compete over limited resources to amend the difficulties brought about by alienation that often leads to conflict between them. This need to compete is systemic and ingrained in the differences created by the state between so-called ethnic groups, which are also often themselves a creation of hegemonic power.

It is on the latter group of American Indian nations that I focus my analysis. In particular, I will focus on the northern plains—because I am most familiar with this region and because many of the issues addressed are most vividly present in this area. Most Indigenous nations in the northern plains do live on often quite large reservations; most are economically depressed; and most are affected by the consequences of historic allotment policies, which have created checkerboarded reservations and contributed to problems stemming from the fractionation of the remaining trust lands (see Ruppel 2008). Thus, while these nations control some land, consequences of historical policies render this control extremely problematic, as it is almost impossible to exercise true sovereignty over both territory and economic production or to translate this control, as it exists, into meaningful sovereignty.

The political and legal frameworks in place are both hindering and supporting Native sovereignty in this situation. Trust lands—those lands that are owned either by individual American Indian citizens or by their national governments but whose titles are held in trust for their owners by the federal government—serve as an example. Trust status prevents owners from exercising truly sovereign decisions over their land. Because owners do not hold titles, the land cannot be sold or put up as collateral for a loan without permission from the federal government. Still, trust lands are those lands, generally speaking, over which tribal governments exercise sovereignty, and it is the trust status that historically often ensured the survival of a national territory for American Indian nations. The federal government is, on the one hand, a colonial agency and, on the other hand, the guarantor of tribes' sovereign rights. It has diminished and is diminishing sovereignty, yet it has also upheld it. Rather than simply rejecting the existing relationships with the federal government, I agree with Stacy Leeds, who "encourages tribes to utilize the Anglo-American legal tools to the tribes' advantage in restoring the tribal land base" (2004, 828), and, I would argue, tribal sovereignty. Because Leeds limited the tribes' goal to restoring the land base, her analysis focused on property law. Yet to restore sovereignty, a nation needs more than territory, and so my approach looks for a broader solution.

The system that perpetuates economic and political dependence on the plains is based on industrial, capitalist agriculture and the idea that ownership and control are disconnected from personal and material relations. It was the concept of alienated ownership and control that "has subjected the country to the rule of the towns" (Marx and Engels 1906,

19). Alienated ownership has been at the core of increasing rural oppression for centuries. It has also been at the core of establishing divisions and competition between the oppressed so that the elites are allowed to expand their control unfettered. While in America it is often only the American Indian reservations that can be seen in this perspective and are characterized as "Third World" islands in one of the richest countries in the world, the political and economic dependency affects off-reservation, non-Native rural counties as well. This has become much clearer with the latest economic depression, which has demonstrated how one of the wealthiest countries in the world might at the same time be a part of what used to be called the Third World (Maharidge 2013). Although there are differences in social health indicators between Indian reservations and their rural neighbors on the plains, both Indians and their non-Native neighbors are subjected to the same systemic oppression (Brown and Swanson 2003; Davidson 1990; Duncan 1992; Edmondson 2003).

The differences between reservations and the neighboring counties stem, on the one hand, from the limitations to and protections from rampant capitalism that federal Indian policies entail. Tribal governments (which are supposed to be sovereign entities), American Indian societies (which are supposed to be culturally different), and Native national economies (which are supposed to operate differently from those of the states in which they are located) exist in an almost schizophrenic negotiation between the active encouragement to partake in American free market ideology and a paternalistic protectionism that prohibits the full participation in this economy. As briefly explained above, American Indian national territories have been diminished through allotment, but saved through trust land status, for example. On rural reservations, a growing number of landless people live in small areas of high population density and are largely prevented from finding jobs. Off reservation, the industrialization of rural agriculture has led to the economic success of the few, often absent, landowners and the forced outmigration or continued impoverishment of those who have lost their lands and share the often seasonal, underpaid jobs. In reservation communities, the difference between supposed cultural connection to the land and the reality of living in postindustrial environments without meaningful employment opportunities is magnified. Non-Native people do not consider their homes a national homeland, although their emotional attachment to the land cannot be underestimated, either. However, such an attachment to land is not highly valued by their national culture and society, except sometimes as a mythical ideal, an imagined repository of the nation's past. Reservation lands, on the other hand, represent American Indian nations' futures.

The economies of non-Indian communities do not represent national economies. Their shortfalls can be made up elsewhere; their population is, at least theoretically, easily integrated into other regional economies; their place within the national society is peripheral, not central. This, of course, contributes to their relative neglect. Such national neglect is amplified for rural areas where American Indians live. Reservations, which have been underdeveloped for at least a century now, are dependent on the surrounding towns for services, so that their national economies are constantly bleeding resources to the outside. Reservations are the country that is dependent on the country that is dependent on the towns—they are the periphery of the periphery. Mary Lawlor framed the situation as follows:

> Native America has come to live beside mainstream American modernity, feeling its effects, framed by its institutional and political structures, but rarely imbued with means to reproduce its wealth. Without this deeper inscription in the modern European American state, tribes continue to exist apart, sustaining a familiarity with the modern as well as certain means of addressing it; but the lack of hegemony has meant that difference itself has been ineluctably sustained. (2006, 27)

This description rings true for most Americans today, who are increasingly joining the ranks of those excluded from the opportunity to reproduce the wealth of "American modernity." It might actually be time to redefine the meaning of the term, to strip it of its association with wealth, well-being, and care-free life. However, this alienation from wealth, power, and health is still more true of "minority" populations in general and Plains Indians in specific.

Failed Solutions: Ethnification, De-nationalization, and De-territorialization

Historically, the attempted solution to the economic problems experienced by Plains Indians has been to integrate them into the "modern European American state." The United States, like any other modern liberal state, has not been ready to give up political, economic, or cultural control within the territory it claims for itself. The purported solution has been to integrate Native Americans into the American mainstream—to de-nationalize them as members of Indigenous nations, but at the same time re-nationalize them as Americans. The two most serious attempts at this were the allotment policies and the Termination policies, one in the context of industrial agriculture, the other in the context of the post-WWII growth in industrial manufacturing. On a larger scale, from the 1819 Civilization Fund Act to the Carlisle Indian Industrial School of the late nineteenth century to recent Supreme Court decisions on federal Indian policies, this strategy and the intent have stayed the same. Forced assimilation and "civilization" might not be the advocated goal, anymore, but American Indian nations and people are still expected to eventually fit into the political, cultural, social, and economic system constructed by the United States. In this sense, that system remains the model for "development," not simply a potential alternative. The solution sought is still cultural integration. The opposition to the existing system, on the other hand, is simply its mirror image if it simply advocates for cultural segregation.

These solutions, in part because they were and still are sought within "a system which perpetuates economic dependence" (American Indian Policy Review Committee 1976, 2), have not been of help to anybody except the existing elites, nonindigenous and indigenous. The status quo has therefore remained the same and has arguably been strengthened. The imagined process of creating a new American society out of many nations has always been hampered by the fact that the new society was never absolutely new, but modeled after one or two of these preexisting cultures, which thereby also acquired status and prestige as upper classes. This was true for policies of open assimilation; it remains true for this age of "diversity." "Others" have to imitate, acculturate, and assimilate, which means in practice that they assumed inferior positions in the political, cultural, and economic hierarchies (Bell and Hartmann 2007).

In addition to these processes undergone and undertaken by "minorities," however, the de-nationalization of American Indians still goes hand in hand with their literal—not only their metaphorical—de-territorialization. This was necessary because Indigenous people were integrated into the American state not as individuals from a specific society, but collectively, with their societies intact. A complete integration thus always depended on the breaking apart of these societies and their territories. The social, economic, and political individualization of American Indians was not only a requisite for their integration into the capitalist culture, but also a requirement for the demise of their status as existing and competing nations. Restricting Native American nations' sovereignty has not been limited to the integration of American Indians into the American mainstream. The limitation of legal sovereignty at the federal level, perhaps because it was never completed, has been accompanied by a strategy of ethnification. American Indians have been made to appear as simply another "ethnic group." As an ethnic group, they are not citizens of nations, but simply another colorful mosaic stone in the famed American diversity. Their legal diversity can thus be ignored while, at the same time, their cultural diversity can be celebrated after having been reduced to harmless elements like food, dance, and music. Once this is accomplished, their claims on their legal rights can be portrayed as the behavior of an ethnicity that unfairly tries to gain a leg up on the majority of hardworking Americans of other ethnicities. Creating and sustaining ethnic conflicts rests on confusing cultural, ethnic, and political identities. This has a long history in American Indian affairs, where certain "American" values, such as individualism, thriftiness, rationality, and Christianity, were used in the late eighteenth and early nineteenth centuries to create divisions between so-called full-bloods and mixed-bloods (Biolsi 1995).

More recent events suggest that this strategy is still actively pursued in and beyond American Indian affairs. The State of Arizona, for example, passed HB 2281 in 2010, which prohibits the teaching of courses that, among other things, "promote resentment toward a race or class of people," that "are designed primarily for pupils of a particular ethnic group," and that "advocate ethnic solidarity instead of the treatment of pupils as individuals." However, the law explicitly allows "the grouping of pupils according to academic performance, including capability in the English language, that may result in a disparate impact by ethnicity." In practice, then, because English proficiency, even outside of English classes, is defined as part of a student's academic performance, the law allows ethnic segregation. However, it threatens to shut down courses that "advocate ethnic solidarity." Ethnic solidarity is fine as long as it is supporting those who supposedly have the right values, namely those who speak English and who value individualism. The law supports a two-tiered education system based on language, and it also makes sure that cultural belonging and individualism are put in opposition to each other. Furthermore, it implies that ethnic solidarity—or perhaps cultural knowledge—is equated with political sedition. The fact that this last point, although politically adept, is irrational should be obvious to anybody who thinks about culture in a nonfundamentalist way. As Terry Eagleton has pointed out, "culture is not inherently political at all" (2000, 122). Culture, he contended, "become[s] political only when [it is] caught up in a process of domination and resistance—when these otherwise innocuous matters are turned for one reason or another into terrains of struggle" (122–123). Thus, culture is political when it is politicized. Speaking Spanish is not a political issue unless it is made one. Including Mexican fighters at the Alamo or ignoring them and only remembering Davy Crockett and Jim Bowie, as in recent proposals for the Texas curriculum, or implying that teaching Ethnic Studies is teaching sedition, creates ethnic politics because it makes culture into a political issue. It creates ethnic differences and takes them to mirror political loyalties.

Another strategy of ethnification is based on the opposite approach. Instead of ascribing political importance to essentialized cultural values—that is, to declare certain constructed ethnicities non-American—it disputes that legal rights are held by certain special groups, recognizing everybody simply as American. This strategy of (de)ethnification can be used to dispute the inherent sovereignty and special legal status of American Indians. For example, it led the Chief Justice of the Supreme Court of the United States to pretend to not understand the fundamental difference between Italian ethnicity and inherently sovereign American Indian political identity and its legal (and sovereign) implications; or, if he did understand the difference as he assured, then completely ignoring it. The following exchange between Chief Justice Roberts and Mr. Frederick, the legal representative of the Respondents, which appears in the transcript of Plains Commerce Bank v. Long Family Land and Cattle, Inc., et al. (2008, 32–35), illustrates this point.

> CHIEF JUSTICE ROBERTS: One of the points you mentioned earlier is that this is an Indian corporation, and that's a concept I don't understand. If Justices Scalia and Alito form a corporation, is that an Italian corporation? (Laughter.)
>
> MR. FREDERICK: I would like to beg the indulgence of the Court in not answering that question specifically. (Laughter.) My point . . .
>
> JUSTICE SCALIA: And do we get special loan guarantees? (Laughter.)
>
> CHIEF JUSTICE ROBERTS: How would a normal—I guess a non-Indian or non-Italian or non-Irish—corporation dealing

with the Long Family Land and Cattle Company know that it was an Indian corporation . . .

MR. FREDERICK: Well, I . . .

CHIEF JUSTICE ROBERTS: . . . putting apart the particulars in this case?

MR. FREDERICK: The difference here, Mr. Chief Justice, is that the bank required BIA loan guarantees as a condition of making the loans.

CHIEF JUSTICE ROBERTS: I'm asking you about: In a general case, let's say they don't require BIA loan guarantees. They require, just as in this case, collateral.

MR. FREDERICK: They did not. They required more, and that's the important point. The facts actually matter.

CHIEF JUSTICE ROBERTS: Well, I am sure the facts here matter. I have a hypothetical question.

This almost poetic exchange shows clearly how American Indians are being constructed as simply another ethnic group. They are here repeatedly compared to other ethnicities, namely Italian and Irish, which are portrayed as not "normal." Then, the facts that would prove their sovereign status are ignored in favor of a hypothetical case. Without context, being American Indian seems to mean the same as being Irish(-American), namely a cultural affiliation, when the point of the matter is exactly that American Indian status has legal implications. Here, the cultural, legal, and political meanings of being Indian are confused, and end up being presented as a codified ethnic affiliation not different from those of other minorities. In this way, the legal status of American Indian sovereign nations can be ignored.

Such ethnification can also be used to further so-called "ethnic conflict" by inducing ignorance of legal frameworks and history. As V.P. Gagnon pointed out in the context of Yugoslavia, "ethnic conflict" is often the consequence of elites trying to conserve their status by creating competition between groups. "The key in politics," Gagnon said, "is to make certain identities more relevant than others, and others irrelevant to politics; and to impute very particular meanings to the relevant ones, meanings that seem to lead 'naturally' to particular policies or outcomes" (2004, 26; quotes in original). On the Plains, those in power in the current system, which relies on the primacy of ethnic distinctions—including Indigenous elites and, to a degree, ourselves in academia—have a vested interest in making "rural" identities irrelevant and instead making "white" and "Indian" identities relevant; in other words, we select certain constructed ethnic boundaries over others, although the community experiences might not do so (Braun 2013a). If these ethnic identities are ascribed meanings that transcend all others, then shared economic, political, environmental, and social interests can be made to disappear. The resulting competition over limited resources will further undermine the visibility and voice of cross-ethnic interests that might prove unsettling to the status quo.

The proposal to reverse national policies and hegemonies is not new. The Alcatraz Declaration, issued during the occupation of Alcatraz Island by Indians of All Tribes from 1969 to 1971, imagined a reversal of fortunes and policies that has stricken many people as ironic. I propose that to liberate Native peoples, we need to get beyond irony and beyond a simple reversion. The image of a Bureau of Caucasian Affairs is ironic in part because we do not accept its possible actualization. For American Indians to gain sovereignty, the possibility of Native nations taking actions as sovereign governments—action that affects and impacts all people within their territories, not only a specific ethnic group—has to become real. A Bureau of Caucasian Affairs would simply reverse the policies. The creation of non-Indians living under the powers of tribal governments as colonized peoples might be tempting as poetically just, yet a simple reversal of oppression would not solve the problem.

A Real Solution: Achieving Sovereignty

All elites are profiting from the existing system, which is why it is being perpetuated. Some American Indian elites—tribal politicians, influential ethno-political leaders, and cultural representatives, for example—are profiting, too: internally by thriving on politics of identity, and externally by preserving ethnic status. However, the persistence of this system is at the same time of great disadvantage to Native communities, as the continued social disparities to their neighboring communities show. The same system that creates political opportunities through ethnic difference uses that same ethnic difference to sustain economic competition that leads to hardened ethnic conflict—jealousy over seemingly unfounded favoritism, sustained racism, and infighting over limited resources. If rural Indian reservations on the plains are to achieve sovereignty and economic well-being, this status quo must be changed. Paradoxically, this can only happen through acts of sovereignty, Native Acts (Barker 2011). In fact, for American Indians to regain sovereignty, changing the system needs to be an extension of American Indian sovereignty. "To be genuine, liberation must not only remain comprehensive in scope," wrote Leonardo Boff, "but it must also and primarily be achieved by the poor themselves" (1997, 108). The problem is, of course, that while American Indian nations are inherently sovereign, in what former Supreme Court Justice John Marshall called the "actual state of things" (*Worcester v. Georgia* 1832) their sovereignty has become more and more limited through consecutive treaties, acts of Congress, and in recent years, the increasingly narrow interpretation of federal Indian law by the Supreme Court. Changing the system thus requires finding the niche in which Indigenous nations can exert enough sovereignty in ways that will change the system in their favor. I do not see how unilaterally rescinding from treaties, for example, would be in their favor, as without treaties the United States could simply declare the Native nations nonexistent and rescind even their theoretical sovereignty.

The one area in which federal courts have consistently argued that American Indian nations retain almost complete sovereignty is the decision over who is and who is not a citizen of a Native nation. As the Supreme Court ruled in *Santa Clara Pueblo v. Martinez* (1978), and as has been reiterated since, for example, by the United States Court of Appeals, Ninth Circuit in *Lewis v. Norton* (2005), this decision belongs to a Native nation alone. Therefore, American Indian nations can impose their own restrictions on citizenship. As the Tenth Circuit Court of Appeals has stated unequivocally in *Ordinance 59 Association v. Babbitt* (1998), "tribes, not the federal government, retain authority to determine tribal membership." Apart from these rulings, the Ninth Circuit Court of Appeals has decided a series of court cases over what constitutes "Indian status." In *US v. Bruce* (2005), the court stated that Indian status relies on both "the degree of Indian blood; and tribal or government recognition as an Indian." However, the court also cautioned that while "[t]he first prong requires ancestry living in America before the European arrived . . . this fact is obviously rarely provable as such." The second prong "probes whether the Native American has a sufficient non-racial link to a formerly [*sic!*] sovereign people"; tribal enrollment is of primary importance here.

In *US v. Maggi and Mann* (2010), the court again stated that Indian status is based on both "the presence of some Indian blood indicating tribal ancestry; and tribal or government recognition as an Indian." The court explicitly did "not decide the novel question whether [somebody's] blood degree is adequate." Instead, it decided that Maggi and Mann, despite having Indian blood, were not enrolled members of a federally recognized tribe, and therefore were not Indian.

What these cases show is that, theoretically, both ancestry and citizenship are considered in determining official Indian identity, but because in practice ancestry is impossible to prove, the emphasis in determining Indian status lies greatly on citizenship in a federally recognized tribe. Once a person is recognized as a citizen of a tribe by that community, that person has, for all intents and purposes, status as an Indian, and his or her biological ancestry cannot be challenged in practice. As Fletcher (2008) demonstrates, the understanding of the status of American Indian nations by the federal government is, and has always been, based on political, not racial categorizations (although in practice, the racial categorization is pervasive) (Fletcher 2012–2013). Joseph Kalt has written that "one of the most fundamental acts of sovereignty is each Native nation, itself, coming to grips with the question [of citizenship criteria]. . . . The pressing challenge for Native nations is to push the boundaries of sovereignty by devising criteria of their own" (2007, 85). Determining who is and who is not a member of a community, a citizen of a nation, is indeed perhaps the most fundamental expression of sovereignty; this has been rightly recognized by the American courts in the decisions mentioned. In the American Indian case, this decision—in part because it is potentially and actually tied to land ownership and land status, and therefore to the territorial expression and enactment of sovereignty—is also a way to break the system of dependency.

Citizenship in a Native nation is tied to land because it involves the possibility that the federal government assumes responsibilities for land as trust land, and that land is under the sovereign control of the Native national government. Although federal agencies and courts have been trying to weaken the legal status of trust lands, the legal principles of trust lands stand just as much as tribes have sovereignty in deciding their citizenship criteria. Tribal sovereignty is connected to trust lands because Native nations have sovereignty over Indian lands, and trust land is unquestionably Indian land. Thus, as tribes expand or lose trust lands, their sovereignty expands or contracts as a consequence. With sovereignty, tribes also increase or reduce their economic self-sufficiency because they, as sovereign nations, can levy taxes on lands in their sovereign domain.

I propose that a way to fight the perception that American Indians are an ethnic group, to re-expand their land base, and to exert sovereignty in a meaningful way, is that Indigenous nations assimilate Americans into their own sovereign entities by changing the basis of membership criteria from ethnicity to citizenship. As Matthew Fletcher argues,

> Indian tribes must evolve into Indian nations. I mean "nation" to mean a legal entity with membership criteria at least somewhat broader than the purely race and ancestry based rules now in place. In other words, I would include at least some non-Indians in the mass of tribal people. It's not such a foreign concept to Indian communities, as that is how it was done historically, and it could be done carefully to preserve the best aspects of tribalism, and therefore Indian culture. (2012–2013, 12)[3]

The young Maori man who walked with Daniel Rosenblatt (2005, 111) was on to something when he said, "Maybe, after a while, if people keep marrying each other, then everyone in New Zealand will have some Maori blood, and that's when we'll have Maori sovereignty." The integration of Americans into American Indian nations would challenge the hegemonic view that only the opposite is possible and has the potential to break the system. This is, as McDougall wrote, a vision "of a kind of sovereignty based not on the right to exclude foreign others but on the right to include them" (2005, 105). I doubt that this vision is "distinctly Pacific," however—it is simply the application of citizenship. While assimilation policies rested on the need to erase ethnicity, termination policies—at least theoretically, if they could be seen as distinct from assimilation— rested exactly on this kind of sovereignty, and so do any citizenship ceremonies. For American Indian nations to adopt this kind of sovereignty, then, would mark them as a liberal state among other liberal states and simultaneously unmark them as an ethnic group. Reversing termination policies into their opposite, American Indian nations could define parts of the state out of existence in some regions. Their territories could be consolidated in a meaningful way, while competing political organizations, such as counties, would be rendered meaningless.

As is the case in all liberal states, citizenship criteria would of course have to include knowledge of and loyalty to the national laws and history. Clearly, the nation will be and remain American Indian. Previously nonenrolled individuals who become citizens of the nation would legally become Indians in the act of acquiring citizenship, just like people who gain American citizenship become Americans. Giving local communities the power to confer citizenship will protect the nation against "wannabes" and ensure that it can build into a cohesive whole. The scope of considerations about tribal membership, wrote Kalt, "mirrors those found in citizenship standards and procedures of nations such as the United States, where the granting of citizenship commonly entails issues of where and to whom one was born, demonstrating potential for positive economic contribution, learning the basics of national history, pledging loyalty, and residency" (2007, 85). Of primary importance, I would argue, are the last four criteria. American Indian nations might want to offer citizenship first to those local people who already live on reservation lands, are integrated into the tribal economy, and are at least familiar with the nation's cultural, social, and political issues. In this way, Native nations could expand their sovereignty, enhance their economic self-sufficiency, and create a larger political interest group to counter outside interests. Imagining a community, a group, a nation in a style that includes those who agree with certain fundamental rules and share a common economic and political interest toward the outside is also the traditional way of imagining communities by most Indigenous peoples in North America, where kinship relations were not merely tied to biology. A community, and ultimately a nation, consists of those who take an interest in it and actively participate in it for the good of the community.

Building New Communities

As Matthew Fletcher has written, the acceptance of citizenship criteria instead of ethnic membership "may not be palatable for a host of reasons. First, the federal government, from Congress to the executive branch to the federal judiciary, might not be ready for such a radical change in how the United States deals with Indian nations. Second, Indian nations might not be ready for this change, either" (2011, 324). Despite the fact that many American Indian nations do accept ethnically non-Indians as members (Fletcher 2011, 324–325; 2012–2013, 14), the currently popularly accepted position on Native identity is definitely that in order to be an enrolled member of a tribe, one needs to be ethnically Native.[4] It is often claimed that Indigenous people face the threat of a dual extinction: blood quantum rules, on one hand, and the appropriation of their identity by people without Indigenous ancestry, on the other. In order to protect against the second, many people accept the first. Some—and ironically the federal government, as well as many of those who see blood quantum rules as a tool of genocide—might object to the proposal of building Native nations based on true citizenship, rather than ethnicity, on the grounds that it opens the doors to citizens without ancestral ties.

Although this is true, it only matters if we assume that ancestry in some way determines culture and culture in some way determines political loyalty. "Native American" is officially already a legal, not a racial or cultural category. Thus, expanding its reach thus would not fundamentally alter its nature. The fear of somewhat diluting a national identity by allowing others to join can be put at rest by clearing up two key points. First, as mentioned above, the community of the nation always restricts citizenship according to some criteria and retains the power to approve or disapprove the inclusion of new members. Second, no community is "pure" or homogeneous in terms of culture or ancestry. As Benedict Anderson has explained, "all communities larger than primordial villages of face-to-face contact (and perhaps even these) are imagined. Communities are to be distinguished, not by their falsity/genuineness, but by the style in which they are imagined" (1991, 6). Re-imagining community and rendering meaningless ethnic conflicts used to keep elites in power and others in economic and political dependency would contribute to the empowerment of those currently oppressed (see also Barker 2011).

Oppression and exclusion of Indigenous groups, as Manuhuia Barcham has pointed out in the Maori context, is based on the "inability of current political and judicial frameworks to recognize the legitimacy of difference not predicated upon the maintenance of a prior identity" (2000, 138). In other words, cultures change, and a continued imagination of cultures as they were a hundred years or longer ago is to delegitimize societies. Eva Marie Garroutte wrote that Elizabeth "Cook-Lynn's analysis suggests that the embrace of a biological (or any other) definition of identity over whatever legal definitions a tribe elects to apply is an insult to tribal sovereignty" (2003, 57; parentheses in original). Thus, the expansion of tribal sovereignty through legal citizenship rather than biological ancestry would not only increase the political and economic reach of tribal nations, but also mark their true nature as inherently sovereign entities.

Citizenship as the formal recognition of a nationality is not tied to ethnic criteria, although the actual political situation in many countries creates second class citizens. Those who do confer all or some privileges of citizenship only to individuals of a particular ethnicity are criticized by the international community. The rule is that anybody can become a citizen of a state. The potential citizen may need to fulfill certain requirements of political assimilation and will need to be loyal to the laws and constitution of the state; yet in principle the modern, liberal state does not operate on ethnic difference. In fact, it overrides ethnic diversity through citizenship, although one might not think so when fundamentalists affirm that no religion other than Christianity or no language other than English should exist in a given state. This, however, is the result of the confusion between ethnicity and nationality stemming from the double meaning of "nation" in the "nation-state." It is the insistence on ancestry—on kinship as a biological instead of a social relation—as a criterion for citizenship as well as for cultural belonging that creates oppressive and homogenizing nation-states.

When discussing identity politics in Africa, Patrick Chabal wrote that the problem of identity divisions "is twofold. First, there is disagreement about who is the original native in the region. Criteria based on chronological history clash with those of control and labour—that is, groups that may have come later but that have invested and transformed the area. Second, the dominant local group expects its party to prevail in the game of representation" (2009, 61). This statement, which can be easily applied to North America, illustrates how the questions of asserting residential primacy and achieving ethnic dominance are related. Both need to be overcome in order to achieve success in community building, but paradoxically, they can only be overcome by building community. The introduction of Native citizenship and its extension to qualified reservation residents could partially overcome these two problems. In fact, the political importance of being "the original native" exists mainly because it is translated into an argument over scarce resources: money, land, political voice, interest, and sympathy. Competition over resources lends itself to and furthers ethnic politics; by supporting ethnic differences, the elites who control and allocate the resources do not have to act responsible but can simply point to, imply, or blame the scapegoat of the Other. The resulting competition creates resource envy across ethnic lines and often manifests itself in racism. Eliminating parts of these hard ethnic boundaries would force the partial abandonment of such arguments. An emphasis on citizenship instead of ethnicity is but a small part in eliminating how people think about each other, but it creates an official signal. At least in local communities, it might result in the perception of a fairer distribution of resources and, as a consequence, dissipate resource envy.

Citizenship in Native nations is not a magic wand, and simply offering citizenship in Native nations does not by itself build communities. In fact, there are no magic wands in community building. This process would take years and would have to be an ongoing effort, as Oliver-Smith makes clear. He writes,

> The kind of community that sustains individual and group life, never perfectly, is not a finely tuned mechanism or a well-balanced organism, but rather a complex, interactive, ingoing process composed of innumerable variables subject to the conscious and unconscious motives of its members. The idea that such a process could be the outcome of planning is ambitious, to say the least. (2005, 56)

However, breaking the official and officious statements about and practices of ethnic identity politics would remove one artificial, political obstacle that stands in the way of successful social and economic communities. The elimination of the rhetoric of ethnic politics helps to build common communities, which rely on the realization and acknowledgment of lived commonalities across limited and constructed ethnic boundaries, and the ability and willingness to compromise. Existing, practical relationships need to be strengthened through symbolic relations, and new relationships need to be built throughout and across communities before these merge into new tribal national communities. These symbolic relationships could also serve the newly formed tribal national communities in practical ways. For instance, an inclusive national service for youth, engaging young people in work in range improvements, environmental services, health care settings, community restoration, and communal gardening would bring different people from the new national community together and, at the same time, could be used to train them in applicable skills, build community projects, install pride in communities, and mark the sovereignty of the nation to the outside and inside.

Overcoming the Obstacles of Ethnified Identity and Culture

Ethnic identity, which embodies the politicization of culture, originates out of a struggle for survival that is very real for the people involved. If some people fear that their ethnic identities would be compromised, they cannot be ignored, overruled, or ridiculed. But these fears can and should be addressed, in part because ethnic markers, especially when reacting to external expectations, too often are likely to hurt communities and misrepresent realities. "The paradoxical imperative," Mikael Kurkiala wrote, "is this: In order to resist encompassment the Oglala must unite under the very label by which they are encompassed in the dominant structure, and they must perpetuate that external definition of themselves by evoking traditional concepts of grouphood" (1997, 233). The discourse "of Native legal status and rights in U.S. politics," writes Joanne Barker, "has made Native rights contingent on a particular kind of Native: a Native in or of an authentic culture and identity. . . . authentic only if absent of Christianity and science, recognizable only if possessing identities and truths beyond colonial and imperial history and politics" (2011, 223). To paraphrase Niezen, once that happens, culture "is expressed in the form of the publicly exhibited artefact" (2009, 47) and authenticity is measured by "a sanitized Paleolithic ideal" (87). These expectations that go to the heart of being will never allow for true liberation and sovereignty. It needs to be challenged by showing that encompassing others in one's nation does not mean that one's culture or society will be encompassed in return. Strict identity boundaries can be relaxed and redefined once the threat to personal, cultural, or political survival is weakened and the agency and confidence to encompass others (without the fear of being the victim of encompassment) is regained.

In terms of ethnic identity, there seem to exist different threat levels for different groups within American Indian societies, and presumably all societies, depending on how secure people feel in their cultural identity (Braun 2008, 76–80). This reflects the general hypothesis that the more secure people are in their cultural identity, the less difficulty they have to accept people with other cultural identities as neighbors, immigrants, or co-citizens. Kurkiala wrote,

> Those individuals who at a later stage in their lives try to 'become' Indian, of necessity approach that identity as an object, a desired state, which they wish to appropriate and embody. Objectification, then, is a symptom of distance and discontinuity. Those individuals who are socialized in a Lakota setting, such as rural Pine Ridge, to a larger extent take their identities for granted and are less inclined to manifest it [sic] either verbally or symbolically. . . . It seems as if those on Pine Ridge who feel that their Lakota culture is most threatened are the ones most likely to hold the most exclusive interpretations of lakotaness. They are the ones most preoccupied with drawing boundaries around the 'purity' of Lakota identity and tradition

and with defending those boundaries from 'outsiders.' (1997, 231–232; quotes in original)

Theresa DeLeane O'Nell (1996, 67, 151) and Loretta Fowler (1987, 141–183) support the idea that insecurity in one's own cultural identity leads to both the drawing of rigid ethnic boundaries and a strict definition of culture. The idea that the ethnification of identity is not only diverging from historic ways of assigning and assuming identity, but also weakening identity overall, might be paradoxical at first. But it makes sense that people who grow up living a culture have fewer needs to patrol the expressive markers of ethnic identity. They are more secure in their culture and do not have to define themselves by living according to or defining themselves by ethnic markers. It is no coincidence that in Jackie Grey's chapter in this volume, it is Anne—rooted in the community, its history, and its (encompassing) culture, and not threatened by the settlement—who argues that the Aquinnah Wampanoags will continue its leadership in the larger community as an integral culture. I would argue that it is not just the "connection to a Wampanoag past," however, that mediated her fear, but fundamentally the connection to a lived Wampanoag present that gave her confidence that there would be a Wampanoag future, whether that included nontribal residents in the community or not.

Many people in communities on reservations already have and live ties across these boundaries; they, like their non-Indian neighbors, are ranchers, members of the same social clubs, dependent on the same climatic conditions and commodity prices, members of the same congregations, and neighbors in the same communities. They still live their own cultures (see Braun 2008, 85–89), but they live them in daily interactions with their neighbors, with whom they share certain values and experiences. It is important to remember that the correlation between ethnic identity and national group is a relatively new one for Native societies, and one that has arguably been imposed on American Indian groups by the dominant society (Barker 2011; Biolsi 1995). In any case, notions about community identity and the criteria that forge such identities can and do change (DeMallie 2009).

If ethnic objectification is related to cultural distance, it makes sense that among those who feel most threatened in their cultural identity are often those who have become a "success story" as measured by the values of the dominant society, although it bears emphasis that this does not imply the inverse. It is entirely possible to be successful while staying grounded and secure in one's culture. If people who for various reasons have experienced the loss of their cultural identity (re-)appropriate ethnic identity, however, those who are in positions to set the discourse about cultural identity probably do so, too. Exclusionary statements about ethnic relations and boundaries do not necessarily reflect the ideas and practices of those who live their culture in communities that often see and seek much cooperation across such constructed ethnic boundaries. A contemporary example of this is provided by the Thunder Valley Community Development Corporation on Pine Ridge, which is trying to build a Lakota community, but sees that Lakota culture not as defined by closed ethnic boundaries. In an interview with Stephanie Woodard (2011), Brett Lee Shelton had the following to say: "Lakota culture is inclusive. The more this project reaches out, the more it honors that. There's room for everyone, including non-Indians living on the reservation. The more, the better."

The lived practices of community members often contradict official notions of culture as ethnicity. Steven Hoelscher wrote,

> Official culture originates in the concerns of cultural leaders and authorities at all levels of society and promotes an interpretation of the past that reduces the threat of competing interests. Official culture tends toward the dogmatic as it presents an ideal or abstract version of public memory uncluttered by complex or ambiguous terms. Vernacular culture, conversely, 'represents an array of specialized interests that are grounded in parts of the whole.' First-hand experience in small-scale communities forms the basis for the defenders of this culture which, by its very existence, threatens the sacred and eternal character of official expressions. (1998, 22; quotes in original)

As such, the official and officious discourses about identity and boundaries do not necessarily reflect the lived reality in local communities, where other boundaries might be emphasized. When local communities hold the power to determine who should and who should not be a part of their community—that is, when they hold the sovereign power to confer citizenship regardless of (officious) ethnicity—they truly enact sovereignty. Social and political cooperation and social and political community are not dependent on cultural (ethnic) unity or sameness, and neither does citizenship imply such cultural unity. This is true in all communities, Native ones included. Every community shows different interpretations of culture, and, as Kurkiala has written, "Culture, then, consists not of shared meanings, but, paraphrasing the title of Fowler's book, of shared symbols and contested meanings" (1987, 231). Current debates in American Indian communities, about tribal sovereignty, economic development, the importance of aspects of traditional culture, and a host of other issues, as well as similar discussions about the right way into the future in every society clearly demonstrate this.

Conclusions

As Frank Sejersen shows in the context of Greenland, creating a space in which sovereignty does "not have to be worked out in relation to land use and occupancy generates totally different preconditions for nation building" because it avoids finding oneself "caught in a geographical, political and ethnic jigsaw puzzle" (2004, 35). Simply the act of eliminating the need to consult a map to read the landscape in all daily interactions would make life much more tolerable and economically efficient. The gains for all involved are difficult to define because, as the term already shows, we are constantly looking for increases in value when what might truly count for the development of a community is rather the symbolic expression of kinship and solidarity, which transcends economic value but ultimately creates it.

American society is dominated by the hegemonic capitalistic discourse that demands economic incentives for actions. So, the question remains: why should both Indians and non-Indians take an approach that, at least in the short term, favors community building over economic and political gains? What incentive is there, considering also that states would certainly appeal further land-into-trust processes and oppose the increase of tribal political and economic power, given that both economics and politics are seen as zero-sum games? Increasing tribal membership entails that Native nations could exert more political power within their states, so that state politicians would have to heed the interests of residents of tribal rural areas. In the current system, in which external reservation boundaries are almost meaningless, county and tribal governments face the need to exhaust their resources to provide services to exclaves in each other's territory. Available economic resources and limited political power are fiercely competed over. Government services are basically doubled. Counties, for instance, face the difficulty of providing services, such as road upkeep, to areas in which only a few of their own taxpayers live.

The expansion of tribal sovereignty through the integration of new citizens would allow for a focused political and economic effort for the well-being of all constituents. It would integrate bordering towns into the tribal national economies, thereby stopping the bleeding of resources to an outside economy and increasing self-sufficiency. Not the least, it would also deal with the feeling of disenfranchisement that many Indian and non-Indian nontribal members living on reservations carry. Integrating these residents, who already share personal, cultural, social, and economic ties with tribal members, as fully recognized citizens with all rights and obligations would build stronger, more efficient communities, economies, and, because of increased, yet more relaxed and secure cultural exchanges, cultures. Indigenous nations could rely on large tax bases; nothing would change in their status as Indigenous nations with whom the federal government has treaties, and for whom it has taken responsibilities that it is obliged to fulfill. Should the government no longer want to fulfill these responsibilities, it would have to give up its stance of being a guardian for these wards and release them into full sovereignty.

In no way would these enlarged nations be uniform or avoid internal struggles over the meanings of values and symbols. However, no society is homogenous.[5] Fault lines of internal debate would not be congruent with ancestry, as they are not now and have never been. A tribalization in the sense of integration of the rural communities within, and perhaps even outside current reservation boundaries into the Native political and economic sphere of action would increase economic self-sufficiency, cooperation, and political power to be projected and used toward further enhancements of sovereignty. Perhaps more importantly, tribes would take hold of the political discourse and shape it, rather than being defined by it. The successful change from ethnic membership to national citizenship would pave the way for the four "Rs" of community development: reconciliation, redistribution, relocation, and relationships (Kemper and Adkins 2005, 93–94). By officially acknowledging and valuing relationships not limited by ethnicity throughout the community, all people within the community would ideally relocate (at least metaphorically) as a new community is being built. Putting themselves into new (although perhaps, at first, threatening) places, people could then reconcile and through that process attempt to redistribute economic, political, and social resources. In practice, many communities are already engaging in relationships across ethnic boundaries, and, as alliances between "cowboys and Indians" remind us, have done so for many years.

American Indian communities, because of their historical notions of community, are in a good position to lead the way in changing the discourse of diversity coexisting with a pervading fear of Otherness to one of political, social, and cultural equality. This is not to say that cultural differences should be erased—absolutely not. However, a nation can withstand the challenges of containing cultural differences. In fact, one might argue, many American Indian nations today already are dealing rather well with internal cultural differences. I have no doubts that states, tribes, and individuals would fight hard to prevent this expansion of Native national sovereignty. However, federal courts themselves have cleared the way. Tribes can set citizenship criteria with sovereign freedom, and once a person is accepted as a citizen, ancestral biology is impossible to disprove and becomes, for all practical purposes, irrelevant. Given the actual realities of ethnic politics, all of this remains, of course, simply a provocation for further thought and to a degree a theoretical exercise in problem solving. I do think, however, that we should not refrain from reimagining realities outside of the boxes we are delivered by hegemonic forces and practices.

Notes

1. Lyons (2010, 184) quotes a translation of Carl Schmitt: "Sovereign is he who decides on the exception." Schmitt (1993, 21) does think that one should depart from the exception to study the general or normal. That quote, however, is much stronger. Schmitt writes, "Souverän ist, wer über den Ausnahmezustand entscheidet"—*sovereign is he who decides on the state of emergency* (1993, 13).

2. Barker reminds us of the Indian Citizenship Act of 1924. She writes that the act "made explicit that citizenship did not negate tribal membership: 'That the granting of citizenship shall not in any manner impair or affect the right of any Indian to tribal or other property'" (2011, 93). Here, however, the difference between membership and citizenship becomes clear: membership is defined through property ownership. No state defines citizenship in that way.

3. As I am revising this text, I have found that Matthew Fletcher proposed the exact same thing (Fletcher 2011, 2012–2013), although from a different perspective. I wrote this text originally in 2010, before I saw Fletcher's papers. Matthew Fletcher is somebody I admire greatly, and we shared some ideas while he was at the University of North Dakota. The fact that both of us came up with this argument is not attributable to diffusion, but to independent invention, or perhaps shared inspiration. It might be a sign that there is something to the idea.

4. An added layer of complexity is raised by instances in which Native nations incorporate other Native nations. Barker's account of the Cherokee inclusion of the Delaware nation comes to mind. She quotes then Cherokee Nation Principal Chief Chad Smith: "The Cherokee Nation never has and never will make an effort to terminate the Delaware language, culture and identity. By law, the Cherokee Nation recognizes these citizens as Delawares, though citizens of the Cherokee Nation" (Smith in Barker 2011, 67). This is exactly the distinction of political and cultural belongings discussed here.

5. When I grew up, Switzerland, culturally and linguistically divided into many small, local groups, and fractured by uncommon histories and socioeconomic inequality between groups, defined itself as a nation of will (*Willensnation*), meaning that it could only exist as long as people have the will to live together (and consequently take the actions required to do so—that is, listen to and respect each other, etc.). That metaphor still seems very important to me; it is when people forget it and take the political unity of any state for granted that they start dominating each other. Historically, Plains Indians were governed by a similar tenet: those who disagreed with decisions would leave the group. It is a rather effective way to remind people that if they want to preserve the group, they have to pay attention to everybody.

References

Anderson, Benedict. 1991. *Imagined Communities. Reflections on the Origin and Spread of Nationalism*. Verso: London.

American Indian Policy Review Committee. 1976. *Report on Reservation and Resource Development and Protection*. Final Report to the American Indian Policy Review Commission. Washington, D.C.: Government Printing Office.

Barcham, Manuhuia. 2000. (De)Constructing the Politics of Indigeneity. In *Political Theory and the Rights of Indigenous Peoples,* edited by Duncan Ivison, Paul Patton, and Will Sanders, pp. 137–151. Cambridge: Cambridge University Press.

Barker, Joanne. 2011. *Native Acts. Law, Recognition, and Cultural Authenticity.* Durham, NC: Duke University Press.

Bell, Joyce M., and Douglas Hartmann. 2007. Diversity in Everyday Discourse: The Cultural Ambiguities and Consequences of 'Happy Talk.' *American Sociological Review* 72: 895–914.

Biolsi, Thomas. 1995. The Birth of the Reservation: Making the Modern Individual among the Lakota. *American Ethnologist* 22(1): 28–53.

Boff, Leonardo. 1997. *Cry of the Earth, Cry of the Poor.* Maryknoll, NY: Orbis Books.

Braun, Sebastian Felix. 2008. *Buffalo Inc. American Indians and Economic Development.* Norman: University of Oklahoma Press.

———. 2013a. Imagining Un-imagined Communities. The Politics of Indigenous Nationalism. In *Tribal Worlds. Critical Studies in American Indian Nation*

Building, edited by Brian Hosmer and Larry Nesper, pp. 141–160. Albany, NY: SUNY Press.

———. 2013b. Against Procedural Landscapes. Community, Kinship, and History. In *Transforming Ethnohistories. Narrative, Meaning, and Community,* edited by Sebastian Felix Braun, pp. 181–200. Norman: University of Oklahoma Press.

Brown, David L., and Louis E. Swanson (eds.). 2003. *Challenges for Rural America in the Twenty-First Century.* University Park: Pennsylvania State University Press.

Chabal, Patrick. 2009. *Africa: The Politics of Suffering and Smiling.* New York: Zed Books.

Davidson, Osha Gray. 1990. *Broken Heartland. The Rise of America's Rural Ghetto.* New York: Doubleday.

DeMallie, Raymond J. 2009. Community in Native America: Continuity and Change among the Sioux. *Journal de la Société des Américanistes* 95(1): 185–205.

Duncan, Cynthia M. (ed.). 1992. *Rural Poverty in America.* Westport, CT: Auburn House.

Eagleton, Terry. 2000. *The Idea of Culture.* Oxford, UK: Blackwell.

Edmondson, Jacqueline. 2003. *Prairie Town. Redefining Rural Life in the Age of Globalization.* Lanham, MD: Rowman and Littlefield.

Fletcher, Matthew L.M. 2007. The Supreme Court's Legal Culture War against Tribal Law. *Intercultural Human Rights Law Review* 2: 93–127.

———. 2008. The Original Understanding of the Political Status of Indian Tribes. *St. John's Law Review* 82(1): 153–181.

———. 2011. Race and American Indian Tribal Nationhood. *Wyoming Law Review* 11(2): 295–328.

———. 2012–2013. Tribal Membership and Indian Nationhood. *American Indian Law Review* 37(1): 1–18.

Fowler, Loretta. 1987. *Shared Symbols, Contested Meanings. Gros Ventre Culture and History, 1778–1984.* Ithaca, NY: Cornell University Press.

Freedman, Eric. 2007. Protecting Sacred Sites on Public Land. Religion and Alliances in the Mato Tipila-Devils Tower Litigation. *The American Indian Quarterly* 31(1): 1–22.

Gagnon, V.P. 2004. *The Myth of Ethnic War. Serbia and Croatia in the 1990s.* Ithaca, NY: Cornell University Press.

Garroutte, Eva Marie. 2003. *Real Indians. Identity and the Survival of Native America.* Berkeley: University of California Press.

Grossman, Zoltan. 2003. Cowboy and Indian Alliances in the Northern Plains. *Agricultural History* 77(2): 355–389.

———. 2005. Unlikely Alliances: Treaty Conflicts and Environmental Cooperation between Native American and Rural White Communities. *American Indian Culture and Research Journal* 29(4): 21–43.

Hoelscher, Steven D. 1998. *Heritage on Stage. The Invention of Ethnic Place in America's Little Switzerland.* Madison: University of Wisconsin Press.

Iverson, Peter. 1997. *When Indians Became Cowboys. Native Peoples and Cattle Ranching in the American West.* Norman: University of Oklahoma Press.

Kalt, Joseph P. 2007. The Role of Constitutions in Native Nation Building. Laying a Firm Foundation. In *Rebuilding Native Nations. Strategies for Governance and Development*, edited by Miriam Jorgensen, pp. 78–114. Tucson: University of Arizona Press.

Kemper, Robert V., and Julie Adkins. 2005. The World as It Should Be. Faith-Based Community Development in America. In *Community Building in the Twenty-First Century*, edited by Stanley E. Hyland, pp. 71–100. Santa Fe, NM: School of American Research Press.

Kulchyski, Peter. 2005. *Like the Sound of a Drum. Aboriginal Cultural Politics in Denendeh and Nunavut.* Winnipeg: University of Manitoba Press.

Kurkiala, Mikael. 1997. *"Building the Nation Back Up." The Politics of Identity on the Pine Ridge Indian Reservation.* Acta Universitatis Upsaliensis: Uppsala Studies in Cultural Anthropology. Uppsala: Sweden.

Lawlor, Mary. 2006. *Public Native America. Tribal Self-Representation in Museums, Powwows, and Casinos.* New Brunswick, NJ: Rutgers University Press.

Leeds, Stacey L. 2004. Borrowing from Blackacre: Expanding Tribal Land Bases through the Creation of Future Interests and Joint Tenancies. *North Dakota Law Review* 80(4): 827–848.

Lyons, Scott Richard. 2010. *X-Marks: Native Signatures of Assent.* Minneapolis: University of Minnesota Press.

Maharidge, Dale. 2013. *Someplace like America.* Updated edition. Berkeley: University of California Press.

Marx, Karl, and Frederick Engels. 1906. *Manifesto of the Communist Party.* Chicago: Charles H. Kerr and Co.

McDougall, Debra. 2005. The Unintended Consequences of Clarification: Development, Disputing, and the Dynamics of Community in Ranonnga, Solomon Islands. *Ethnohistory* 52(1): 81–109.

National Indian Gaming Commission. 2011. NIGC Tribal Gaming Revenues 2005–2009. Available online at http://www.nigc.gov/Gaming_Revenue_Reports.aspx (accessed September 2015).

Niezen, Ronald. 2009. *The Rediscovered Self. Indigenous Identity and Cultural Justice.* Montreal: McGill-Queen's University Press.

Oliver-Smith, Anthony. 2005. Communities after Catastrophe. Reconstructing the Material, Reconstituting the Social. In *Community Building in the Twenty-First Century*, edited by Stanley E. Hyland, pp. 45–70. Santa Fe, NM: School of American Research Press.

O'Nell, Theresa DeLeane. 1996. *Disciplined Hearts. History, Identity, and Depression in an American Indian Community.* Berkeley: University of California Press.

Rosenblatt, Daniel. 2005. Thinking Outside the Billiard Ball: Cognatic Nationalism and Performing a Maori Public Sphere. *Ethnohistory* 52(1): 111–136.

Ruppel, Kristin T. 2008. *Unearthing Indian Land. Living with the Legacies of Allotment.* Tucson: University of Arizona Press.
Schmitt, Carl. 1993 (1922). *Politische Theologie. Vier Kapitel zur Lehre von der Souveränität.* Berlin: Duncker & Humboldt.
Smith, Dean Howard. 2000. *Modern Tribal Development. Paths to Self-Sufficiency and Cultural Integrity in Indian Country.* Walnut Creek, CA: AltaMira Press.
Thornton, Thomas F. 2008. *Being and Place among the Tlingit.* Seattle: University of Washington Press and Juneau: Sealaska Heritage Institute.
Wagoner, Paula L. 2002. *"They Treated Us Just Like Indians." The Worlds of Bennett County, South Dakota.* Lincoln: University of Nebraska Press.
Woodard, Stephanie. 2011. Pine Ridge Rising: Community-Based Development Project Gets Underway. *Huffington Post,* 01/31/2011. Available online at http://www.huffingtonpost.com/stephanie-woodard/pine-ridge-reservation_b_816089.html (accessed September 2015).
Wuttunee, Wanda. 2004. *Living Rhythms. Lessons in Aboriginal Economic Resilience and Vision.* Montreal: McGill-Queen's University Press.

Legal Cases

United States Court of Appeals, Ninth Circuit. 2005. *Lewis v. Norton.* 424 F.3d 959.
United States Court of Appeals, Ninth Circuit. 2005. *United States v. Bruce.* 394 F.3d 1215.
United States Court of Appeals, Ninth Circuit. 2010. *United States v. Maggi and Mann.* 598 F.3d 1073.
United States Court of Appeals, Tenth Circuit. 1998. *Ordinance 59 Association v. Babbitt.* 163 F.3d 1150.
United States Supreme Court. 1832. *Worcester v. Georgia.* 6 Pet. 515.
United States Supreme Court. 1978. *Santa Clara Pueblo v. Martinez.* 436 U.S. 49.
United States Supreme Court. 2008. *Plains Commerce Bank v. Long Family Land and Cattle, Inc., et al.* No. 07-411. April 14. Argument Transcript. Available online at http://www.supremecourt.gov/oral_arguments/argument_transcripts/07-411.pdf (accessed September 2015).

CHAPTER 2

The Antics of Anticipation in an Odyssey of Self-Rule

Jackie Grey

> I am suddenly aware of the changes in the earth's surface, especially when I find that I must change the trail that leads to my little house, because a ravine has been gradually eating toward it practically unnoticed. When it comes within a few feet of my road, I must do something immediately, or one day I shall find my road to town blocked.
>
> —John Joseph Mathews (1945, 83)

This chapter concerns itself with anticipation and what anticipation does and does not do in the preservation of juridical and territorial self-rule in a Southern New England, tribal homeland. This is a narrative, a narrative that traverses thirty years of contestation, documenting the struggles of a small tribal community and its intimate engagement with what is known in legal nomenclature as a "settlement agreement." Anticipation throughout this account can be observed in a state of contextual and ideological fluctuation, as tribal and nontribal regimes seek to affix conflicting desires, interests, *and* anticipations onto the settlement document. I am about to argue that though seemingly destabilizing in its effects, the antics of anticipation as represented here are not altogether a bad thing. Rather, they beckon new openings and create new tensions in a reassertion of tribal rights and the political prowess of tribal governments. This chapter, then, invokes the sentiments of other contributors to this volume who demonstrate through particular histories an enduring and adaptable commitment to indigenous relationships to nation, power, and place.

As a reconstruction, this chapter does not aspire toward chronological simplicity but meanders both systematically and spasmodically across a field of juridical and political events, most of which are propelled by the fear of loss. The narrative starts in the twilight years of the twentieth century, jumps back some three centuries, and then jettisons forward to moments of critical contemporaneity. The saga of how anticipation intervenes in a tribal project of political preservation begins in 1983 in the Indigenous island community of Aquinnah, Massachusetts, known at the time—and even now—as "Gay Head." The ancestral territory of Aquinnah is perched on the southwestern tip of Noëpe, known by its colonial name, "Martha's Vineyard," a one hundred-square-mile acreage of shrub, vine, and dune that sits like a humpback whale seven miles off the coast of mainland Massachusetts. This story of Aquinnah ends without finality, reflecting the ongoing, never-ending labor in the reaffirmation of tribal nationhood and self-rule.

Strategies of "Will"

When Anne, president of the Wampanoag Tribal Council of Gay Head, Inc., signed a settlement agreement in November 1983 with the town of Gay Head, with a nontribal citizens' rights group calling itself the Gay Head Taxpayers Association, and with the Commonwealth of Massachusetts, her people had been acquainted with the vagaries of juridical texts for more than 300 years.[1] One of the most dramatic of these historical texts was Mittark's "will." As archival records tell it, it was in the late seventeenth century when Mittark, sachem of the Wampanoags of Aquinnah, declared that Aquinnah's territorial sovereignty would remain sovereign "forever." The declaration, believed to have been uttered by Mittark in a speech two years before he died in 1683, allegedly was committed to textual form, bearing the date September 11, 1681. The document was resurrected some years later when the Aquinnah Indians sought redress in the Massachusetts General Court in an effort to halt English expansionism and exploitation (C. Banks 1966, 9; Silverman 2005, 143).

In *Native Writings in Massachusett*, Ives Goddard and Kathleen J. Bragdon published a translation of the document, which originally had been written in a Romanized alphabet superimposed on what had been an Indigenous oral language.

> I am Muttaak, sachem of Gay Head and Nashaquitsa as far as Wanemessit. Know this all people. I Muttaak and my chief men

and my children and my people, these are our lands. Forever we own them, and our posterity forever shall own them. . . . I Ummuttaak say this, and my chief men: if any of these sons of mine protects my sachemship, he shall forever be a sachem. But if any of my sons does not protect my sachemship and sells it, he shall fall forever. And we chief men say this and our sachem: if any of these sons of ours protects our chieftainship, he shall forever be a chief man. But if any one of our sons does not protect our chieftainship and sells it, he shall fall forever. I Umuttaag, sachem, say this and my chief men; this is our agreement. We say it before God; it shall be forever. I Ummuttaak, this is my hand (X), on the date September 11, 1681. . . . (Goddard and Bragdon 1988, 97)

Arguably, it was anticipation, as much as anything else, that provoked Mittark to craft what was essentially a will and testament. Aquinnah at the time was a small peninsula, separated from the rest of Noëpe by a body of water. Not long after the explorer Bartholomew Gosnold landed on Noëpe in 1602, the Indigenous designation of the island was displaced by the English name, "Martha's Vineyard" (C. Banks 1966, 59). The name stuck, and Noëpe over time evolved into what it is now, a signifier of nonindigenous leisure, wealth, and prestige. But at first contact with the English, Noëpe was the home of an estimated three thousand or so Wampanoags spread across four major sachemships or kingdoms, one of which was Aquinnah, an island within an island (C. Banks 1966, 39; Jennings 1976, 26; Manning 2001; Mayhew 1694, 24).[2] In the years surrounding the period in which Mittark produced his "will," colonial and European imperial interests competed for proprietary control over Aquinnah and so, too, did other Natives (C. Banks 1966, 80; Silverman 2005, 17). Not surprisingly, Mittark's document forebodingly reflects the anxiety of a set of indigenous leaders worried over territorial alienation of their homeland.[3]

As historical interpretation suggests, anticipation in this moment of juridical confrontation performed in what was essentially a parroting of English textual practice mixed with Native tradition of that era. Observing English legal custom, the Aquinnah Wampanoags no doubt expected Mittark's declaration—which was, after all, a written document—to safeguard the geopolitical integrity of their sachemship and keep outsider hands off of Aquinnah land into perpetuity. We can only surmise what Mittark's people had in mind, strategically, when they presented the document to a colonial court. Perhaps, as historian David J. Silverman speculates, "the

Indians were shrewdly playing the colonists' old game of manipulating the printed word" (2005, 144). Or having accepted or at least *professed* acceptance of Christianity and the promise of redemption through faith and literacy, Mittark and his lieutenants might have anticipated, naively, a favorable outcome from a document crafted for another kind of salvation. Neither strategy succeeded. The general court dismissed Mittark's will as a forgery.

Three centuries later, in the waning years of the twentieth century, the signing of a 1983 settlement agreement would add yet another chapter to an ongoing, seemingly eternal epic narrative in the political assertions of indigenous Aquinnah. Like the maneuvers of a dying sachem, anticipation stands at the epicenter of this ongoing, contemporary struggle, a struggle that remains, to date, unresolved. This chapter examines the ways in which anticipation, articulated through legal form, simultaneously reaffirms and constrains an indigenous relationship to self-government over a thirty-year period that began in the early 1970s and extended into the start of the twenty-first century.

This study is the result of four years of ethnographic and ethnohistorical research, focusing primarily but not exclusively on Wampanoag-settler relations in the tiny Indian town of Aquinnah. During my tenure on Noëpe from 2000 to 2004, I lived year-round on the island, floating from one living situation to another because of the high cost of island living. I was employed off and on by the Aquinnah Tribe, working mostly as a clerk and administrative assistant and at times as an assistant in the Tribe's shellfish hatchery.

My experience on the island during those years is indelible, etched in the raw brittleness of small-town, intercultural politics. I witnessed firsthand the social and political tensions that erupted when tribal officials decided in the spring of 2001 to ignore a key provision of the settlement agreement by refusing to ask town officials for permission to build a shed at the Tribe's newly constructed shellfish hatchery. I witnessed, as well, the dismay of nontribal seasonal and year-round Aquinnah residents who, on a number of public occasions, articulated the sentiment that tribal people in a tribal town wielded unfair advantage in matters of land rights and economic resources, including the question of who should be able to lease souvenir lots at the Gay Head Cliffs. For a core group of these nontribal complainants, the settlement agreement represented a way in which nontribal citizens' rights could be championed, if not always assured.

My interest in "anticipation" evolved a few years after my field experience, when I began researching the history of the settlement agreement itself. The research revealed, among other points, that the settlement process embodied three sets of political actors and three diverging sets of anticipations. As suggested above, the nontribal people who engineered and favored the settlement sought and anticipated constraints against future assertions of tribal self-governance. Within the tribe itself, the agreement signified two oppositional trajectories: the anticipation of loss—that is, the loss of tribal power—and a mode of anticipation that would remain securely moored to the political formidability of an Indigenous past, no matter what. So, some tribal people wanted the settlement, believing it would bring good things to the Tribe in spite of its defects. Others adamantly opposed the settlement, fearing and anticipating its lethal hold on tribal sovereignty.

This chapter tries to work through some of these conflicting anticipations, but it also reveals much about the challenges and performances of tribal nationhood. A few key arguments stand out. At the outset, this chapter underscores the historical fact that the Aquinnah Wampanoags possess a sense of nationhood that predates colonial intrusion and certainly a relationship to nationhood that predates a document crafted a mere thirty years ago. Tribal relationships to governance, however, have changed by necessity. Writing in separate essays in the text, *Rebuilding Native Nations: Strategies for Governance and Development*, Stephen Cornell and Alutiiq scholar Sarah L. Hicks saliently observe the ways in which the tools of tribal nationhood and governance have adapted under the political and legal manipulations of federal and state regimes (Cornell 2007, 59; Hicks 2007, 251).

What has remained constant, though, is what I am calling a "sense" of tribal nationhood, an Aquinnah Wampanoag political identity that understands itself as enduring. Mittark epitomized durability some three hundred years ago when he proclaimed Aquinnah to be the land of his people "forever." This enduring sense of tribal nationhood and self-governance arguably has never faltered in Aquinnah, which may explain, to an extent, the fearlessness of signing onto a settlement arrangement that would, if it could, endanger the very core of an Indigenous identity. In their anticipations, tribal leaders who favored the settlement remained steadfast in their belief that no settlement document, however determinate its intent, could dismantle what has been sustained in Aquinnah for centuries.

Dualities

This interest in anticipation and its encounter with what is typically called tribal sovereignty is complicated all the more by the geopolitical context of the place itself. As a contemporary signifier, Noëpe has been remarkably fluid across time. Popularized over the last two centuries as a small island community that attracts eclectic Americans wanting to escape America, long known for its appeal to African-Americans and Jewish-Americans wanting to elude the worst articulations of racism and anti-Semitism, and recognized as a venue for bird watchers and conservationists, Noëpe in its most recent articulation seems irrecoverably enchanted by the force of material and symbolic wealth and prestige: money and class.

When I was on the island in the opening years of the twenty-first century, beachfront land was selling at nearly a million dollars an acre, if not more, in some locations. I recall a woman boasting to me of summering in "the Hamptons" and then declared that she now was thinking about building a home on Noëpe. I knew of not-rich islanders who lived outdoors in tents during the summer, while they rented out their homes for $3,000 a week or more. The commodification of the island was so extreme in the opinion of some islanders that a down-island shopkeeper and friend of mine intoned one day, "We've got to save this place. We can't let it go the way of the bucks."[4]

Yet, even more intriguing than the social performance of money is the way the isle performs as an icon for the liberal, Democratic aristocracy (Appadurai 1988; Bourdieu 1993). As heads of state, both U.S. President Barack Obama and former U.S. president Bill Clinton have made ritual appearances on Noëpe. The Kennedys have sustained a long though sometimes tragic relationship with the island, and it was the late Jacqueline Kennedy Onassis who pursued privacy on Noëpe, retiring to Aquinnah. An exhaustive list of public personas linked to "Martha's Vineyard"—people like African-American writer and journalist Dorothy West, U.S. Senator Edward W. Brooke, Pulitzer Prize-winning novelist John McCullough, and actors Patricia Neal and Michael J. Fox—would weigh down this chapter (Hayden and Hayden 1999).

Indeed, so dense is "the Vineyard" as a signifier that the reanimation of "Noëpe," a Wampanoag place, would be a daunting and implausible endeavor, if not for the active presence of the Aquinnah Tribe, a federally recognized tribal nation of some eleven hundred members, whose administrative and ancestral headquarters remain situated in Aquinnah. With less than three hundred and fifty year-round residents, Aquinnah is the second smallest town in the Commonwealth of Massachusetts. Not so long ago, Aquinnah was listed on state records as "Gay Head." Then, in 1997, members of the island tribe successfully petitioned the state to resurrect the sachemship's indigenous name.[5]

Aquinnah itself is poised so far west on the island that the sun can be seen sinking into the cold Atlantic like a giant, sizzling orange. Being so close to the ocean, Aquinnah understandably is a wet place, a place of bog, dune, and thick, enshrouding fog, all of which accentuate its petulant beauty and stubborn simplicity. There are wild orchids and a menagerie of fauna in Aquinnah—egrets, raccoons, and an overabundance of deer. Yet even at the beginning of the twenty-first century, there is no gas station, no post office, no place to buy eggs and milk in Aquinnah. It is this lonely, brooding hinterland that the island Wampanoags and a nontribal, local, regional and state regime fought over from 1974 to 1986 and again in the spring of 2001 during my tenure of fieldwork on Noëpe.

Another Mittark Moment

If Mittark imagined enduring tribal nationhood through the invocation of a written "will," tribal inhabitation of legal textuality would make an even more dramatic statement when the Aquinnah Wampanoags sued for the return of unoccupied, communal tribal land in 1974. The Wampanoag Tribal Council of "Gay Head" officially filed the suit in a U.S. district, federal court. Representing the council was a feisty, white lawyer, Tom Tureen. Tureen was working then for the Native American Rights Fund, which offered legal services pro bono for struggling tribal communities seeking the recovery of ancestral land. In 1974, Tureen was making a name for himself by deftly invoking a two-hundred-year-old piece of federal legislation—the 1790 Trade and Intercourse Act—on behalf of the Passamaquoddy and Penobscot nations in the state of Maine (Eisler 2001). Typically called the "Indian Nonintercourse Act," the Trade and Intercourse law gave Congress, not the states, the exclusive power to sanction land transactions with Native peoples.

Tureen's legal strategy was welcomed news for tribes throughout Southern New England. Many of the indigenous land dealings with settlers and settler polities in the region were carried out within the political domains of states or colonial versions of states, not with the U.S. federal government. Indeed, when Southern New England sachems engaged in seventeenth-century and early eighteenth century land deals with European colonials, or when early settlers expropriated unoccupied Indian lands outright for private use and profit, there *was* no federal government.

Like a ghost reinvigorated for battle, the resurrected Nonintercourse Act gave Tureen what he needed. In 1972, the lawyer successfully maneuvered a reluctant U.S. Justice Department into suing the state of Maine on behalf of the two tribes there. By the time the suit was settled in 1980, the Passamaquoddies and Penobscots jointly were awarded $81.5 million and the authority to purchase 300,000 acres in Maine's "unorganized" territories (Clifford 1988, 278; Eisler 2001, 74).

The Wampanoags on Noëpe must have been buoyed by the legal gyrations coming together in Maine, but Tureen's coup d'etat may not have been the only thing that stirred political resistance in Aquinnah. A wave of refashioned American Indian resistance enveloped Indian Country in the 1960s and 1970s. Known popularly as "Red Power," Native activism during this period sought redress through nationally publicized political theatricality, much of it articulated in the form of marches and occupations. Indians were not alone in the deployment of such strategies. As Joane Nagel has noted, Red Power "did not emerge in a social vacuum" but was immersed in an era that also belonged to the Black Panthers, Cesar Chavez's National Farm Workers, the turbulent protests over the Vietnam War, and youthful resistance to "Establishment" hair, politics, and gendered identities (Nagel 1996, 130).

One of the earliest demonstrations of American Indian activism were the fish-in protests organized in the early 1960s by the Pacific Northwest tribal nations, among them the Nisqually, Puyallup, and Duwamish peoples of Washington (Smith 2007, 152). Notably, tribal organizers of the fish-ins enlisted the support of actor-activist Marlon Brando in 1964, and in 1966 the Survival of American Indians Association (SAIA) invited the thirty-three-year-old African-American comedian Dick Gregory to "fish the Nisqually River" (Smith 2007, 149). Brando was especially effective in attracting national attention to the protests for the limited time he was associated with them, but fish-in leaders were dismayed by Gregory's participation, contending that Gregory primarily played to Southern black activism, exhibiting far less interest in Indian fishing rights. When the relationship with Gregory fizzled out, the SAIA invited actor Jay Silverheels to support their cause. Silverheels portrayed the character Tonto in the *Lone Ranger* television series (Smith 2007, 150).

Native activism would shift to an occupation mode in the late 1960s. In the early morning hours of November 20, 1969, eighty-nine Native

Americans college students, identifying themselves as "Indians of All Tribes," landed on Alcatraz Island in San Francisco Bay and for nineteen months claimed the island by "right of discovery." The young activists demanded clear title to the island and called for the establishment of an American Indian university, an American Indian cultural center, and an American Indian museum. Indigeneity has a long history with Alcatraz. Thousands of years before European contact, a diversity of indigenous groups used the rocky, barren island alternately as a way station in their canoe travels, as a designated holy place, and as a place of ostracism and isolation for violators of laws and taboos (Johnson 2008).

Interestingly, Alcatraz Island in the mid-twentieth century would perform as a site of isolation of a different sort when it became a prison for some of America's most notorious violators, felons like Al "Scarface" Capone and Robert Stroud, the "birdman of Alcatraz." Alcatraz operated as a prison for some thirty years before being closed by U.S. Attorney General Robert Kennedy in 1963. After its doors were shut down, the prison captured the attention of Texas business developer and oil tycoon Lamar Hunt, who dreamt of transforming a "warehouse for the living dead" into a capitalist venture about the size of Texas (Mankiller and Wallis 1993, 186–189). Hunt's dream would install manicured gardens, an underground space museum, and a futuristic tower topped off with a revolving restaurant; but the prison's main cellblock would be preserved for the enjoyment of tourists. Hunt's memorial to Alcatraz would have completely ignored and obliterated Indigenous history. In a memoir recounting her days as a protestor at Alcatraz, Wilma Mankiller, a former principal chief of the Cherokee Nation of Oklahoma, lamented:

> For a year after the last inmate was removed, Alcatraz sat like an aging derelict surrounded by water, a symbol of past punishment and acts of brute force. Visitors to San Francisco stood on Fisherman's Wharf and gazed at "the Rock." Some of them circled it in tour boats. In the dying sunlight when the fog moved in, it seemed to be only a mirage. The island was no longer as it had been centuries before, when free-spirited native people stopped there as nature's guests. (Mankiller and Wallis 1993, 187)

Native activism would continue to escalate, becoming increasingly bold. In 1971 and again in 1972, members of the American Indian Movement (AIM) organized an occupation of the U.S. Bureau of Indian Affairs building in Washington, D.C. Then, in 1973, AIM members, as well as Natives from as far away as Mi'kmaw country in Nova Scotia, shared hunting rifles and powdered orange juice with Oglala Lakotas in a seventy-one-day siege at Wounded Knee on the Pine Ridge Reservation in South Dakota. Gunfire was exchanged during the siege, leaving two Indians dead and a U.S. Marshall wounded (D. Banks 2004; Cobb and Fowler 2007; Crow Dog and Erdoes 1995; Nagel 1996).

Eventually, Indian activists and their nontribal supporters would turn away from highly publicized protests and look to lawyers and the courts, seeking and receiving help from the Seattle Legal Services, the Native American Rights Fund, and finally the U.S. Justice Department, which in 1974 affirmed the rights of Washington Indians to half of the harvestable fish and mandated co-management by the tribes and the state.[6] These legal interventions, born of a climate of life-threatening activism, produced important developments on behalf of Native treaty and land rights (Smith 2007, 156). Aquinnah's 1974 lawsuit against the town of Gay Head and the anticipation of recovery and preservation of tribal, ancestral land represented, then, both the spirit of an age and a pivotal moment in Native American pride and agency.

Anticipating "Forever Wild"

There were other anticipations astir during the 1970s, anticipations linked to another concept of preservation. In 1973, U.S. Senator Edward M. "Ted" Kennedy of Massachusetts introduced the *Nantucket Sound Islands Trust* bill, a revised version of a bill Kennedy had introduced a year earlier. The 1973 bill S.1929 would have placed a significant portion of beachfront land in Aquinnah, under the protectorate of a national preserve. The ethnographic analysis of Gloria Levitas, whose 1980 dissertation describes this period of anticipation in detail, suggests that Kennedy introduced the bill for reasons that seem connected to an intense period of lobbying by a well-placed coterie of "Vineyard" seasonal residents and other island enthusiasts, a group calling itself "Friends of the Island."

One of the charter members of the "Friends" was Anne W. Simon, described by Levitas as the "ex-wife" of a well-known developer responsible for the conception and construction of the planned community of New Town in Reston, Virginia (Levitas 1980, 537).[7] In her 1973 conservation memoir, "No Island is an Island," Simon self-identified as one of the charter members of "Friends" and listed a number of other founding members in what adds up to be an enumeration of public figures, such as Jerome Wiesner of the Massachusetts Institute of Technology and a member of John F. Kennedy's cabinet during the Kennedy presidency; Leona Baumgartner, a retired Commissioner of Public Health; Richard Pough, the "well-known" conservationist and officer of the Audubon Society; Michael Straight, novelist and former editor of the *New Republic*; John Oakes, then editorial page editor of the *New York Times*; actress Katharine Cornell; and artist Thomas Hart Benton, whose family thirty years later would join a lawsuit against the Aquinnah tribe (Simon 1973, 21).

The discursive fervor of Simon's conservationism is organized around an argument in which local islanders on Noëpe, acting alone, were perceived as ineffectual in their ability to protect the island from future incursions of overdevelopment. Championing the idea of federal intervention and the Kennedy initiative, in particular, Simon wrote, "The Vineyard can no longer plead innocence or trust in its insularity for protection" (1973, 79). Much of Noëpe still remained pristine and virginal in the public imagination of the early 1970s and thus was perceived by Simon and the other "Friends," as worth saving.

So, if the locals could not protect and preserve this island paradise from the scourge of development, then a partnership with the federal government, "jointly conceived and carried out," clearly was called for. "Without a working partnership, even the wish to protect will not survive" (Simon 1973, 80). Simon admitted that the future of the Kennedy bill could not be assured when she said, "It may become a law or it may serve its purpose by inspiring other action" (1973, 203). However, what was perhaps more critical for Simon was the way in which the visions of conservationists and their local, state and nation-state "friends" brought the conservation issue before "the people."

As the legislation worked its way through public review, island detractors complained indignantly at the prospect of losing "home rule."[8] In Aquinnah, Wampanoags and nontribal, island residents alike reportedly were "infuriated" by that part of the Kennedy bill that would have designated the "entire coastline" of Aquinnah "forever wild." Levitas wrote,

> "Forever wild" lands were to be free of all building or development, owners of homes on this land would be allowed to keep them until they died, or to sell them to the government at any time for a fair market valued. If they failed to sell during their lifetimes, the government had a right to make a payment to the heirs and take the land. In no other town was privately owned beachfront property designated as "forever wild." (1980, 546; quotes in original)

The Kennedy legislation never was enacted. Rather, in its place, Noëpe islanders accepted the imposition of state land-use laws—the Wetlands Act—and the 1978 creation of the Martha's Vineyard Commission, an island-wide regulatory body, charged with the oversight of island preservation and development.

Wampanoag Intervention

It was within this intersection of disparate and conflicting relationships to anticipation, punctuated by a politicized atmosphere of heightened Indianness and bourgeois sensibilities seeking desire in legislation, that members of the Aquinnah Wamopanoag community succeeded in gaining a state charter in 1972, codifying the already structured Wampanoag Tribal Council of Gay Head. The formation of an officially incorporated tribal council, a legal entity, allowed the island Wampanoags to pursue more effectively their own strategies for protection. What mobilized the Aquinnah natives, wrote anthropologist Christine Grabowski, was the prospect of losing their "common lands," a discontinuous acreage of beach, bog, creek, dune, and the once-multicolored shoreline cliffs fronting the Atlantic Ocean (Grabowski 1994, 5). The cranberry bogs, in particular, are infused with symbolism as a place in which Aquinnah Wampanoags still gather communally to harvest cranberries in a private annual ceremony.

The Aquinnah Wampanoags worried over the possibility that, once declared "forever wild," the common lands of their ancestors would be removed from tribal control. Once again invoking legal formality, the Aquinnah natives initially tried to transfer the common lands to the newly incorporated Tribal Council. The effort was foiled by an injunction filed by a group composed largely of nontribal, "summer people," a collective of financially advantaged, urban lawyers and business people organized under the "Gay Head Taxpayers Association."

The transfer of the common lands already had been approved by the three town selectmen, all of whom were tribal members. The Taxpayers, however, successfully asserted through their injunction that the selectmen were unfairly safeguarding only the interests of Wampanoag residents in the 'town" and thus were ignoring the interests of nontribal, townspeople (Grabowski 1994, 8). Tribal strategies shifted. With the transfer plan blocked, Tribal Council members turned to lawyer Tom Tureen, and in December 1974 the council filed suit against the town of Gay Head for the return of what eventually would add up to roughly 485 acres of tribal land, a fraction of the 3,400-plus acres Mittark tried to protect with another juridical document three hundred years earlier.[9]

In Pursuit of Stasis

The Aquinnah lawsuit initiated in 1974 tried to manage a field of multiple, unruly elements—anticipation, human agency, market forces, desire, and fear—none of which seemed at all inclined to perform the role of the fixed object. That did not stop people from trying. The desire for fixity appeared especially pronounced within the Taxpayers Association. A couple of years after the Aquinnah Tribal Council filed its lawsuit, the Taxpayers officially intervened in the litigation. Panicked by the lawsuit underway in Maine, fearing that white islanders would lose their year-round and seasonal homes and worried that the tribe eventually would put a hotel or casino on "the Vineyard," the Taxpayers pressed for out-of-court, settlement negotiation as a means by which the tribe's lawsuit could be brought to closure expeditiously and with minimal damage to nontribal economic and political interests. No less consequential was the desire to produce a legal instrument that would constrict tribal anticipation into an unspecified future.

Tribal Council members for their part did not immediately embrace the first round of proposals. Indeed, negotiations grew so tense and embittered that in 1977 Massachusetts Governor Michael S. Dukakis appointed Albert M. Sacks, dean of Harvard Law School, to mediate a settlement package acceptable to all parties. The mediation attempt failed. Negotiations broke down in the spring of 1979 when a tribal faction resisted a plan that would grant tribal title to common lands in exchange for relinquishing all other titles and claims to tribal lands and natural resources (Grabowski 1994, 352).[10]

By 1983 differences on both sides of the proposed settlement debate seemed irreconcilable (Grabowski 1994, 360). On August 5, 1983, the Taxpayers Association placed an ad in the *Vineyard Gazette*, seeking island-wide support of the settlement and blaming the Tribal Council for the lack of progress in the lawsuit. Fueled by anticipation, the ad read,

> What is at stake?
>
> The answer to this question is simple. For the residents of Gay head (sic), the loss of the case could mean loss of our property.

> Like most Americans, our homes represent our major asset in our lives. We view the possible takeover of our property with alarm. (*Vineyard Gazette*, August 5, 1983)[11]

Popular discourse during the settlement talks reflected, as well, the now familiar sentiment of nontribal citizens' rights groups whose relationship to equality and indigenous rights claims, as Alyosha Goldstein (2008) observed, conveniently detaches itself from historical inequities. Indulging in the cant of temporal innocence, one defense lawyer for the Taxpayer's Association remarked in 1986,

> Consider for a moment who the people are whose rights are threatened by the assertion of this ancient (land) claim. The vast majority of them are homeowners who have acquired land and homes in Gay Head within the last twenty or thirty years, completely unaware of any ancient legislation or conveyance which forms the basis of the plaintiffs' claims. (United States Senate 1986, 149)

The defense lawyer quoted above was a member of the Boston law firm Hale and Dorr, the same firm that successfully derailed the Mashpee Wampanoags in the 1977 Mashpee land-recovery lawsuit filed against the town of Mashpee on Cape Cod. The sister tribe to the Aquinnah people on Noëpe, the Mashpees lost their land-recovery suit when a nonindigenous jury ruled that the Mashpees no longer constituted a "tribe" (Campisi 1991; Clifford 1988). Hale and Dorr not only represented nontribal interests in the Mashpee and Aquinnah cases of the 1970s and 1980s but would litigate on behalf of nontribal landowners in the hatchery lawsuit filed against the Aquinnah Indians in 2001.

Given the ideological divides evident in the settlement talks in the late summer of 1983, it seems all but incredulous that a settlement proposal was endorsed by Tribal Council and approved in a majority vote within the tribe's general membership by mid-November.[12] The final document, the one signed by Anne in November 1983, returned to the tribe 238 acres of tribal common lands, another 175 acres of negotiated land of a bankrupted private estate, known as the "Strock" estate, plus a controversial, seven-acre coastal parcel known as the Cook Lands.[13] In exchange for these lands, the tribe agreed to the extinguishment of all other "aboriginal" land claims.

Settlement agreements must at least *appear* magnanimous. Thus, there are moments when the document teasingly gestures toward tribal autonomy, only to rip it away in the next discursive breath. For instance, the Tribal Land Corporation, created in the settlement process, was to have established safety and protection regulations that would apply to hunting on settlement lands. Tribal regulation, however, would extend only to hunting carried out by means "other than firearms or crossbow," which as defined in the settlement only would allow tribal regulation of hunting methods such as trapping or, taken to a ludicrous extreme, something like stone throwing. Yet, even within the tribal corporation's narrow domain of jurisdiction, tribal oversight still was regulated. The tribal corporation's standards of safety and protection were subject to state and local "judicial review for reasonableness."[14]

Unbounded

As previously indicated, the discursive labor that constructed a local agreement from a field of conflicting anticipations was distinctly not local. About a decade after he introduced the Islands Trust legislation, the "forever wild" bill, Senator Ted Kennedy intervened once again in island politics, this time sponsoring Senate bill S.1452, which would ratify the proposed Aquinnah settlement agreement and provide up to three million dollars in federal and state funds to purchase the Tribe's common lands. In effect, congressional approval would transform a local agreement into a federal "act," a federal law. Kennedy's settlement legislation also foreshadowed federal recognition, which would be granted to the Aquinnah Tribe in April 1987, a few months before the enactment of S.1452.[15]

In its immediacy, the legislation purported to "remove all clouds" on land titles in Aquinnah (United States Senate 1986, 3). What had become standard, metaphoric discourse of that period was the assertion that the unresolved, 1974 Aquinnah lawsuit had disrupted land transactions in the town, creating "clouds" that had disabled a lucrative real estate market. The "clouds" metaphor even appears in the preamble to the S.1452 settlement "bill" and survives verbatim in Section 2, paragraphs 2 and 3, of the congressionally approved settlement "act:"

> (2) The pendency of this lawsuit has resulted in severe economic hardships for the residents of the town of Gay Head by

clouding the titles to much of the land in the town, including land not involved in the lawsuit.

(3) The Congress shares with the Commonwealth of Massachusetts and the parties to the lawsuit a desire to remove all clouds on titles resulting from such Indian land claim. (United States Congress 1987)[16]

Tribal members who opposed the proposed settlement critiqued the "clouds" rhetoric as a "scare tactic" and "false argument" (United States Senate 1986, 201). However, as noted above, these counterarguments lost their potency against an apparent fear that the Aquinnah Natives would replicate the phenomenal land acquisition of the Passamaquoddy and Penobscots in Maine.

As a matter of procedure, congressional intervention demanded the airing of all sides of the debate. In early April 1986, a number of Aquinnah tribal members traveled to Washington, D.C., and personally testified before the Senate Committee on Indian Affairs, arguing why the settlement agreement should and should not be ratified by Congress. The hearing was conducted on April 9, 1986. While much of the testimony was oral, a number of tribal testifiers also submitted written statements to the committee. My reconstruction of these testimonies is derived from both written accounts and transcribed oral accounts.

Schisms of Anticipation

The settlement deal, as proposed and eventually enacted, is represented in this chapter as a saga of anticipation embodied in texts. During the thirteen-year period in which the settlement agreement was negotiated, drafted, and codified, anticipation makes its appearance from within a temporal field of conflicting perceptions and interests. As the Taxpayers Association activated its own agenda, attempting to forestall and foreclose tribal anticipation through a settlement process, the Aquinnah Tribe itself split into a factional field that would be sustained for more than a decade. The split calcified around those tribal members who championed the proposed settlement and detractors who opposed the land deal as an affront and threat to the future of tribal sovereignty.

Based on the Senate testimony, as well as legal archival documents obtained from the National Archives office in Waltham, Massachusetts,

Aquinnah tribal members opposing the settlement over the life of the 1974 lawsuit made several attempts to intervene in the settlement process and reconstruct many of the settlement's key features. During the Senate hearings themselves, members of the antisettlement group—sometimes referred to as the "James" faction or the "James Group," and at other times more generally referenced as the "dissenting faction" or simply the "dissenters"—cast the settlement as shortsighted, offensive, and a lethal blow to the future of tribal power. "The settlement is an insult to any intelligent thinking human being," one tribal member wrote in a pithy piece of 1986 testimony (United States Senate 1986, 213).

In another piece of oppositional testimony, another tribal member singled out the settlement provision that required the tribe to relinquish all "aboriginal" land claims and titles. The tribal member characterized the provision and the proposed settlement act in its entirety as "disastrous" for the tribe, "legally and morally." She argued further that "federal trustship" over the settlement lands should be granted "before" any land settlement was made. "Then and only then can we be assured that the Gay Head Wampanoag Tribe interest will be secure" (United States Senate 1986, 227).

Members of the antisettlement group prolifically articulated their concerns and grievances, the result of which is a near volume of memos, letters, and legal texts produced across more than a decade of legal and political wrangling. One of the documents lists certain provisions the opposition leaders said they would require of any acceptable settlement. The proposed features, which for the most part were ignored, would have modified the settlement to provide:

- Conveyance to the tribe of the Cook lands without restriction;
- Conveyance to the tribe of all the beaches as part of the common lands;
- Conveyance to the tribe of all unclaimed lots in Aquinnah, with the right of access to those lots;
- Recognition of Wampanoag hunting and fishing rights;
- Right of refusal to redeem land "put up by the town" for tax sale, giving the tribe the right to obtain land before land was made available to other potential buyers;
- Land owned by the tribe "to be held without restriction";

- Conveyance of immediate areas surrounding a number of sacred and cultural sites and access by tribal members to those sites, including sacred sites located on private property occupied by nontribal residents.

The list of requisite items appears in a separate, stand-alone document and is also incorporated in a letter written by a member of the dissenting camp.[17] Dated April 5, 1986, the letter is addressed to Senator Mark Andrews, then chairperson of the Select Committee on Indian Affairs. In the letter, a tribal member criticizes the settlement for not going far enough to accomplish what was originally intended to "preserve and maintain Wampanoag culture and heritage for our future generations." The letter identified the settlement detractors not as a collection of tribal "dissidents" but as "reconstructionists" seeking to recast the negotiation in a manner "which will strengthen our Indian heritage and not bury it."

Yearnings

In contrast to the angry prescience and argumentation of tribal opposition to the settlement, Anne, the tribal co-signer of the settlement document, installs temporal and political coherence as a foundational argument against which tribal members so inclined were able to justify their support of the settlement process and its congressional codification. In both her written and oral statements at the Senate hearing, Anne argued that her people would be able to sustain the political integrity of the Tribe across time, a position of confidence that refuses to capitulate to the increasing presence and intervention of nontribal residents in Aquinnah. She noted in her testimony,

> At present, all three selectmen—the town clerk, the tax collector, both constables, the chief of police, and the shellfish warden—are all Gay Head Indians, and, with a few exceptions, have always been Indian. If this legislation is enacted, the tribe, with a land base and the opportunity to develop economically and socially, will continue its control (*sic*) of the leadership position in the Gay Head community. (United States Senate 1986, 99)

Anne's relationship to anticipation seems anchored to a historically familiar politics in which the Aquinnah Wampanoags, even when under the colonial gaze, have been able to maintain a politically coherent community across the centuries. Indeed, during my fieldwork, I came to understand that Anne proudly traced her lineage to Zachariah Howwaswee, an Aquinnah preacher and tribal leader born in 1738 (Silverman 2005, 179–182). Anne herself served many years in tribal government and is credited for being largely responsible for shepherding the Tribe through the lengthy federal recognition process. Anne's immediate family members also have been involved in local politics. Her brother, Donald F. Malonson, was long-time chief of the Tribe. After his death in 2003, he was succeeded by the current chief, his son Ryan. All three of Anne's sons—Marc, Donald, and Carl—were involved in tribal and town politics over the last two decades, maintaining positions such as tribal chair and town selectmen. Anne died in 2012 at the age of 97.

Beyond Anne's own kinship ties, Edwin D. Vanderhoop, a member of the expansive Vanderhoop family, is cited in historical records as the first Wampanoag to be elected to the state legislature, representing Dukes County in 1888 (Manning 2001, 54). A politically engaged family, two members of the Vanderhoop line have served as tribal chair in recent years: Beverly Wright, who was tribal chair at the start of the shellfish hatchery litigation in 2001, and Tobias Vanderhoop, who is tribal chair at this writing. Other tribal family names often cited in Aquinnah Wampanoag history are the Jeffers, the Smalleys, and the Belains.

I argue that Anne's connection to a Wampanoag past, a past of political achievement, creates, as plausible, a tribal relationship to identity and power that mediates the fear that any settlement agreement (that any mere text, in fact) can or will displace self-rule for her people. Still, some imperfections of the settlement were too glaring to ignore. Anne, for instance, was well aware of the settlement's "limited provision for tribal jurisdiction" (United States Senate 1986, 91). In her written testimony, she noted that at the time the 1974 lawsuit originally was filed, the tribe was advised "by our attorneys" that if the suit for the common lands was successful, "there could be a similar claim for the entire town" (United States Senate 1986, 91). Overall, though, Anne seemed to find a secure refuge in customary practice and the historical facticity of tribal cohesion and control.

A Matter of Practicality

If faith in the sustainability of Wampanoag power, in large part, rationalized tribal support of the settlement, so, too, did more practical interests.

What emerges in the testimony as a compelling selling point in the acceptance of the settlement is the prospect of setting aside land that would allow more off-island tribal members to return to their ancestral homeland, an anticipation that would be fulfilled, at least partially, in 1996 with the construction of a limited number of tribal housing units.

Prosettlement testifiers in the 1986 Senate hearing spoke of the need to obtain a protected land base that would not succumb to financial pressures in the escalating island real estate market. The creation of tribal housing, as well as the preservation of undeveloped common lands, signified for prosettlement tribal members a means by which political and communal continuity would be secured.[18] In the discourse of preservation, the settlement document becomes a bulwark against the vagaries of increasingly aggressive, capitalist encroachment. As one prosettlement tribal member testified, "All we are asking is the chance for us, including our children, as a Wampanoag Tribe, to be granted the right to remain in Gay Head, where our people's heritage lies and will forever" (United States Senate 1986, 41). Invoking the language of reason, one tribal member offered this statement at the hearings:

> I know there are people within the tribe who oppose this settlement, but I have listened to their objections and arguments at tribal and town meetings and find them, in my mind, to be unquestionably wrong.
>
> This settlement preserves the town common lands for the tribe, which has been a major objective from the start of the suit. It also provides that the tribe will require land that can be used for affordable housing. This will ensure that our people are not driven out of Gay Head by the forces of the marketplace.
>
> As a tribe, we have considered the terms of this settlement time and time again. We have conducted open tribal meetings and discussed the settlement at numerous town meetings. I believe that any tribal member who is interested has complete knowledge of the terms of the settlement and is aware that, although not perfect, it achieves our basic tribal goals. I have no doubt that a substantial majority of the tribal members want and need this settlement.
>
> We Indians of Gay Head have always been a tribe. We have always believed that. We have always taken care of our own and have conducted our own affairs. This bill will ensure that our way of life will not be lost. (United States Senate 1986, 24)

Interestingly, tribal yearnings for fixity, for an enduring trajectory of promise, find an awkward resonance with nontribal aspirations. For nontribal social and legal actors unsettled by the potential of tribal power, the settlement text performs as an energizing source of infinite containment. Similarly, tribal supporters of the settlement sought their own version of lasting assuredness in the body of a text. I contend, however, that the settlement document cannot offer concrete guarantees, even in its most determined performances. Rather, it is the land itself that becomes the settlement's material underpinning. Tribal land effectively grounds a textual artifact crafted from the cravings of hope and fear. What will endure, perhaps longer than the settlement itself, is Aquinnah land.

Consider yet another segment of oral testimony from the 1986 Senate hearings. What seemed of particular concern to members of the Senate committee was the position of some Aquinnah tribal members who would seek not just the reclamation of the tribe's common lands but all or nearly all of the 3,400 acres of the entire town of Aquinnah and thus a full recovery of territorial sovereignty. What follows is a transcribed version of the dialogue between the moderator of the hearings, Peter S. Taylor, and R. James, one of the "dissenting" members of the tribal James Group.

> MR. JAMES: I am (R.) James, and I am a member of the Gay Head Wampanoag Tribe. . . . I come before you today to speak in opposition to the passage of this bill. Since the dates and figures have been stated over and over again in the many legal documents that have been filed by all parties during the 12 years this settlement proposal has been debated, and, as we all know, statistics can be manipulated to bolster any side one takes in an argument, I do not feel they need to be repeated today. Instead, I am going to speak of the negative impact this bill's passage will have on my people . . . I believe that the one thing that disturbs me most, if you allow this legislation to pass, is never again, and I say never again, will Gay Head Wampanoags, whether singularly or as a tribe, will be able to sue for land, land which is rightfully owned by my people . . . I feel very strongly that it is wrong for any of us, Indian or non-Indian, to feel that we have the right to negotiate or legislate away the rights of unborn generations. . . . The State (*sic*) corporation has told people that if the settlement, as written, goes through, they will be able to use land as they see fit, perhaps to build homes or make a living. This sounds pretty good on

the surface. . . . We should all realize that once government, be it State or Federal, gets involved, one cannot even build a doghouse without having to go through endless paper drills, impact studies, conferences, meetings, and the like; in short, loss of control forever. . . . If this bill is allowed to pass, we will have a little less than 5 percent of our land, and land that we can never hope to get. . . . I am also disturbed . . . *(James is interrupted)*

MR. TAYLOR: Mr. James let me ask a question on this.

MR. JAMES: Yes.

MR. TAYLOR: Is it your contention that the land that is currently in private ownership is, in fact, Indian land?

MR. JAMES: I believe strongly that the 3,400 acres that was originally the reservation down there is Indian land; yes, sir.

MR. TAYLOR: That encompasses the entire township of Gay Head, does it not?

MRS. (I): Yes. May I add to that please? I am sorry. I was with (my) aunts at the county courthouse, looking up the land sales that were made between 1974 and 1986. After the lands were described, the lot numbers, and so forth, they all say Indian land. That is how they are described.

MR. TAYLOR: Well, I think the question or the point I am driving at—let's take Jackie Kennedy's estate (in Aquinnah). The estate has come up two or three times today. She owns a title from the State of Massachusetts, or at least the county that has jurisdiction in the Gay Head area. What I am trying to get at is, what are we looking at here as an alternative to what is before us? Are you saying that Jackie Kennedy's estate, as well as all other properties that are within these 3,400 acres, the title has currently been issued to by the State of Massachusetts, that that land should be taken from the current owners and returned to the tribe? Is that what you are recommending?

MR. JAMES: No.

MRS. (I): No; I have never said that.

MR. JAMES: I believe it was brought out before, when someone mentioned that it could be put into a Federal trust, like the National Seashore on Cape Cod, where these people would be allowed to stay there, and they could will the house to their future generations, and if they decided to sell it, the tribe would get first refusal. I think that was brought out here before. (United States Senate 1986, 69–71)

As moderator of the hearing, Taylor is empowered to determine how much can be said by testimony participants, a role he seems to command readily in his dialogue with James. At a critical transition in the testimony, the moment in which James stated, "I am also disturbed," Taylor interrupted him and began to rehearse a conversation that had been recorded earlier in a testimony of another member of the James family (United States Senate 1986, 64). The previous testimony explained the strategy by which Wampanoag-owned land could be inhabited by nontribal occupants and how that land might return to the tribe by a process of "first refusal." Taylor's revisitation of the earlier testimony prompted James to remark: "I think that was brought out before."

Taylor, however, pressed for elaboration on the issue of occupation, this time invoking the estate of Jacqueline Kennedy Onassis, who purchased about 375 acres of Aquinnah land in 1978 in pursuit of privacy.[19] In Taylor's dialogue with James, it is as if the Onassis estate—the land holdings of a legendary American aristocrat, former White House "First Lady," and the widow of a slain, nationally adored U.S. president—becomes the discursive boundary against which no testimony can pass. Taylor did not seem satisfied until he pressed James against that boundary:

Are you saying that Jackie Kennedy's estate, as well as all other properties that are within this 3,400 acres (of Aquinnah) . . . that that land should be taken from the current owners and returned to the tribe? (United States Senate 1986, 70)

James could only reply, "No," as did Mrs. (I), another tribal member disaffected by the proposed settlement. So potent is the invocation of Jacqueline Kennedy Onassis that it is barely noticeable that James never completed the comment that would have identified the other matter that "disturbs" him.

The Taylor-James dialogue all but crumbles from a kind of Bakhtinian dissonance, as the ideologically colliding speakers compete in a textual space produced by transcription. To the extent that the dialogue is ideologically cohesive, it is the mediation of prescience that becomes the binding element. Both sides represent diverging interests but both sides anticipate a similar species of loss. James worries over the loss of tribal control "forever," and Taylor seeks assurances again and again that nontribal property owners, if placed under the control of the island Wampanoags, would not lose the land holdings upon which a nontribal land and power base is implicitly sustained. Here, the nuances of an intercultural relationship of cohabitation elude nontribal, political actors who remain fixed on a solution of fixity, wanting to produce a text that will perform indefinitely as a legal talisman against nontribal dispossession and loss of power.

Renegotiating "Forever"

Vine Deloria, Jr., and Raymond J. DeMallie have characterized the settlement process as the "modern equivalent of treaty making," a process by which Indigenous nations and their representatives are directly involved in negotiation, consent, and, ideally, renegotiation (Deloria and DeMallie 1999, 563). Under the settlement process, a settlement document is produced through a collaboration of interested parties. Like the Aquinnah case, the resulting settlement document then is enacted as law in Congress.

Between 1971 and 1996, Congress approved thirty-eight such settlement acts for Indian tribes. The earliest of these acts was the Alaska Native Claims Settlement Act of 1971. Deloria and DeMallie noted that the Alaska settlement act, widely known to be flawed, has been "amended several times since its passage" (1999, 563). The amendments are the result of strong and persistent criticism from within a base of what is now more than 100,000 Alaskan Natives.[20] I am unaware, however, of any legislated mandate, federal or state, that actually requires periodic reassessment of settlement terms and conditions.[21] In the Aquinnah case, the provision that comes closest to a periodic review is the requirement that any change to the Aquinnah settlement agreement would require a majority vote of the tribe, a vote of the state, and a vote of the town, which would include some of the very people who anticipate and fear tribal power.

As of this writing and to my knowledge, neither the language of the settlement "agreement" nor the language of the settlement "act" has been altered. Locally, tribe and town officials in Aquinnah worked out a revised land use agreement in 2007, but tribal officials have since exited the agreement. The local pact laid out a plan designed to avoid the bitter litigation and community divisiveness that characterized the hatchery litigation, but the 2007 agreement did not supersede the original settlement measure approved in 1983 and codified as federal law in 1987.[22]

Conclusion

In this chapter I have explored collisions of anticipation embodied in legal texts. I started out with a brief examination of the deployment of Mittark's "will" in the late seventeenth century and then examined more extensively Aquinnah Wampanoag participation in the creation of a 1983 settlement agreement, as well as tribal resistance to the agreement. In each of these episodes, an Indigenous nation seeks, across time, to secure and protect geopolitical self-rule through the inhabitation of juridical, textual practice.

In my examination of the 1983 settlement, I have tried to demonstrate that the settlement document emerged from a temporal field of discord and political theatricality. As detailed above, the 1974 tribal land case and the eventual 1983 settlement evolved from a set of events and developments that coagulated at specific historical moments in the 1970s and 1980s: sizeable, Indigenous land recovery in Maine, a heightened period of Indigenous pride and activism, tribal fear of losing land to Native peoples, island resistance to a federal attempt to legislate "forever wild," and more than a decade of intercultural and intratribal dispute over the settlement process and content. The end result was a text crafted to anticipate conflicting agendas and impulses.

Despite the destabilizing conditions of its genesis, the settlement text would feign coherence. Like many juridical instruments, the document wants to strip away historical, social, and political variance in favor of a transcendent language that would override any change in context or circumstance. I witnessed such a move toward coherence, when, in the winter of 2003, lawyers for the nontribal plaintiffs in the hatchery case stood before a judge and recited verbatim the language of the 1983 settlement. The lawyers argued that the Aquinnah Wampanoags could not justify a claim of sovereign immunity in the case because they wrote away their sovereignty when they signed the settlement document. Legal maneuvers like the ones deployed in the hatchery case perhaps are what the tribal "reconstructionists" had in mind when they fervently and steadfastly opposed the signing of the 1983 settlement, grounding their opposition in visions of tribal disempowerment made possible by the legal interventions of the state and a support base of financial elites.

Kanienkehaka Mohawk scholar Taiaiake Alfred has foreclosed the kind of courtroom scenes I witnessed in 2003. Alfred has advised Indigenous communities and nations to "challenge," rather than emulate, the "destructive and homogenizing" manipulations of the state. For Alfred, Indigenous inhabitation of deals associated with settler rule dangerously compromises Indigenous values and relationships to Indigenous nationhood, relationships that cannot be reduced to mere mimicry of Western models of coercive governance. Such inhabitation, Alfred has contended, entails entrapment. He added,

> By allowing indigenous peoples a small measure of self-administration, and by foregoing a small portion of the money derived from the exploitation of indigenous nations' lands, the state has created incentives for integration into its own sovereignty framework. Those communities that cooperate are the beneficiaries of a patronizing false altruism that sees indigenous peoples as the anachronistic remnants of nations, the descendants of once independent people who by a combination of tenacity and luck have managed to survive and must now be protected as minorities. By agreeing to live as artifacts, such co-opted communities guarantee themselves a role in the state mythology through which they hope to secure a limited but perpetual set of rights. In truth the bargain is a pathetic compromise of principle. (Alfred 1999, 60)

Alfred made his points convincingly. Still, I would argue that in the Aquinnah case anticipation complicates this scenario. The writing-in of constraints against anticipated demonstrations of tribal power does not always produce pure containment. Rather, these attempts at prohibition in a settlement text can open up new possibilities for tribal assertiveness and resistance. In the Aquinnah hatchery case, not only did Tribal Chair Beverly Wright and other tribal officials refused to seek approval from the town to build a shed for their hatchery—the refusal that triggered the lawsuit in 2001—but as the litigation moved toward closure, the tribe started building a new community center, also without obtaining a town permit.[23]

More recently, Aquinnah tribal officials, at this writing, are legally challenging a decision by former Massachusetts governor Deval Patrick, who refused to give the Tribe permission to build a casino on tribal land in Aquinnah. Patrick argued that the Tribe cannot move ahead with plans to build a casino without state permission, noting that the Tribe entered into a settlement that insisted that tribal officials abide by all local and state laws.

While settler anticipation embedded in the 1983 settlement clearly seeks to constrain, anticipation also seems to release impulses of conflict on the level of political practice, giving substance to one of the big social dilemmas of authoritarian law.[24] Anticipation, as Pierre Bourdieu suggested in his construction of time, often may fulfill social expectations, but it also can invite the destabilizing force of rupture (1995 [1977], 211). Without question, the Aquinnah Wampanoag decision to inhabit settler law through a policing settlement has troubled tribal self-rule on Noëpe.[25] Yet, conversely, inhabitation might in some ways *fortify* Indigenous self-governance, creating new engagements in Indigenous-settler relationships, engagements that can find strength, power, and purpose in the inherent instability of anticipation.

Acknowledgments

This chapter evolved from a 2010 presentation I made at the Theorizing Native Studies symposium, organized at Columbia University by Kahnawake Mohawk scholar Audra Simpson, associate professor of Anthropology at Columbia, and Andrea Smith, associate professor of media and cultural studies at the University of California, Riverside. Much of what appears in this chapter is indebted to the critique I received from that presentation. The chapter has benefited, as well, from the peer review associated with the publication of this volume. I am also grateful to the enduring support of my colleagues Richard Kernaghan and Khaled Furani.

Notes

1. Because of the sensitivity of some of the material in this chapter, I have chosen to change the names of tribal individuals or use only partial names.

2. The use of the term "kingdom" in this context is intended to represent an approximate comparison only. Sachemships were populated, geopolitical

territories under the guardianship of a sachem. Sachems, however, were not absolute rulers or monarchs in the European sense. Rather, their power was dependent on persuasion and performance and thus was continually reaffirmed. Men typically inherited the position of sachem from their fathers, but women also served as sachems among the mid-Atlantic Indigenous peoples. See Bragdon 2009; Robert Steven Grumet, "Skunksquaws, Shamans and Tradeswomen: Middle Atlantic Coastal Algonkian Women During the 17th and 18th Centuries," in *Women and Colonization: Anthropological Perspectives*, edited by Mona Etienne and Eleanor Leacock, 1980, 46–53.

3. Prior to Puritan, colonial intervention, the Wampanoags had no written language. By the time Mittark and his people crafted the will, however, Mittark had been Christianized and would have been familiar with the Puritan insistence of salvation through the written word in the Bible.

4. My friend's remark was made in a casual conversation with me, while I was working in a jewelry shop in the down-island town of Edgartown. The statement was recorded and archived after the conversation. The person quoted is not tribal. The designation "down-island" is a nautical term. Down-island on Noëpe is north; up-island is south. There are six towns on Noëpe. Two of them are up-island: Aquinnah and neighboring Chilmark. The town of West Tisbury is centrally located, although it is sometimes cast as up-island. Vineyard Haven, Edgartown, and Oak Bluffs are down-island towns situated in the northern half of the island.

5. All historical documents refer to Aquinnah as "Gay Head," and for centuries the Aquinnah Wampanoags were known as the "Gay Head Indians." Indeed, "Gay Head" even appears in the official name of the tribe, the "Wampanoag Tribe of Gay Head (Aquinnah)." For the purposes of this study, however, I privilege the Indigenous designation, "Aquinnah." According to one translation, "Aquinnah" roughly translates into "land under the hill" or "land at the end of the shore." See Manning 2001. Helen Manning, now deceased, was an Aquinnah tribal member and educator.

6. See *United States v. Washington*, 384 F. Supp. 312 (W.D. Wash. 1974).

7. This is probably a reference to developer Robert E. Simon.

8. See United States Senate, *To Establish the Nantucket Sound Islands Trust: Hearing before the Subcommittee on Parks and Recreation of the Committee on Interior and Insular Affairs,* United States Senate, Ninety-Third Congress, first session, on S.1929, July 16, 1973 (Nantucket and Tisbury, MA).

9. Four hundred and eighty-five acres is what the tribe now officially claims as the size of its tribal land base. The acreage includes unoccupied common lands, as well as approximately 160 acres of private land. See the Wampanoag tribe official website at http://www.wampanoagtribe.net (accessed September 2015). In Mittark's day, however, Aquinnah was significantly larger. Aquinnah tribal members continue to complain that the neighboring town of Chilmark encroached on Aquinnah land, thus reducing its original size.

10. The extinguishment of land claims only affects the status of tribal landholdings, not that of tribal members' individually owned parcels.

11. Cited in Grabowski 1994, 360.

12. In testimonies made at Senate hearings in 1986, opposing tribal factions concurred that the general membership of the tribe approved the final settlement by a vote of 164 to 29 in November 1983. What was debated, though, was the extent to which tribal members were sufficiently informed of the settlement provisions and the extent to which the general membership understood the provisions. For a discussion on the vote, see United States Senate 1986, 53 and 95.

13. These figures vary from one source to another. The 238 acres of common lands and 175 acres of private "Strock estate" lands are listed in a September 23, 1983, version of the settlement. The originally negotiated tribal lands were expanded once the tribe became federally recognized. The current figure, 485 acres of federal "trust land," includes parcels added from the isle of Chappaquiddick and from Christiantown, the site of what was once a seventeenth-century Noëpe village set aside for "praying Indians."

14. See *Building Inspector and Zoning Officer of Aquinnah [FN1] & others [FN2] vs. Wampanoag Aquinnah Shellfish Hatchery Corporation & another [FN3]* SJC-09211. (Transcript from proceedings in Dukes County Superior Court, Richard F. Connon, Superior Court Justice, February 12, 2003.)

15. Federal recognition was in itself another grueling process, a process that took more than ten years to complete. The U.S. Bureau of Indian Affairs (BIA) initially rejected the tribe's bid for recognition in a preliminary finding but the decision was reversed after receiving additional input from tribal officials. Anne, then president of the Tribal Council, was cited as a key participant in the recognition process. For an in-depth analysis of Aquinnah's federal recognition odyssey, see Grabowski 1994.

16. See also United States Senate 1986, 3.

17. The original letter is located in the National Archives office in Waltham, MA.

18. In recent years, tribal officials have expressed the desire to expand the size of tribal housing. Not only would this allow more tribal people to return to their ancestral home, but theoretically, an increase in the size of the tribal population on Noëpe would strengthen the voting power of tribal residents in the "town."

19. For updates and history of the Aquinnah estate of Mrs. Onassis, see *Vineyard Gazette,* "At the Kennedy compound," June 8, 2001, and "Caroline B. Kennedy files land plan to create limited family subdivision," Nov. 4, 2005. Mrs. Onassis bought the Aquinnah land in 1978 for $1.1 million. In recent years, the estate has been valued at $12 million. Mrs. Onassis died in 1994.

20. The 2010 U.S. Census lists the Native population of Alaska at 138,312, for people who either claim Alaskan Native identity alone or in combination with other identities. For Alaskans who claim Native identity alone, the population figure is 104,871. See http://www.census.gov/prod/cen2010/briefs/c2010br-10.pdf (accessed September 2015).

21. An email inquiry to the Office of the Solicitor of the U.S. Department of the Interior confirmed that no law exists mandating periodic reviews for settlement agreements. I received the email confirmation on January 13, 2012, at 5:20 p.m. Eastern Time.

22. For a discussion of the revised land use agreement, see "Abandoning Draft Pact, Town, Tribe Call Summit," *Vineyard Gazette*, 19 January 2006, available at http://vineyardgazette.com/news/2006/01/19/abandoning-draft-pact-town-tribe-call-summit?k=vg54bed6e553e05 and "Tribe Approves Land Use Pact," *Vineyard Gazette*, 11 January 2007, available at http://vineyardgazette.com/news/2007/01/11/tribe-approves-land-use-pact?k=vg54bed6e553e05. (Both accessed September 2015.)

23. See "Tribe Issues Community Center Permit; $1.2 Million Project Impacts Wetland," *Vineyard Gazette*, 15 April 2004, available at http://vineyardgazette.com/news/2004/04/15/tribe-issues-community-center-permit-12-million-project-impacts-wetland?k=vg54bed6e553e05 and "Town, Tribe Pact on Land Use Nears Decision; Attorneys Press for Accord," *Vineyard Gazette*, 16 November 2006, available at http://vineyardgazette.com/news/2006/11/16/town-tribe-pact-land-use-nears-decision-attorneys-press-accord?k=vg54bed6e553e05. (Both accessed September 2015.)

24. Much has been written about the extent to which dominant regimes attract resistance. Classic works on this topic are Aihwa Ong's *Spirits of Resistance and Capitalist Discipline: Factory Women in Malaysia* (Albany: State University of New York Press, 1987) and James C. Scott's *Domination and the Arts of Resistance: Hidden Transcripts* (New Haven, CT: Yale University Press, 1990).

25. For an insightful debate on Indigenous inhabitation of settler legality, see Taiaiake Alfred, Sovereignty: An Inappropriate Concept, in *Sovereignty, Colonialism and the Indigenous Nations: A Reader*, Robert Odawi Porter, ed., 67–72 (Durham, NC: Carolina Academic Press, 2005); Mark Rifkin, Introduction: Self-Determination, Subaltern Studies, and the Critical Remapping of U.S. Empire, in *Manifesting America: The Imperial Construct of U.S. National Space*, 3–36 (New York: Oxford University Press, 2009); and Dale Turner, *This Is Not a Peace Pipe: Towards a Critical Indigenous Philosophy* (Toronto: University of Toronto Press, 2006).

References

Alfred, Gerald R. (Taiaiake). 1999. *Peace, Power, Righteousness: An Indigenous Manifesto*. Don Mills, ON: Oxford University Press.

Appadurai, Arjun. 1988. *Social Life of Things: Commodities in Cultural Perspective*. Cambridge: Cambridge University Press.

Banks, Charles E. 1966. *The History of Martha's Vineyard*. Edgartown, MA: The Dukes County Historical Society. vol. 1.

Banks, Dennis, with Richard Erdoes. 2004. *Ojibwa Warrior: Dennis Banks and the Rise of the American Indian Movement*. Norman: University of Oklahoma Press.

Bourdieu, Pierre. 1993. *Field of Cultural Production*. Cambridge: Polity Press.

———. 1995 [1977]. *Outline of a Theory of Practice*. Cambridge: Cambridge University Press.

Bragdon, Kathleen J. 2009. *Native People of Southern New England, 1650–1775.* Norman: University of Oklahoma Press.

Campisi, Jack. 1991. *The Mashpee Indians: Tribe on Trial.* Syracuse, NY: Syracuse University Press.

Clifford, James. 1988. *Predicament of Culture: Twentieth-Century Ethnography, Literature, and Art.* Cambridge, MA: Harvard University Press.

Cobb, Daniel M., and Loretta Fowler. 2007. *Beyond Red Power: American Indian Politics and Activism since 1900.* Santa Fe, NM: School for Advanced Research.

Cornell, Stephen. 2007. Remaking the Tools of Governance: Colonial Legacies, Indigenous Solutions. In *Rebuilding Native Nations: Strategies for Governance and Development,* edited by Miriam Jorgensen, pp. 57–77. Tucson: University of Arizona Press.

Crow Dog, Leonard, and Richard Erdoes. 1995. *Crow Dog: Four Generations of Sioux Medicine Men.* New York: Harper Collins.

Deloria, Vine, Jr., and Raymond J. DeMallie. 1999. *Documents of American Indian Diplomacy: Treaties, Agreements, and Conventions, 1775–1979. Volume I.* Norman: University of Oklahoma Press.

Eisler, Kim Isaac. 2001. *Revenge of the Pequots: How a Tiny Native American Tribe Created the World's Most Profitable Casino.* New York: Simon and Schuster.

Goddard, Ives, and Kathleen Bragdon. 1988. *Native Writings in Massachusett, Part 1.* Philadelphia: The American Philosophical Society.

Goldstein, Alyosha. 2008. Where the Nation Takes Place: Proprietary Regimes, Antistatism, and U.S. Settler Colonialism. *South Atlantic Quarterly* 107: 833–861.

Grabowski, Christine Tracey. 1994. *Coiled Intent: Federal Acknowledgment Policy and the Gay Head Wampanoags.* PhD dissertation. DAI, 55(7): 2024A. City University of New York.

Hanks, William F. 2005. Pierre Bourdieu and the Practices of Language. *Annual Review of Anthropology* 34: 67–83.

Hayden, Robert C. and Karen E. Hayden. 1999. *African-Americans on Martha's Vineyard & Nantucket: A History of People, Places and Events.* Boston: Select Publications.

Hicks, Sarah L. 2007. Intergovernmental Relationships: Expressions of Tribal Sovereignty. In *Rebuilding Native Nations: Strategies for Governance and Development,* edited by Miriam Jorgensen, pp. 246–271. Tucson: University of Arizona Press.

Jennings, Francis. 1976. *The Invasion of America: Indians, Colonialism and the Cant of Conquest.* New York: W.W. Norton.

Johnson, Troy R. 2008. *Red Power and Self-Determination: The American Indian Occupation of Alcatraz Island.* Lincoln and London: University of Nebraska Press.

Joint Memorandum of Understanding Concerning Settlement of the Gay Head, Massachusetts Indian Land Claim. September 28, 1983.

Lefebvre, Henri. 1991. *The Production of Space*. Oxford, UK: Blackwell.
Levitas, Gloria. 1980. *No Boundary is a Boundary: Conflict and Change in a New England Indian Community*. PhD dissertation. Rutgers University.
Mankiller, Wilma, and Michael Wallis. 1993. *A Chief and Her People: An Autobiography by the Principal Chief of the Cherokee Nation*. New York: St. Martin's Press.
Manning, Helen. 2001. *Moshup's Footsteps*. Aquinnah, MA: Blue Cloud Across the Moon Publishing.
Mathews, John Joseph. 1945. *Talking to the Moon*. Chicago: University of Chicago Press.
Mayhew, Matthew. 1694. *A Brief Narrative of the Success which the Gospel hath had, among the Indians, of Martha's Vineyard (and the Places Adjacent) in New-England, With some remarkable curiosities, concerning the numbers, the Customes, and the present circumstances of the Indian*. Boston in N.E.: Printed by Bartholomew Green, sold by Michael Perry, under the Exchange.
Nagel, Joane. 1996. *American Indian Ethnic Renewal: Red Power and the Resurgence of Identity and Culture*. New York and Oxford: Oxford University Press.
Silverman, David J. 2005. *Faith and Boundaries: Colonists, Christianity, and Community among the Wampanoag Indians of Martha's Vineyard, 1600–1871*. Cambridge: Cambridge University Press.
Simon, Anne W. 1973. *No Island Is an Island: The Ordeal of Martha's Vineyard*. Garden City, NY: Doubleday.
Smith, Sherry L. 2007. Indians, the Counterculture, and the New Left. In *Beyond Red Power: American Indian Politics and Activism since 1900*, edited by Daniel M. Cobb and Loretta Fowler, pp. 142–160. Santa Fe, NM: School for Advanced Research.
United States Congress. *Wampanoag Tribal Council of Gay Head, Inc., Indian Claims Act*. Land Claims, Pub. L. 100-95, Aug. 18, 1987, 101 Stat. 704 (25 U.S.C. 1771 et seq.).
United States Senate. 1986. *Indian Land Claims in the Town of Gay Head, MA: Hearing before the Select Committee on Indian Affairs, United States Senate, Ninety-Ninth Congress, Second Session, on S. 1452*. April 9, 1986. Washington, D.C.
Walsh, John F. 1985. Settling the Alaska Native Claims Settlement Act. *Stanford Law Review* 38(1): 227–263.

CHAPTER 3

The Mi'kmaw Path to First Nationhood

A Roadmap, Some Strategies, and a Few Effective Shortcuts

Simone Poliandri

In the last few decades, "First nationhood" and "First nationalism" (the terms that I use to define and highlight the peculiarity of Native Americans' expressions of nationhood and nationalism) have characterized the political, social, and cultural actions of many Native communities in Canada and the United States. Such actions have been undertaken both by single First Nations (or tribes) and extended beyond tribal boundaries. Nationhood represents one of the newest frontiers where Native North American peoples have been searching for sources of self-determination. The use of the frontier image, one of the strongest ideological and territorial elements of North American colonialism, in this context aims purposely at highlighting the virtual inversion of the colonial march whereby Native peoples are now pushing back in the ever-growing attempts to regain their rights to self-define, self-identify, and self-rule. First nationalism and nation *re*-building embody some of the strongest attempts to achieve these goals going through the second decade of the twenty-first century.

In this chapter, I discuss Mi'kmaw[1] First Nationhood and nation *re*-building as they have being concurrently developing in three different sociopolitical contexts and dimensions: First, Mi'kmaw First Nationhood and First Nationalism are tribal sentiments, thus expressed by people from the entire Mi'kmaw territory, also known as Mi'kma'ki,[2] about the entire territory. The Mi'kmaw powwow circuit and the annual celebrations of

St. Anne, the Mi'kmaw patron saint, portray Mi'kmaw nationhood as a sentiment gluing people from the entire Mi'kmaw territory. Similarly, the Mi'kmaw people's experiences in the Church-run Shubenacadie Indian Residential School have contributed to create a shared new layer of identification that has reached First national dimension in Mi'kma'ki.

Second, Mi'kmaw First Nationhood and First Nationalism are expressed distinctively by single bands (or communities). It has recently become customary for the single Canadian bands, the tribal subgroups created by the Indian Act that usually occupy the space of one reserve, to identify singularly as First Nations. Using the example of the Millbrook First Nation, a small band located in central Nova Scotia and part of the larger Mi'kmaw nation, this paper portrays First Nationhood as both a further layer in the Canadian Aboriginal people's perceptions of community and a foundation of sovereignty at the local level. Furthermore, the Nova-Scotia-based Membertou First Nation's pioneering political and administrative efforts toward the definition and implementation of Aboriginal governance and citizenship in twenty-first-century Canada also exemplify this expression of First Nationhood and nation building from a single community standpoint.

Finally, First Nationhood and First Nationalism, as well as the devising and implementation of Mi'kmaw nation-building strategies, have recently become a provincial affair, thus involving all the bands from single provinces—Nova Scotia, in this case. The example of the Made in Nova Scotia Process—a tripartite forum to discuss treaty and Aboriginal rights that includes the Mi'kmaw First Nations of Nova Scotia, the government of Nova Scotia, and the Canadian federal government—illustrates how Mi'kmaw First Nationalism and nation-building efforts have been recast in a more prolific and manageable context to become pillars of the bands' collective strategy to achieve visibility and voice in the provincial social and political arenas.

Mi'kmaw First Nationalism and nation building are undoubtedly grounded on territory. Yet, the extent of such territorial base is different according to whether nationalism and nation building are expressed prevalently in economic, political, administrative, social, or cultural terms. On the one hand, legal and political discussions and actions toward the recognition and implementation of Mi'kmaw treaty and Aboriginal rights have played out in supra-tribal (read, Mi'kmaw national), provincial, and local (read, single bands) contexts. The Marshall case and the Made in Nova Scotia Process, both discussed later, illustrate this diverse territorial span of the current Mi'kmaw nation-building efforts. On the other hand, the social and cultural Mi'kmaw expressions of First Nationhood and First National sentiments embodied in the powwow circuit, the St. Anne Day celebrations, and the emergence of the Shubenacadie Indian Residential School survivor figure extend beyond band, provincial, and even international contexts (one Mi'kmaw band is located in Maine, and many Mi'kmaw people have lived and traveled across the United States–Canada border).

The inclusion of Aboriginal social and cultural elements in the Mi'kmaw people's definitions of nationhood and nation-building strategies presented here somewhat resonates with Taiaiake Alfred's vision, which portrays a community-level Native nationhood based on elements such as kinship, culture, and Aboriginal language rather than (and differing from) the Western model based on territorial boundaries and key Western values (1995). Similarly, Mi'kmaw lawyer and scholar Pamela Palmater traced an Indigenous nation-building path that must bypass the colonial restrictions imposed by the registration under the Canadian *Indian Act* and blood quantum in favor of more inclusive criteria. Specifically, Palmater envisioned broadening the set of principles determining Mi'kmaw (and, more extensively, Indigenous) identity and citizenship to include "ancestral connection . . . commitment to the Mi'kmaq Nation . . . and respect for Mi'kmaq language, traditions, customs, and practices" (2011, 208). This chapter complements and builds on these lines of investigation and those that I laid out extensively in the book's introduction.

As a sociocultural anthropologist specializing in Native American/First Nations Studies, my research path among the Mi'kmaw people has developed from issues of tradition and traditionalism in the accessing and harvesting of natural resources (Poliandri 2003) to broader questions on the contemporary formation, transformation, and maintenance of Indigenous identity (Poliandri 2011). Much of my work with the Mi'kmaq has necessarily addressed questions of power and inequality, as well as inclusion/exclusion dynamics. From here, the leap toward addressing issues of Mi'kmaw nation-building perspectives and efforts was small and virtually seamless. This chapter is part of a larger new project on contemporary Mi'kmaw nation-building visions and strategies that I have recently started and will focus mostly on the Nova Scotia communities. It is informed by participant observation in numerous Mi'kmaw communities of Nova Scotia and, more broadly, the Canadian Maritimes; many observations of and interviews about Mi'kmaw relations with the Canadian federal government and provincial governments, as well as reserve boundaries and relations with surrounding non-Native communities; informal conversations with Mi'kmaw and non-Mi'kmaw people on the nature and development of Mi'kmaw band communities; and use of academic and nonacademic secondary sources (such as local news, including regular monitoring of the Mi'kmaw/Maliseet Nations News, the official newspaper of the Mi'kmaq and Maliseet). Finally, this chapter benefits from numerous discussions on Indigenous nationhood and nation building that I have engaged in with U.S. and Canadian-based Native and non-Native scholars both privately and in the context of academic conferences, such as the already-mentioned NAISA meetings, over the last four years.

First Nation

Let me start by offering a brief background on the concept of First Nation. The phrase "First Nation" represents the ultimate expression of sovereignty among the Aboriginal peoples of Canada. The phrase was coined by members of the National Indian Brotherhood (NIB), the institution created in 1968 to represent the status and treaty Indians of Canada, while participating in the discussions that led to the federal recognition of Treaty and Aboriginal Rights under section 35 of the Constitution Act in 1982. In the weeks following this major achievement, the National Indian Brotherhood changed its name to Assembly of First Nations (AFN) and reorganized to acquire its current structure. Today, the AFN represents more than six hundred Canadian First Nations.[3]

Some academics, such as conservative political scientist Tom Flanagan, argued that the change of name did not reflect either the desire to simply renovate the public image of the institution or an exercise in syntax. Rather, Flanagan highlighted how such an act constituted a semantic transformation mirroring a much deeper change in the political strategy of the Canadian Aboriginal peoples. In his work *First Nations?, Second Thoughts,* published in 2000, arguably one of the most controversial recent studies on First Nations affairs, Flanagan underscored that whereas the term "national" in National Indian Brotherhood referred explicitly to Canada, the term "nations" in Assembly of First Nations refers explicitly to the Aboriginal nations. The rationale behind this small but significant change, Flanagan contested, must be traced in the renewed purpose of the Assembly and its constituency, as "Aboriginal nationalism in practice has oriented itself resolutely towards achievement of political power" (2000, 80). As a matter of fact, it has. But rightfully so, in my opinion, after generations in which such power was restricted or denied to them by governmental Indian politics and policies, and even came close to extinction with the failed *White Paper* termination attempt of 1969 (Miller 2004).[4]

The Mi'kmaw Nation

The Mi'kmaw people responded to the *White Paper* policy—aimed at eradicating Indian status, canceling all land claims, and abolishing all federal Indian legislation—with a drive toward retribalization. In 1969, the thirteen Mi'kmaw bands of Nova Scotia sought collective representation by creating the Union of Nova Scotia Indians (UNSI), a tribal entity merging the bands' political forces. UNSI joined all the other tribal unions of Canada in the National Indian Brotherhood (Larsen 1983). In 1986, a few bands of mainland Nova Scotia left the Union and formed the Confederacy of Mainland Mi'kmaq, the tribal council that today represents six communities: Annapolis Valley, Bear River, Glooscap, Millbrook, Paqtnkek (Afton), and Pictou Landing.[5] Similar tribal institutions were created to represent the bands in the other provinces of Mi'kma'ki.

The 2007 Mi'kmaw Resource Guide—the official publication of the Union, the Confederacy, and the Native Council of Nova Scotia, the three tribal institutions representing status and nonstatus Mi'kmaq—describes the Mi'kmaw Nation as the sociopolitical entity containing and representing all the Mi'kmaw people. In its historical overview, the guide states, "The Mi'kmaw Nation has lived and occupied the area now known as the Atlantic Provinces and the Southern Gaspe Bay Peninsula since time immemorial. This area is known to Mi'kmaw people as *Mi'kma'ki*" (UNSI, CMM, NCNS 2007, 3, italics in original). Similarly, Aboriginal scholar James (Sákéj) Youngblood Henderson opened his historical account on the Mi'kmaw people saying, "While no explanation of the origin of the Aboriginal peoples in Atlantic Canada has been universally accepted, the Putús or Míkmaq story keepers or historians say the Míkmaq Nation forged its origins thousands years before the rise of the great civilizations of Mesopotamia and Egypt" (1997, 30).

References to the Mi'kmaw nation are found in several historical works, including the reports of Roman Catholic priest Pierre Maillard, who worked as a missionary among the Mi'kmaq from 1735 to his death in 1762 and served them as a counselor and negotiator with the British. Despite his representation of the Natives as savages, in accordance with the customary and widely shared perspective among European colonial personnel of the times, Maillard nevertheless acknowledged the national character of the tribes of Eastern Canada when he said, "The original inhabitants of this country are the savages, who may be divided into three nations, the Mickmakis, the Maricheets, or Abenaquis, (being scarcely different nations) and the Canibats" (1758, 24). Although the product of Maillard's choice of words, such a portrait, when coupled with the political services that the missionary provided to the Mi'kmaq, hints at a perception of the national character of the local tribes that he may have very well acquired and come to respect through the long-lasting and careful observation of the Natives' institutions and sociopolitical life.

In the same period, the minutes from a council held at the house of Peregrine Thomas Hopson, the newly appointed Governor of Nova Scotia, on 14 September 1752, report a discussion about an attempt to bring the ". . . tribes of the Mickmack nation . . ." to a conference with the Governor himself in the near future (Akins 1869, 671). Again, both the colonial administrators' choice of word to describe the entire Mi'kmaw collectivity and their belief in the possibility to address such a collectivity (or, likely, its representatives) in a single meeting reveal a perception allegedly based on the existence of an overarching national entity encompassing and binding the tribes of Mi'kma'ki.

More than a century later, Nova Scotian physician and artist John Bernard Gilpin, a member of the Nova Scotian Institute of Natural Science, produced a small account on the original inhabitants of the Province, titled *Indians of Nova Scotia*, that he read at the Institute on 12 March 1877. Filled with scanty information and quasi-racist descriptions, the document mirrors the assimilationist views of many contemporary policymakers and administrators of Indian affairs. In a significant passage, Gilpin wrote, "They will die out as Mic-Macs . . . It is evident that the time has long passed to consider them a nation, in approaching them for their good. The sooner all national feeling, language and traditions are gone the better" (1877, 275). Such a statement provides evidence of the existence of a national sentiment that was under attack on several fronts, often unfortunately with successful results.

In the 1950s, Mi'kmaq connoisseurs Wilson and Ruth S. Wallis verified the disappearance (or lack) of national sentiment among the Mi'kmaw people. Although the Wallises acknowledged the deep knowledge that Mi'kmaw adults had of all Mi'kmaw groups across Mi'kma'ki as well as the binding role of the Mi'kmaw language, they nevertheless recognized that "there is no Micmac nationalism" (1953, 120).

Such a historic development is reflected also in the changes that the Mi'kmaw leadership underwent during colonial times. The Mi'kmaw

Resource Guide describes the Grand Council as the Mi'kmaw Nation's precontact government. The tribal Grand Council supervised the chiefs of all local bands, which had existed for centuries as loose subtribal groups (UNSI, CMM, NCNS 2007). Sákéj Henderson presented a comparable portrait when he described the Mi'kmaw leadership in the traditional seven districts of Mi'kma'ki. When speaking about the seven regional *sakamowit* (chiefs), who worked under the direction of a *sakamow* (the Grand Chief), Henderson stated, "These leaders formed one *national* council, the Santé Mawiómi (Holy Gathering or Grand Council), to advise the Míkmaq and defend the country under the general leadership of the great chief and their chief spiritual leaders" (1997, 31, italics added).

With the ratification of the Indian Act in 1876, the "band" was institutionalized as a form of political organization of First Nations peoples under the Canadian law. The Indian Act made bands a legal unit, with membership lists, assigned reserves, and elected leaders with administrative and political powers. The Indian Act chiefs and council system favored the fragmentation of the Mi'kmaw nation (in fact, all Aboriginal nations) and undermined the traditional leadership role of the Grand Council. The political role of the Mi'kmaw Grand Council rapidly faded out, and its function has been reduced to mere representation devoid of any authority. Today, band chiefs and councils *de facto* govern the Mi'kmaq and, more broadly, the Aboriginal peoples all over Canada. In fact, even more "modern" political and administrative institutions such as the tribal councils (CMM, UNSI) work for the band chiefs and councils, who are the real repository of political power and authority.

A few years ago when speaking to me about Mi'kmaw leadership, John (pseudonym), the former chief of a Nova Scotia Mi'kmaw band, was very clear about the relationship between the traditional and current forms of government. "Tribal councils are not above the bands," he told me. "They work for the bands and administer programs for their bands. The Grand Council has no political power . . . I don't know really [what the role of the Grand Council is today]. They're not chosen by the people."[6]

Some Mi'kmaq have underlined the detrimental effects of such a political artifact which, they contend, often leads to disagreements among Mi'kmaw people and communities. When I discussed the issue of Mi'kmaw community boundaries with Anna (pseudonym), a Mi'kmaw woman in her mid-forties, she was prompt to underscore the customary divide-and-rule First Nations policy employed by the Canadian government to address Aboriginal affairs. "The government made each band a First Nation, rather than the whole Mi'kmaq population under one Mi'kmaq Nation," Anna said. "This divides the people, and the government has always looked for that. The reserves became more and more the only place that people would feel as familiar places. The spatial continuity of people's presence on the territory was definitively broken."[7]

In the course of a telephone interview, Victor, a Mi'kmaw individual working in the Kwilmu'kw Maw-klusuaqn (KMK; Mi'kmaq Rights Initiative)[8]—the tripartite forum involving the Mi'kmaq bands of Nova Scotia, the government of Nova Scotia, and the government of Canada—mentioned that it was only in the 1960s that Canada began to allocate diverse resources to different bands. "Before then," Victor said, "we were considered one band."[9]

These points of view resonate with the words of law- and education-trained Wet'suwet'en leader Satsan (Herb George), Hereditary Chief of the Frog Clan and the President of the National Centre for First Nations Governance, a First Nations controlled nonprofit organization created to help Aboriginal peoples achieve their right to self-government. Cited by sociologist Stephen Cornell in a discussion on the reserves as the inherited political framework within which Native nations must act in Canada, Satsan criticized the weakening fragmentation of the Canadian Natives into single First Nations (or bands) by the government.[10]

Mi'kmaw Nationalism at the Tribal Level

Still, it is mainly at the tribal level that until recently the Mi'kmaw people have employed First nationalism to claim sovereignty and to address political and legal issues before the provincial and federal governments. The events and discussions that led to and immediately followed the 1999 Marshall case—in which the Mi'kmaq challenged the Canadian government over their Aboriginal right to fish beyond federal regulations, and which resulted in a historic Supreme Court decision in their favor—are a well-known example of this (Coates 2000; Isaac 2001; Poliandri 2003; Wicken 2002).

Although centered on the case of late Donald Marshall Jr., a Nova Scotia Mi'kmaq accused of illegal fishing and selling of eels in 1993 and found guilty in the lower courts, the issue became a shared battleground for all Mi'kmaq as it related to the infringement of centuries-old treaty rights to resource access and use. The repeatedly declared interest shared by all Mi'kmaw bands to preserve their rights originating from the Treaties of 1760–1761, signed between the Governor of the British Colony of Nova Scotia and the Mi'kmaq, hints at a "Mi'kmaw nationwide" common determination to face the adversity. Furthermore, the heated responses from the non-Native commercial fishing industry, worried by the possible development of a Supreme Court decision upholding Aboriginal rights to fish outside regulations (although only to sustain "a moderate livelihood," an ambiguous phrase that the Supreme Court used but never clarified), and the Department of Fisheries and Oceans (DFO), interested in maintaining power and control over national marine resources, led to episodes of tensions and violence in 1999 and 2000. This favored the coalescence of the Mi'kmaq into a unified body characterized by both a sentiment of "national" solidarity for all tribal members, who were equally perceived as under attack from external forces, and the necessity to offer a strong communal front in the face of such attacks.

Yet, in this particular case, the mutual efforts to face the government and the DFO as a single national entity progressively gave way to the concerns (and interests) of the single bands, which struck individual and customized interim agreements with the government and the DFO, which outlined the regulation of their own fishing activity. When discussing the Marshall case and its developments, Albert (pseudonym), a former official of a Mi'kmaw band, illustrated this process in succinct but clear terms. "When the Marshall case happened," he said, "all the chiefs said that we were going to stick together and do something about it. Then, one by one they all signed agreements."[11]

Such a scenario reflects and exemplifies the difficulties that the Mi'kmaw leaders and communities have had in constituting a national front before an external challenge; yet the unanimous concern toward preserving treaty rights that belong to all the Mi'kmaq of the present and the future—the seventh generation, as phrased by innumerable leaders and common individuals from many Mi'kmaw communities—speaks of a vision of bound destiny (albeit not translated into facts in this occasion) held by a large number of Mi'kmaq.

In the social sphere, the powwow trail and the St. Anne celebrations of late July evoke a larger Mi'kmaw community extending beyond reserve and provincial boundaries, which represents precisely this tribal national entity. As customary among many Native North American groups, the Mi'kmaw powwow season takes place each summer. During the course of almost each weekend of the season, the bands take turns in hosting their powwows, which are attended by Mi'kmaw people from the entire Maritime region as well as occasional local non-Natives. Carpooling, temporary residence in homes of family and friends from the hosting communities, and scheduled and unscheduled visits to relatives and acquaintances living afar are integral parts of the powwow routine. The Mi'kmaw people's high degree of mobility on the powwow trail contributes to create and strengthen a network of kinship and friendship relations, which is essential for the social and cultural life of individuals, families, and communities.[12] Anthropologist Harald Prins acutely remarked, "Individuals who do not form part of this informal network of kith and kin are effectively cut off from their social identity as Mi'kmaq Indians" (Prins 1996, 192). When discussing the powwow and, more in general, the thick fabric of kin relations linking Mi'kmaw people throughout Mi'kma'ki, John confirmed this scenario. "There are a lot of family connections throughout the Atlantic Provinces," he said.[13] In fact, family names like Googoo, Francis, Marshall, and Paul (just to cite a few) can be found in virtually all Mi'kmaw communities throughout the Maritimes.

In the course of my residence in and several visits to Nova Scotia since 2003, I have had multiple opportunities to attend powwows all over Mi'kma'ki with Mi'kmaw friends and acquaintances from the Nova Scotia reserves (particularly Millbrook, Sipekne'katik-Indian Brook, Paqtnkek-Afton, and Eskasoni). Whether people travel to participate in the powwows as dancers or drummers, to meet with friends and family members living elsewhere, to sell their crafts and food (Indian tacos and fry bread are the powwow staple foods), or simply to attend for fun, distance and the extra-provincial nature of many trips are secondary to reconnecting with loved ones and supporting the hosting communities.

Such a scenario fits Helen Ting's paradigm for the social construction of nationhood. Building on the work of sociologist Dorothy Holland et al. (2001) on "figured worlds"—the socially produced, culturally constructed systems of values, norms, and related behavior that provide the contexts of our social activities and are sites of identity production—Ting discussed the "figured world of nationhood or nationalism" (2008, 463). National identity, Ting argued, is produced and reproduced through the appropriation of "the nation" in concrete life experiences, more specifically, interactions with others. As "the figured world of nationhood is only one among many other figure worlds that ordinary citizens encounter in their daily lives . . . the (re)production of a particular figured world takes place through social activity. . . . Social practice is the medium through which the symbolic world of nationhood is reenacted" (Ting 2008, 464–465). Powwows are a pivotal social practice for many Mi'kmaq (at least for part of the year), one that extends their range of action and interaction across the entire Mi'kma'ki with people from all the Mi'kmaw communities. In this sense, they contribute to recreate and renovate the Mi'kmaw Nation over and over again.

The festivity of St. Anne, which takes place every year on July 26th, serves a similar purpose. Introduced by the French Jesuit missionaries in the early to mid-eighteenth century as the Mi'kmaw patron saint in order to facilitate their evangelization, the figure of St. Anne has had a strong integrating force in the postcontact history of the Mi'kmaq (Hornborg 2002, 2004; Poliandri 2011). Her yearly celebration features processions in every Mi'kmaw community reserve, among which stands the week-long gathering at the St. Anne Mission on Chapel Island (Mniku, in Mi'kmaq), a two-square-kilometer National Historic Site of Canada located in the southeastern part of the Bras d'Or Lake on Cape Breton Island, Nova Scotia. Mniku is part of the Chapel Island First Nation (Potlotek), which rests about three hundred meters across the water, and is home to the Mi'kmaw Grand Council. The mission on the island was established by Abbé Pierre Maillard, a Roman Catholic missionary who arrived in Mi'kma'ki in 1735 and relocated his post to the small Isle de Sainte Famille (later renamed Chapel Island) by 1750 (Chute 1992; Prins 1996).

Since the mid-1700s, Mi'kmaw people have traveled to Chapel Island from all over Mi'kma'ki to attend the mission. Still today, hundreds of Mi'kmaq from different bands own cottages or shacks on the island and relocate to the island on the week of July 26 to participate in the festivities, which include religious functions as well as social interaction. Many of these temporary residences are part of family heirlooms and serve as points of reference for the families' summer life. The celebration offers the Mi'kmaq an opportunity to reconnect with family and friends who reside in different locations, thus contributing to recreate and strengthen the larger Mi'kmaw community, the Mi'kmaw Nation, extending across the entire Mi'kmaw territory.

The national character of St. Anne's Day developed arguably since the early colonial era, when French-introduced Catholicism became a powerful element of cultural, social, and political resistance available to the Mi'kmaq against the dispossessing and assimilationist British (Protestant) colonial enterprise (Jaenen 1976; Reid 1995). The association of religion with tribal independence and survival contributed to make St. Anne and her yearly celebration a pillar of Mi'kmaw shared sense of destiny, which has endured until today. Similarly to the powwow trail, St. Anne's Day has become a source of First National identification for the Mi'kmaq, who often speak of it as the proof of larger Mi'kmaw national entity. In a sense, the July 26 festivity embodies a Mi'kmaw national holiday, a day of shared meaning that holds its own special place on the Mi'kmaw people's calendars.

If Catholicism provides a positive source of national identification for most Mi'kmaq, it is equally associated with one of the darkest pages in the recent history of the Aboriginal people of Mi'kma'ki—one that has contributed to offer yet another basis for collective identification at the tribal level, albeit marked by tragedy. The Catholic Church was responsible for running the government-sponsored Shubenacadie Indian Residential School from 1930 to 1967. Located near the Shubenacadie village in central Nova Scotia, just a few kilometers from the Indian Brook (Sipekne'katik) reserve, the institution was responsible for heavily disrupting or compromising the cultural, social, familial, physical, and psychological life of thousands of Mi'kmaw individuals (Knockwood 2015 [1992]; Poliandri 2011, 2016).

The goals and methods of the Shubenacadie School were similar to those employed in comparable institutions scattered across Indian country in North America and, more broadly, among Indigenous populations worldwide. They often involved the use of both physical and psychological violence, as well as a straightforward system of rewards and punishments in order to achieve conformity to the religious and mainstream values instilled in the Native students.

Although attended by roughly two thousand Mi'kmaw youngsters, who were affected directly by the educators' inhumane and occasionally humane teaching practices, the Shubenacadie School extended its effects indirectly to the descendants of the former students. Many school survivors and their family members have suffered from the byproducts of a disruptive education system that include loss of Mi'kmaw language and culture, lack of parenting skills, inability to engage in healthy marital life, alcohol and drug abuse, the use of physical and psychological violence as common child-rearing practices, low self-esteem and, for some, suicidal tendencies.

It is certainly along these perspectives, focusing on cultural disruption as well as psychological and social problems, that the connection between surviving the school, on the one hand, and a sense of shared destiny as Mi'kmaw (and even First Nations) people, on the other hand, can be understood. The experiences in the Shubenacadie School resulted in the emergence of an additional layer in many Mi'kmaw people's sense of identity: the Shubenacadie residential school survivor. The common challenges, sufferings, and the few moments of normalcy endured in the school by children from all over Mi'kma'ki contributed to create a shared sense of fate in the face of colonial assimilation that translated into a collective form of identification for Mi'kmaw people of different generations, gender, and provenience (see Poliandri 2016).

If, on the one hand, residential schools operated all over Canada (and the United States) thus making the residential school survivor a pan-Indian form of identification rather than a tribal one, the peculiarity of the Shubenacadie School experiences endured by the Mi'kmaw people, on the other hand, allows to speak of this as a tragedy for the Mi'kmaw Nation.

The Shubenacadie School was the only residential institution in Mi'kma'ki (and the rest of eastern Canada, for that matter). The overwhelming majority (if not the totality) of its students were Mi'kmaq who were all "instructed" by the same religious personnel over many generations. Father Mackey, Father Brown, Sister Superior, Sister Mary Leonard (also known as Wikew, which means "fatty"), Sister Paul of the Cross, and Sister Adrian are some of the common names recurring in the survivors' innumerable stories of the school days (see Knockwood 2015 [1992]). The shared nature of the Mi'kmaw survivors' experiences and memories, as well as those of their family members and friends, makes the legacy of the school and its contribution to individual and collective identification a "national" affair. Being a Shubenacadie Indian Residential School survivor means (or implies) being a member of the Mi'kmaq nation before anything else. It provides a unique designation for people who reside in or originate from Mi'kma'ki, at the same time as it relates them to all the Aboriginal survivors of Canada (and, ideally, the world).

Such a connection surfaces also from another important aspect, namely, the sense of community and the empowerment generated by the shared struggles that many Mi'kmaq (as well as Natives across the country) have been fighting against the government and the former educational institutions to obtain both the recognition of their status as abused people and compensation for those abuses.

The case of the late Nora Bernard, the former director of the Shubenacadie Indian Residential School Association that has been operating on behalf of more than nine hundred Mi'kmaw survivors since 1995, is representative of this empowerment. Through her work in the association, Nora, who spent five years in the Shubenacadie School in the 1940s, provided a sense of social belonging to many Mi'kmaw survivors who identified themselves with a community of people sharing similar experiences. This sense of community—represented by the association, its meetings, its bonding significance, as well as by the legal struggles fought alongside First Nations people from all over the country—has provided many of these men and women also with a sense of strength and empowerment. Being a residential school survivor has become a way, and for many the principal way, in which former students identify as Mi'kmaq (and, by extension, First Nations people). Being a survivor means having gone through one of the "national tragedies" marking the recent history of the Mi'kmaq. In fact, it reflects the formation of a significant piece of the Mi'kmaw national memory and consciousness. Sharing a common destiny and struggle with other Mi'kmaw people from across Mi'kma'ki has contributed to replace what is perceived as "lost Mi'kmaqness," which was measured mostly in emotional and cultural terms, with a somewhat stable sense of identity, this time gauged in emotional and political terms. Shared by people across the entire Mi'kmaw nation, this process of identification highlights the existence of a Mi'kmaw national community.

Nora Bernard was also the person behind the class-action suit of 2000, which threatened four religious denominations (Roman Catholic, Anglican, United, and Presbyterian) with bankruptcy (Paul 2006). Tens of thousands of claims were filed by survivors of many First Nations of Canada. Unfortunately, the Canadian government's delay strategy allowed many survivors (especially the older ones who were in the schools in the early and rougher times) to die off before they could receive compensation. Supported by the Assembly of First Nations, the lawsuit has finally come to a resolution. On December 15, 2006, the Canadian courts approved a four billion dollar settlement in favor of more than eighty thousand living residential school survivors. The compensation procedure was formally structured in September 2007.[14]

Reserve as Nation

A new sociopolitical phenomenon has added another dimension to the Mi'kmaw (and Canadian Aboriginal) people's expressions of nationality. In recent times, the single bands making up an Aboriginal nation, the Mi'kmaw Nation in this case, have started to introduce themselves singularly as First Nations. This appears in the language of their public communications as well as on visual elements, such as reserve signs and band councils' letterhead (see figures 3.1 and 3.2).

FIGURE 3.1. Indian Brook (now Sipekne'katik) First Nation's band council former official letterhead (scanned by author).

FIGURE 3.2. Eskasoni First Nation's sign at the northern entrance of the reserve along Shore Road (Route 216) on Cape Breton Island, NS. (Author photo)

Lisa Valentine (1994) was among the first scholars to highlight such a phenomenon when she discussed the recent use of the term "nation" among the southwestern Ontario Algonquian communities and its usual association with the name of a single reserve rather than the entire tribe. Similarly, Heidi Kiiwetinepinesiik Stark (2013) recently pointed to the national character of individual Anishinaabe bands, and its distinction from Anishinaabe (collective) nationhood, in her broader discussion of the dynamics of Anishinaabe nationhood in the context of treaty-making with the United States and Canada.

It is worth to keep in mind that most Mi'kmaw bands, as well as most Canadian First Nations, occupy the space of one (often small) reserve which, in some cases, may have one or more minuscule separate appendixes. Both reserve residents and the neighboring non-Native populations usually envision these reserves as stand-alone communities, with variable degrees of cohesion and participation in the life of their surrounding region.

Millbrook, for instance, has a current band membership of about 1,800 (half of whom live on the reserve) and is located within the town borders of Truro, which has a total population of roughly 12,500, in central Nova Scotia. Although vexed by many of the problems that characterize the life of a large number of Native reserves (as well as inner-city and low-income areas) in North America—including alcohol and drug abuse, violence, teen pregnancy, suicide, and petty crime—Millbrook has succeeded in curtailing some of these problems and today looks different from most Mi'kmaw reserves in the region (and, more broadly, in North America). In fact, it does resemble many neighborhoods of its hosting town and, in most cases, actually looks better. The state of residences and infrastructures is more than adequate due to the band's financial success after the opening of the Truro Power Centre, Millbrook's commercial district, in 2001. Located alongside Highway 102—the main transportation artery connecting Halifax, Nova Scotia's capital and largest city, to the rest of the province—and thus benefiting from the high-volume traffic, the Power Centre leases land to many companies in different business categories, including hospitality, entertainment, retail, and fuel vending. These enjoy the favorable fiscal and regulatory benefits of reserve territory and, in exchange, pay leasing money and make Millbrook a preferred destination for regional shopping and entertainment. Needless to say, the revenues generated by the Power Centre have changed the outlook of Millbrook radically and increased both the opportunities available to band members and their overall quality of life, safety included. Furthermore, as one of the main job providers in the region, Millbrook's Power Centre offers employment to many local non-Mi'kmaw people.

All this might give the impression (and the expectation) that Millbrook, more than many other struggling and more isolated reserves, represents a case of excellent integration in the regional social environment. Yet, when discussing the relationship between Millbrook and Truro with

Mi'kmaw and non-Mi'kmaw people, I received a similar portrait of the actual state of things. "There is a line around the reserve," most of them said. "It is not a real line, but a psychological one that divides Native and non-Native territory."[15] I managed to identify a tangible evidence of this "unreal line" in a street sign which, until very recently, was located within the Truro city limits, thus offering a topographic representation of such a separation (see figure 3.3).

In many of their public and private communications, Millbrook leaders express this divide using the national discourse. In a casual conversation about the relationship between town and reserve, Millbrook's former chief told me, "The reserve used to be in the area of today's downtown Truro and was relocated to its present location in the early 20th century." Then, he added, "Now the Millbrook Nation is here to stay and we will expand."[16] Victor provided confirmation to such a perception when he said that for the Mi'kmaq "the band is a distinct layer of nationality."[17]

FIGURE 3.3. Until very recently, this sign was located on Willow Street, one of the main arteries of Truro, at the intersection with the McClure's Mills Connector Road, which provides access to and from Provincial Highway 102. (Author photo)

It is interesting, for instance, that almost every Mi'kmaw powwow (in Millbrook and elsewhere) features the formal display of the Mi'kmaw flag, the Nova Scotia flag, the Canadian flag, and the U.S. flag. Every day at Grand Entry, elders and notable individuals carry these flags into the ceremonial grounds and place them onto the poles of the drummers' harbor. In the many occasions I attended the Millbrook powwow, I could not avoid noticing that the Master of Ceremonies, the microphone-holding individual responsible for explaining and guiding the powwow activities, extended the hosting Millbrook Nation's official welcome to the members of all First Nations and the nations represented by the flags.

Millbrook's commemoration of Remembrance Day, which celebrates the veterans of all wars on November 11th, offers another example of this First National discourse at the band level. When I participated in the ceremonies in 2003, I noticed the band leaders carrying the Mi'kmaw, Canadian, Nova Scotia, and American flags in a single line, while marching behind representatives of the Royal Canadian Mounted Police, Canada's national police force. After the parade settled on the arranged commemorative site, the Mi'kmaw Honor Song, the unofficial anthem of the Mi'kmaw people, and "O Canada," Canada's national anthem, were performed in sequence. Then, Mi'kmaw leaders and veterans delivered official speeches celebrating "the veterans of the Millbrook Nation."

These examples highlight the widespread narrative found among the Mi'kmaq that portrays the Millbrook band, which overlaps the Millbrook reserve, as an independent First Nation. This suggests the presence of a further layer in the Mi'kmaw people's perception of their community, namely the national level. Speaking from a national standpoint certainly provides a sense of empowerment.

The national character of single Native communities has recently emerged in several initiatives set up by some bands to configure and promote their First national efforts. This has been the case with a series of workshops on governance and citizenship where single First Nations share their nation-building efforts and create forums to learn from one another, although maintaining autonomy of action. In most cases, these initiatives have been coordinated by the *National Centre for First Nations Governance*, a nonprofit organization devoted to support the Native communities' efforts toward developing independent governance.[18] Among the Mi'kmaq, the financial powerhouse Membertou First Nation, located in the Nova Scotia town of Sydney, promoted a series of six nation rebuilding workshops and two community engagement sessions between October 2010 and March 2011. Furthermore, Membertou scheduled a series of five Emerging Leaders workshops on nation rebuilding in early August 2011.

The purpose of these events was to promote community awareness and to develop internal guidelines for governance development, as well as to offer hands-on examples of nation-building efforts to other First Nations.[19] Membertou has also been at the forefront in the study and development of a new concept of Aboriginal citizenship, one that will hopefully rectify the injustices and shortcomings of the *Indian Act* offering a new instrument for First Nations self-government and community self-regulation.[20]

Province-Based First Nationhood

So far, I have illustrated how Mi'kmaw First Nationhood is both a tribal and single-band phenomenon that combines political, cultural, social, and economic aspects. Yet there is another context where Mi'kmaw First Nationhood and Nationalism have recently emerged. When gauging political and administrative efforts to implement Mi'kmaw governance and, more broadly, to improve the lives of the Mi'kmaw people and communities, First Nationalism and nation building seem to work more effectively at the provincial level.

Again, Victor, explained this phenomenon clearly. "Dealing with just Nova Scotia is easier and more effective than dealing with several provinces all together," he said. "Also the Nova Scotia Mi'kmaw nations have a history of dealing with Nova Scotia." He then added,

> There was a time when the Mi'kmaw people wrote an 'Atlantic process,' but many people including myself opposed it as ineffective. The problem with [a multi-provincial effort] is that issues of different bands [belonging to different provinces] overlap. So, negotiation processes may get stalled for some, waiting other people's issues to get resolved with their province. Nova Scotia band have been so far in advance compared with those in other provinces. Thus, it made sense to act at the provincial level.[21]

And, indeed, it has. In June 2002, the Mi'kmaq of Nova Scotia approached the governments of Nova Scotia and Canada to discuss treaty rights. After several conversations, the three parties signed an Umbrella Agreement stating the willingness to work together to resolve treaty issues in Nova Scotia. This officially started the Made in Nova Scotia Process. The Mi'kmaw people are represented by the Assembly of Nova Scotia Mi'kmaw Chiefs (ANSMC), the organization including the chiefs of all the thirteen Nova Scotia bands.[22]

On February 23, 2007, the Nova Scotia Mi'kmaq, through ANSMC, signed a Framework Agreement with the governments of Canada and Nova Scotia. This agreement signals the start of a formal negotiations process "to create stable and respectful relationships and to reconcile the respective interests of the Parties through a Mi'kmaq of Nova Scotia Accord that sets out the manner in which the Mi'kmaq of Nova Scotia will exercise constitutionally protected rights respecting land, resources and governance, to the extent the issues are dealt with in the Accord."[23] The Made in Nova Scotia Process is expected to produce a Final Agreement, which will regulate the future relationship of the Mi'kmaq of Nova Scotia with the Province and Canada, to be ratified sometime after 2011. As of August 2015, a Final Agreement had not yet been ratified.

Also, on October 1, 2008, the Assembly of Nova Scotia Mi'kmaq Chiefs released the *Mi'kmaq of Nova Scotia Nationhood Proclamation*, a national declaration at the provincial level. The Proclamation reads:

> Two hundred and fifty six years ago the Mi'kmaq signed the Treaty of 1752. This is one within a Covenant Chain of Treaties signed between the Mi'kmaq of Nova Scotia and the Crown from 1725 to 1761. We recognize and affirm that our Treaties are made Nation to Nation by their respective governments. The Chiefs of Nova Scotia hereby come together to proclaim and assert Nationhood of the Mi'kmaq of Nova Scotia over our traditional lands and waters. We, the Chiefs and Councils of Nova Scotia, as the elected representatives of the Mi'kmaq, agree to work together to develop a Mi'kmaw governance structure that unites and empowers our Nation to enhance the quality of life and well-being of our people.[24]

This Proclamation represents an historic milestone for the Mi'kmaq of Nova Scotia seeking to implement their rights in the province. The Proclamation also reasserts the nation-to-nation relationship established by the treaty signing processes in the 1700s.

It is significant that the Proclamation was issued on October 1, which every year marks the celebration of Treaty Day. The festivity was established in 1986 in result of the landmark 1985 ruling in *Simon v. The Queen*, where the Supreme Court of Canada upheld the validity of the Treaty of 1752 between the Mi'kmaq and the British.[25] The creation of Treaty Day was intended to celebrate the unique and longstanding relationship between the Mi'kmaw people and the British Crown (McMillan 1996, 118–124; UNSI, CMM, NCNS 2007). Interestingly and fittingly, Treaty Day is celebrated only in the province of Nova Scotia and marks the beginning of Mi'kmaq History Month, featuring a month-long series of initiatives aimed at promoting awareness of Mi'kmaw affairs to the non-Native population of the province. On Treaty Day, Mi'kmaw leaders, led by members of the Grand Council, meet and exchange gifts with members of the provincial government. The provincial character of this event surfaces from the Mi'kmaw people's perception of it, which is epitomized by the informative statement on the Union of Nova Scotia Indians' official website reading:

> People continue to gather in Halifax on October 1st to enjoy various events in celebration of Treaty Day. It's a reunion for many Mi'kmaq and a time for non-aboriginals to learn a part of Nova Scotia's 12,000-year-old history."[26]

Since 2008, the Kwilmu'kw Maw-klusuaqn (KMK; Mi'kmaq Rights Initiative), the tribal agency representing all the Nova Scotia band chiefs, has been coordinating the Mi'kmaw efforts in the Tripartite Forum. In a public statement accompanying the release of the 2008 Nationhood Proclamation, Chief Morley Googoo of the Waycobah First Nation, then co-chair of the KMK Governance Advisory Committee, said,

> Kwilmukw Maw-klusuagn means we are seeking out consensus. The Mi'kmaq of Nova Scotia through the Mi'kmaq Rights Initiative are trying to seek consensus on how we implement our Mi'kmaq rights today and for future generations. The Proclamation represents a first step on our journey toward Mi'kmaq Nationhood.[27]

On March 24, 2011, Mi'kmaw leaders from all Nova Scotia First Nations participated in the third annual Chief and Council Nationhood Conference in Halifax, Nova Scotia. The purpose of the two-day event, hosted by the Assembly of Nova Scotia Mi'kmaq Chiefs with KMK Negotiation Office personnel, was to discuss the next steps toward the building of Mi'kmaw nationhood. The successes and challenges of this task were presented and updated in the fourth annual conference the following year and, lastly, in its fifth edition on October 2 and 3, 2013.[28]

Yet another historic agreement marked the Mi'kmaw nation-building process at the provincial level. On August 31, 2010, the Assembly of Nova Scotia Mi'kmaq Chiefs and the provincial and federal governments signed the Mi'kmaq-Nova Scotia-Canada Consultation Terms of Reference. Ratified in Millbrook, this agreement formally established a consultation process that includes the Mi'kmaq in any legal discussion and government activities that have the potential to impact Mi'kmaw interests and rights.[29]

Finally, on June 15, the Nova Scotia cabinet and the Assembly of Nova Scotia Mi'kmaq Chiefs met for the third time in 2011 to review the progress of the government-to-government relations between the province and the Mi'kmaw communities of Nova Scotia.[30] This has been the last installment in the developing government-to-government relations between the Mi'kmaq and Nova Scotia at the provincial level. As the two parties agreed to meet again in the near future, it is clear that the Mi'kmaq, and seemingly the provincial and federal governments, have a positive outlook on the present and future potential and efficacy of this provincial-based Aboriginal nation-building process.

Conclusion: The Citizenship Path toward Mi'kmaw Nationhood

Victor told me that the Mi'kmaw Rights Initiative has been recently working at a definition of "Mi'kmaw citizenship," a concept upgrading and, at the same time, departing from Indian Status, by which the federal government still regulates Aboriginal rights and policies. The question asked within KMK is: What are the common principles that the Mi'kmaw people have that would make up a definition of citizenship? Such a query must take band autonomy into consideration, as it is key to establish where autonomy ends for each individual band, or First Nation, and begin for the collective Mi'kmaw Nation. The identification of parameters to establish and confer Mi'kmaw citizenship also affects rights, privileges, and benefits that come with band membership, which instead is managed by the individual bands. The larger issues shaping and affecting beneficiary rights are: who belongs to the Mi'kmaw Nation? and, who belongs to the individual Mi'kmaw First Nations?

One hopes these questions will lead to measures that will address the broader concern for the current and future state of Indigenous or First Nations concepts of citizenship, a topic on which little information is currently available. In fact, Lynn Chabot stated, "It is difficult to determine whether First Nations have adopted the theoretical underpinnings of the western concept of citizenship in developing their concepts, or are looking at citizenship from another perspective" (2007, 39). It is possible, Chabot maintained, that overly applied foreign concepts have taken deep roots in the First Nations determination of their constituency. "As of July 2006," Chabot reported,

> . . . 350 bands fell under the *Indian Act* rules for membership and 240 Bands exercised authority under section 10 of the Indian Act and developed custom membership codes. . . . Of those communities who have enacted custom membership codes, an overwhelming 70.8 per cent of custom membership Bands, use *Indian Act*, or *Act*-equivalent rules to determine membership. (2007, 38)

Such a scenario has given some academics and nonacademics (particularly, but not exclusively, of Native heritage) reason to question the efficacy as well as the conceptual integrity of First Nations citizenship. Alfred (2009), for instance, opposed the path leading to a (re)definition and implementation of Aboriginal citizenship. In fact, he claimed such a path as misleading in the construction of Aboriginal national visions modeled after Aboriginal worldviews and cultures. When searching for collective Indigenous identity from an Indigenous perspective, rather than from the point of view of First Nations people who work to develop institutions and philosophies modeled after Canadian and European models, Alfred contended that "the term citizenship is highly problematic" (2009, 13).

Alfred's point of view resonates as well as opposes those of many others, and it is likely to remain a part of the current and future discussions about the developments of First Nationhood and First Nationalism. Yet many Aboriginal communities have been planning and implementing strategies toward their own actualization of First Nationhood. For instance, Mi'kmaw citizenship was among the main items in the agenda of the 2011 Chief and Council Nationhood Conference, where the Mi'kmaw leaders posed and discussed the question "Who is a Mi'kmaq?" In his opening address, Membertou First Nation Chief Terry Paul, also Co-Chair of the ANSMC, touched on this issue, saying, "We are reaching a point in our history that we will have to define ourselves. Currently Indian and Northern Affairs of Canada defines who we are. We must develop our own consensus and definition of Mi'kmaq Citizenship."[31] A significant part of this work has been to survey and solicit the input of community members from all the Nova Scotia bands in search of a consensual response. When invited to elaborate on the scope and significance of this issue, Victor said, "so far, the data we collected shows that Mi'kmaw citizenship is a national issue among the Mi'kmaw people."[32]

Other First Nations have recently undertaken a similar task. In 2009, the Nipissing First Nation of Ontario presented the results of its community discussions about a proposed Anishinabek Nation citizenship law that would affirm the right of First Nations to determine their own citizens.[33] These consultations have involved members of forty-two Anishinabek communities, which are looking for a concept that would replace Indian Status and band membership for good.

It seems, therefore, that a large part of the recent developments of Mi'kmaw and, more broadly, Native nation building and nationalism in Canada points at First Citizenship as one of the main goals that would guarantee full political and administrative self-determination. This aligns and resonates with Sebastian Braun's point (in this volume) about the achievement of true sovereignty being intrinsically dependent on the power of tribal nations to self-define their paths of action in an interrelated world.

In a broader context, it must also be remembered that Indigenous Nationalism has become an officially recognized right, according to the United Nations' "Declaration on the Rights of Indigenous Peoples" of 2007. Ironically (and significantly), Canada was one of the only four governments that originally refused to sign the Declaration. The others were the United States, Australia, and New Zealand. Australia and New Zealand have changed their stance and recently endorsed the Declaration, respectively in 2009 and 2010, while in Canada only the Province of Québec timidly expressed interest in doing so. In 2010, the United States government announced that it will take steps to review its original position regarding the Declaration, although it failed to provide any detail on what will be done, how, and when. Similarly, in March 2010, the government of Canada revised its official position on this matter and announced its willingness to take steps toward endorsing the Declaration "in a manner fully consistent with Canada's Constitution and laws."[34] Finally, Canada at long last endorsed the Declaration on November 12, 2010.[35] For many, this long delay sends somewhat mixed signals about Canada's interest in considering First Nations peoples as equal nation-to-nation interlocutors at any table of negotiations.

In some way, such a development represents an official sanction and a striking examples of the kind of resistance that North American and other nation-states offer, as cleverly illustrated by Rebecca Tsosie (2003). When discussing the Aboriginal quest for sovereignty, Tsosie said,

> The United States and other colonial powers [which include Canada] continue to resist the notion that Indigenous peoples share the same attributes of political sovereignty as the Western nations that have been conquered and involuntarily annexed by other Western nations. These nations . . . reject the ideals of political self-determination that would guarantee strong territorial rights. (2003, 11)

This has been the case despite the clear and longstanding objective of most, if not all, North American Aboriginal peoples to rise to full sovereign status without challenging the sovereignty of their "hosting" nation-states. Michael Asch was already illustrating this vision two decades ago when discussing Aboriginal self-government and nation-to-nation relationships in Canada. "Aboriginal nations," Asch said, "have repeatedly asserted that their goal is to achieve recognition of their sovereignty and not to overturn the sovereignty of the Canadian state" (1993, 51). Such a notion is still embedded in the nation-building efforts of the Mi'kmaq and, arguably, all First Nations. Whether at the tribal, community, or provincial level, Mi'kmaw nation building in the twenty-first century has taken a complementary rather than a confrontational character toward the state and the provinces. In Nova Scotia, the Mi'kmaw First Nations' vibrant participation in the all-inclusive Made in Nova Scotia Process is one testimony of this attitude. Yet, both in and out of this forum, the Mi'kmaq have been keen to remind state and provincial governments that such complementarity needs to be grounded on the premise (and promise) of equal and leveled power status, rather than representing the concession to a reduced form of sovereignty, one where Mi'kmaw control and convenience are only allowed to exist as inversely proportional.

Notes

1. This paper utilizes the Francis/Smith orthography according to which the variant form *Mi'kmaw* plays two grammatical roles: (1) it is the singular of Mi'kmaq and (2) it is an adjective in circumstances in which it precedes a noun (e.g., Mi'kmaw people). See UNSI, CMM, NCNS 2007, 2.

2. The territory of Mi'kma'ki includes the current provinces of Nova Scotia, New Brunswick, Prince Edward Island, as well as part of southern Quebec, part of Newfoundland, and part of northern Maine. In precontact times, Mi'kma'ki was divided into seven traditional districts. See Poliandri 2011 and Prins 1996 for more information.

3. See the Assembly of First Nations website at http://www.afn.ca (accessed September 2015).

4. The full text of the *White Paper*, proposed by Jean Chrétien, then Minister of Indian Affairs and Northern Development in the cabinet of Prime Minster Pierre Trudeau, is available online on the Department of Aboriginal Affairs website at http://www.ainc-inac.gc.ca/ai/arp/ls/pubs/cp1969/cp1969-eng.asp (accessed September 2015).

5. See the Union website at http://www.unsi.ns.ca, and the Confederacy website at http://www.cmmns.com (both accessed September 2015). Recently, the Sipekne'katik First Nation (http://sipeknekatik.ca)—formerly known as Indian Brook First Nation—has left the Union of Nova Scotia Indians and has joined the Confederacy of Mainland Mi'kmaq.

6. Interview with John, 14 November 2003. Parentheses added.

7. Conversation with Anna, 3 October 2003.

8. See the KMK website at http://www.mikmaqrights.com (accessed September 2015).

9. Telephone interview with Victor, 27 October 2007.

10. Stephen Cornell, *Reconstituting Native Nations: Fragmentation and Response in Canada and the United States*, paper presented at the second annual meeting of the Native American and Indigenous Studies Association in Tucson, AZ, 20 May 2010.

11. Interview with Albert, 10 April 2004.

12. See Mattern 1999 for a discussion of the unifying role of the powwow.

13. Interview with John, 14 November 2003.

14. The deal recognized a compensation of $10,000 for the first year spent in a residential school and an additional $3,000 for each subsequent year. Survivors who suffered physical and sexual abuse are also entitled to additional $5,000 to $275,000. Now survivors can opt out (and choose to sue the government and the churches) or accept compensation and give up rights to sue. The Court website for the settlement is available online at http://www.residentialschoolsettlement.ca (accessed September 2015). See Niezen 2013, 43 and ff. for a detailed illustration of the settlement agreement and the compensation structure.

15. Fieldnotes.

16. Conversation with the Millbrook Chief, 29 August 2004.

17. Telephone interview with Victor, 27 October 2007.

18. See its official website at http://fngovernance.org (accessed September 2015).

19. See the Maupeltu T'an Telsutekek/Membertou Governance website, the official informative portal of the Membertou Governance Committee, at http://maupeltutantelsutekek.webs.com (accessed September 2015).

20. See "A World Beyond the Indian Act," *Global News*, 14 July 2011, available online at http://globalnews.ca/news/126133/a-world-beyond-the-indian-act (accessed September 2015).

21. Telephone interview with Victor, 27 October 2007.

22. Recently, the Sipekne'katik (Indian Brook) First Nation's band council voted to withdraw from the Made in Nova Scotia Process for all treaty-related matters, which the band now negotiates individually with the federal and provincial governments. The Sipekne'katik First Nation remains at the table of negotiations alongside the other Nova Scotia Mi'kmaw bands for all non-treaty-related matters.

23. This statement is contained in the Framework Agreement document, under paragraph 10, and it is available online on the KMK website at http://mikmaqrights.com/uploads/FrameworkAgreement.pdf (accessed September 2015).

24. The Proclamation is available online at http://mikmaqrights.com/uploads/NationhoodProclamation.pdf (accessed September 2015).

25. For more information on the Simon ruling, see Coates 2000, 87 and Isaac 2001, 54–55. The full text of the Supreme Court decision is available online at http://scc.lexum.org/en/1985/1985scr2-387/1985scr2-387.html (accessed September 2015).

26. Available online at http://www.unsi.ns.ca/treaty-day (accessed September 2015).

27. This statement is available in a KMK media release dated 1 October 2008, found online at http://mikmaqrights.com/uploads/procmediaadvisoryOct108.pdf (accessed September 2015).

28. See "Chief and Council Nationhood Conference 2011," *Mi'kmaq-Maliseet Nations News*, 22 (April 2011), 14–15 and "5th Annual Nationhood Conference," *Mi'kmaq-Maliseet Nations News*, 24 (November 2013), 25.

29. See the details of the agreement on the Nova Scotia Office of Aboriginal Affairs website at http://www.gov.ns.ca/abor/office/what-we-do/consultation, and the Office of Aboriginal Affairs and Northern Development Canada website at http://www.ainc-inac.gc.ca/al/ldc/ccl/agr/nsf/nstrcp-eng.asp (both accessed September 2015).

30. See "Cabinet Sets Priorities with Assembly of Nova Scotia Mi'kmaq Chiefs," *Mi'kmaq-Maliseet Nations News*, 22 (July 2011), 1.

31. Cited in "Chief and Council Nationhood Conference 2011," *Mi'kmaq-Maliseet Nations News*, 22 (April 2011), 15.

32. Telephone interview with Victor, 27 October 2007.

33. See "Anishinabek conference discusses citizenship law," CNW Group, 20 April 2009, available online at http://www.newswire.ca/en/releases/archive/April2009/20/c3235.html (accessed September 2015).

34. See the Governor-General of Canada's Speech from the Throne of 3 March 2010, available online at http://www.parl.gc.ca/Parlinfo/Documents/ThroneSpeech/40-3-e.html. A video recording of the speech is also available online at http://www.cbc.ca/video/#/undefined/ID=1430608778 (both accessed September 2015).

35. See "Canada Endorses The United Nations Declaration on the Rights of Indigenous Peoples," published on the governmental Aboriginal Affairs and Northern Development website at http://www.aadnc-aandc.gc.ca/eng/1292354321165/1292354361417 (accessed September 2015).

References

Akins, Thomas B., ed. 1869. *Selections from the Public Documents of the Province of Nova Scotia*. Halifax, NS: Charles Annand.

Alfred, Gerald R. (Taiaiake). 1995. *Heeding the Voices of Our Ancestors: Kahnawake Mohawk Politics and the Rise of Native Nationalism*. Toronto: Oxford University Press.

———. 2009. *First Nation Perspectives on Political Identity*. First Nation Citizenship Research and Policy Series, Building Towards Change. Ottawa, ON: Assembly of First Nations.

Asch, Michael. 1993. Aboriginal Self-Government and Canadian Constitutional Identity: Building Reconciliation. In *Ethnicity and Aboriginality: Case Studies in Ethnonationalism*, ed. Michael D. Levin, pp. 29–52. Toronto: University of Toronto Press.

Chabot, Lynn. 2007. *The Concept of Citizenship in Western Liberal Democracies and in First Nations: A Research Paper*. Prepared for the Governance Policy Directorate Lands and Trusts Service, INAC.

Chute, Janet E. 1992. Ceremony, Social Revitalization and Change: Micmac Leadership and the Annual Festival of St. Anne. In *Papers of the Twenty-Third Algonquian Conference*, ed. William Cowan, pp. 45–62. Ottawa: Carleton University.

Coates, Ken. 2000. *The Marshall Decision and Native Rights*. Montreal & Kingston: McGill-Queen's University Press.

Flanagan, Thomas. 2000. *First Nations? Second Thoughts*. Montreal and Kingston: McGill-Queen's University Press.

Gilpin, J. Bernard. 1877. Indians of Nova Scotia. *Proceedings and Transactions of the Nova Scotian Institute of Natural Science* 4(3): 260–281.

Henderson, James (Sákéj) Youngblood. 1997. *The Míkmaw Concordat*. Halifax, NS: Fernwood.

Hornborg, Anne-Christine. 2002. St. Anne's Day: A Time to Come Home for the Canadian Mi'kmaq Indians. *International Review of Mission* 91(361, April): 237–255.

———. 2004. Ritual Practice as Power Play or Redemptive Hegemony: The Mi'kmaq Appropriation of Catholicism. *Swedish Missiological Themes* 92(2), 169–193.

Isaac, Thomas. 2001. *Aboriginal and Treaty Rights in the Maritimes: The Marshall Decision and Beyond*. Saskatoon, SK: Purich Publishing.

Jaenen, Cornelius J. 1976. *Friend and Foe: Aspects of French-Amerindian Cultural Contact in the Sixteenth and Seventeenth Centuries*. New York: Columbia University Press.

Knockwood, Isabelle. 2015 [1992]. *Out of the Depths: The Experiences of Mi'kmaw Children at the Residential School at Shubenacadie, Nova Scotia*. Fourth Edition. Black Point, NS: Fernwood Publishing.

Larsen, Tord. 1983. Negotiating Identity: The Micmac of Nova Scotia. In *The Politics of Indianness: Case Studies of Native Ethnopolitics in Canada,* ed. Adrian Tanner, pp. 37–136. St. John's: Memorial University of Newfoundland.
Maillard, Pierre Antoine Simon. 1758. *An Account of the Customs and Manners of the Micmakis and Maricheets Savage Nations, Now Dependent on the Government of Cape-Breton.* London: S. Hooper and A. Morley.
Mattern, Mark. 1999. The Powwow as a Public Arena for Negotiating Unity and Diversity in American Indian Life. In *Contemporary Native American Cultural Issues,* ed. Duane Champagne, pp. 129–143. Walnut Creek, CA: Altamira Press.
McMillan, Leslie Jane. 1996. *Mi'kmawey Mawio'mi: Changing Roles of the Mi'kmaq Grand Council from the Early Seventeenth Century to the Present.* Unpublished Master's Thesis, Dalhousie University.
Miller, James R. 2004. *Lethal Legacy: Current Native Controversies in Canada.* Toronto: McClelland and Stewart.
Niezen, Ronald. 2013. *Truth and Indignation: Canada's Truth and Reconciliation Commission on Indian Residential Schools.* Toronto: University of Toronto Press.
Palmater, Pamela D. 2011. *Beyond Blood: Rethinking Indigenous Identity.* Saskatoon: SK: Purich Publishing.
Paul, Daniel N. 2006. *We Were Not the Savages: A Mi'kmaw Perspective on the Collision between European and Native American Civilizations.* Third Edition. Halifax, NS: Fernwood Publishing.
Poliandri, Simone. 2003. Mi'kmaw People and Tradition: Indian Brook Lobster Fishing in St. Mary's Bay, Nova Scotia. In *Papers of the Thirty-Fourth Algonquian Conference,* ed. H.C. Wolfart, pp. 303–310. Winnipeg: University of Manitoba.
———. 2011. *First Nations, Identity, and Reserve Life: The Mi'kmaq of Nova Scotia.* Lincoln: University of Nebraska Press.
———. 2016. Surviving as Mi'kmaq and First Nations People: The Legacies of the Shubenacadie Indian Residential School in Nova Scotia. In *Re-storying Indian Residential Schools in the Age of Reconciliation in Canada,* eds. Brieg Capitaine and Karine Vanthuyne. Vancouver: University of British Columbia Press.
Prins, Harald E.L. 1996. *The Mi'kmaq: Resistance, Accommodation, and Cultural Survival.* Fort Worth, TX: Harcourt Brace College Publishers.
Reid, Jennifer. 1995. *Myth, Symbol, and Colonial Encounter: British and Mi'kmaq in Acadia, 1700–1867.* Ottawa: University of Ottawa Press.
Stark, Heidi Kiiwetinepinesiik. 2013. Marked by Fire: Anishinaabe Articulations of Nationhood in Treaty-Making with the United States and Canada. In *Tribal Worlds: Critical Studies in American Indian Nation Building,* eds. Brian Hosmer and Larry Nesper, pp. 111–140. Albany: SUNY Press.
Ting, Helen. 2008. Social Construction of Nation: A Theoretical Exploration. *Nationalism and Ethnic Politics* 14(3): 453–482.

Tsosie, Rebecca. 2003. Land, Culture, and Community: Envisioning Native American Sovereignty and National Identity in the Twenty-First Century. In *The Future of Indigenous Peoples: Strategies for Survival and Development*, eds. Duane Champagne and Ismael Abu-Saad, pp. 3–20. Los Angeles: UCLA American Indian Studies Center.

Union of Nova Scotia Indians (UNSI), Confederacy of Mainland Mi'kmaq (CMM), and Native Council of Nova Scotia (NCNS). 2007. *The Mi'kmaw Resource Guide*. Fourth Edition. Truro, N.S.: Eastern Woodland Publishing.

Valentine, Lisa Philips. 1994. Performing Native Identities. In *Actes du Vingt-cinquième Congrès des Algonquinistes*, ed. William Cowan, pp. 482–492. Ottawa: Carleton University Press.

Wallis, Wilson D., and Ruth Sawtell Wallis. 1953. Culture Loss and Culture Change among the Micmac of the Canadian Maritime Provinces, 1912–1950. *Kroeber Anthropological Society Papers* 8–9: 100–129.

Wicken, William C. 2002. *Mi'kmaq Treaties on Trial: History, Land, and Donald Marshall Junior*. Toronto: University of Toronto Press.

CHAPTER 4

The Boundaries of Indigenous Nationalism

Space, Memory, and Narrative in Hualapai Political Discourse

Jeffrey P. Shepherd

Introduction

Fred Mahone had grown tired of seeing white ranchers running cattle on his reservation. A member of the Mahone Mountain Band and nephew of Indian scout Jim Mahone, Fred served in World War One, walked across France, and pursued a college education. When he returned to Hualapai country in 1919 from his years abroad, Mahone was angered by ten thousand non-Indian-owned cattle on the reservation. Voicing concerns expressed by many Hualapais about their economic, political, and legal status in northwestern Arizona, Mahone wrote the Commissioner about the "dictatorial" Superintendent who controlled the reservation. He told the Commissioner he wanted "freedom from 'restrictions or wardships' under which Indians exist" and demanded cancellation of all leases on the reservation. He wanted to "be as Americans are, free to develop our resources, as a community and to hold our reservation land for future generations."[1]

Not all Hualapais possessed Mahone's rhetorical flair, but he gave voice to a growing Indigenous nationalism that tied the common grievances of Pai bands to the abuses of the Indian Bureau, as epitomized in its failure to protect the Hualapais from ranchers and the Santa Fe Railway.

Mahone's nationalism emerged from a hybrid political culture situated at the historical cusp of "traditional" and "modern" discourses that symbolized the colonial conditions for Hualapais and Indians across the West in the early twentieth century: land allotment, second-class citizenship, reservation tensions, boarding schools, and religious discrimination.

The stories of Fred Mahone and his contemporaries are central to Hualapai history and the experiences of Native people caught in the maelstrom of empire. They stand in contrast to meta-narratives of immigrant achievement, the progressive impulse to protect the weak, the ever-expanding access to voting and civil rights, and the liberal vision of a multicultural nation. Heroic themes of westward expansion, the growth of democratic institutions, and the trope of rugged individualism reveal an American imagination that accepts violence as a necessary byproduct of "settling" the West. The notion that this violence was inevitable is tightly interwoven with the denial of sovereign peoplehood and the existence of Native nations as historical actors (Blackhawk 2006, 2; Guidotti-Hernandez 2011, 3; Ostler 2004, 2).

Recent scholarship has unmasked these myths to foreground how colonialism radically altered life for Indigenous peoples in the Americas. Colonization and empire building were central characteristics of American society, and as Matthew Frye Jacobson (2001), Amy Kaplan (2005), and Noenoe K. Silva (2004) have shown, much of U.S. history has been characterized by the dispossession of Indigenous peoples. To analyze the impact of U.S. colonialism upon Indigenous peoples, one must foreground Native communities and evaluate how they have negotiated the multifaceted nature of empire. Doing so reveals how Native people have employed a sense of space and place, drawn upon their cultural memories, and crafted political narratives about who they are as a people to directly engage the nation-state. The points of interaction where space, memory, and discourse collide with empire serve as useful sites of articulation for Indigenous efforts at nation building in the wake of conquest and in reaction to ongoing settler colonialism (Rifkin 2009, 31).

Historicizing these zones of violence and resistance yields insights into theories of nationhood that complicate the hegemony of "the nation." The frameworks of "the nation," nation building, and nationalism describe how modern structures of governance and social organization have arisen across Indian Country, but these concepts reflect Euro-American epistemologies. Many scholars have assumed that their research neutrally tracked the progression of societies from tribalistic and feudalistic, and ultimately to modern nation-states. While some scholars have acknowledged that these developments were fraught with upheaval, they have uncritically applied these units of analysis to non-Western peoples. They built theories of history from a fraction of humanity and concluded that these were universal processes of development (Alfred and Corntassel 2005, 600).

Applying these frameworks to peoples outside of the Western tradition challenges scholars seeking to interpret the ways in which those people organize themselves in light of European colonialism. Interpretation is complicated by the pollination of concepts tied to the Enlightenment, liberal individualism, and the cluster of ideals enshrined in the American and French Revolutions. Without delving into the critiques of glorifications of these events and the "American Democracy" they gave birth to, Independence and the "postcolonial" nation-building project were marked by myriad complexities that problematized the "American experiment." As the United States engaged Indigenous peoples the discourse of American politics worked its way into the treaty-making process and the larger array of relationships that comprised "Indian affairs." These ideas filtered into Indigenous communities and influenced their internal political identities. This is important for my purposes here because any analysis of Hualapai nationhood and nation building must confront the acceptance of "non-Hualapai" notions of identity that moved across the permeable cultural boundaries between Natives and non-Natives (Chakrabarty 1992, 3; Chatterjee 1993, 12; Cherniavsky 1996, 87; Hobsbawm 1997, 9; Prakash 1995).

By drawing on Indigenous, postcolonial, and subaltern studies, this chapter evaluates how thirteen decentralized bands confronted American colonialism and in the process forged the modern Hualapai nation. This sense of "being national" was a layered and performative identity fraught with ambivalence about and debate over three key issues: band and family identities that cut against a centralized and externally imposed notion of a unified Hualapai nation; the cultural, physical, and discursive complexities of associating "Hualapai-ness" with the colonial site of the reservation; and the tensions emanating from a "third space" of Indigenous sovereignty, that is, Hualapais' attempt to move through history as a people with rights to their land and culture while an imperial nation-state sought their absorption into the greater body politic (Bruyneel 2007, xiii). By embracing the discursive points of convergence between ideas such as "the Hualapai nation, tribe, or people," I demonstrate how the Hualapais confronted conquest and social marginalization to challenge the rhetoric of disappearance and forge an Indigenous discourse of belonging. Anchoring that sense of belonging were memoires of violence, reactions to the colonial/Native space of the reservation, hybrid political groups that represented multiple bands of Pais, and the crisis of legitimacy faced by the Hualapai government in the mid-twentieth century. These themes helped establish the discursive parameters of the highly contested notion of the Hualapai nation (Deloria 2004, 12; Denetdale 2007, 15; Smith A. 2005, 7; Smith L. 1999, 7).

Nations are products of powerful internal and external historical forces, which in the case of the Hualapais involved their reorganization from decentralized bands into more centralized yet layered identities. This process involved painful transformations that linked together nations, nation building, and nationalism. Nations are modern constructs that gain power from their ability to explain the world as it is perceived by groups subscribing to the threads binding them together. This sense of being a nation is tied to nationalism, which is a politicized movement employing the rhetoric of the nation and the implicit commonality of interests to mobilize people for various purposes. Finally, nation building is the complex process of gaining control over the cultural, human, and natural resources of a people and using them in ways that further the survival of that nation (Anderson 1983; Hobsbawm and Ranger 1983).

Whereas the fields of American Indian history and ethnohistory address these issues through the lenses of cultural adaptation and persistence, scholars of Native American and Indigenous studies tackle them head on. For instance, Taiaiake Alfred and Jeff Corntassel problematize nationhood with the concept of "peoplehood," which is rooted in an "oppositional, place-based existence, along with the consciousness of being in struggle against the dispossessing and demeaning fact of colonization by foreign peoples. . . . [This] fundamentally distinguishes Indigenous peoples from other people in the world" (Alfred and Corntassel 2005, 601). As such, Hualapais have faced modernity through colonial law, liberal democracy, capitalist development, and Western time to construct identities that reflect and reimagine preconquest relations with the land. This is an organic sense of peoplehood articulated in lived experiences and ongoing struggles to hold onto land, history, and culture. These concerns are tied to debates about postcolonialism, decolonization, and subaltern studies. I am intrigued by the arguments of scholars such as Ann Laura Stoler (2006, 21), Jennifer Denetdale (2007, 29), and Jodi Byrd (2011, 33), who observe that the United States maintains a colonial relationship with its subjects. Their work situates Indigenous peoples across the United States within a global framework of ongoing Indigenous-colonial interactions. Indeed, the United States subjugated nonwhite peoples and relegated their land and labor to marginality as part of the expansion of capitalism, individualism, and liberalism (Prakash 1995, 1481).

Interpreting Hualapai history as a subaltern confrontation between colonialism and nation building provides a different vantage point for understanding the Hualapai community. The same forces that sought to strip them of their land and culture were central to shaping their common historical memories and the symbolic and real boundaries around them and their landscape. Their sense of peoplehood was and is rooted in a preconquest world when the Pais differentiated themselves from others *and* retained band autonomy. As a colonial settler state invaded their lands, the federal government labeled the Pais as "Hualapais," set aside a reservation for them, and then made resources and recognition contingent on acceptance of that identity. Thus, the notion of being Hualapai rather than Pai deepened. Some people rejected the notion, while others fleshed it out with the creation of political institutions, legal codes, and cultural cues and behaviors. Band differences and family rivalries persisted but within common experiences and solutions to community problems. In short, the Hualapai nation today could not have evolved as it did without a preexisting sense of peoplehood, ties to the land, and a shared set of memories, all of which shaped Hualapais political discourse and interactions with the U.S. Empire (Gooding 1994, 1190).

The Conquest of Aboriginal Homelands and the Restructuring of Hualapai Space

Pai origin stories, which place their emergence at Spirit Mountain, west of Kingman, Arizona, anchor the Hualapai nation along the Colorado River, a place of spiritual sustenance. One story recounts how the ancestors of the Pai left the banks of the Colorado River, migrated to the east and south, and populated what became their cultural homeland of six million acres in northwestern Arizona (Figure 4.1). This landscape is a striking combination of rugged desert, windswept plateaus, mountains covered in pine trees, and deep canyons feeding into the Grand Canyon and Colorado River. These features characterized a borderland shared with Mohaves and Chemehuevis to the west, Paiutes to the north, Hopi to the east, and Yavapai to the south. These relationships tied them to a larger trade network extending from the Pacific Ocean to New Mexico and from Nevada to Mexico. Such relationships enabled the thirteen Pai bands comprised of extended families to survive on a range of wild game

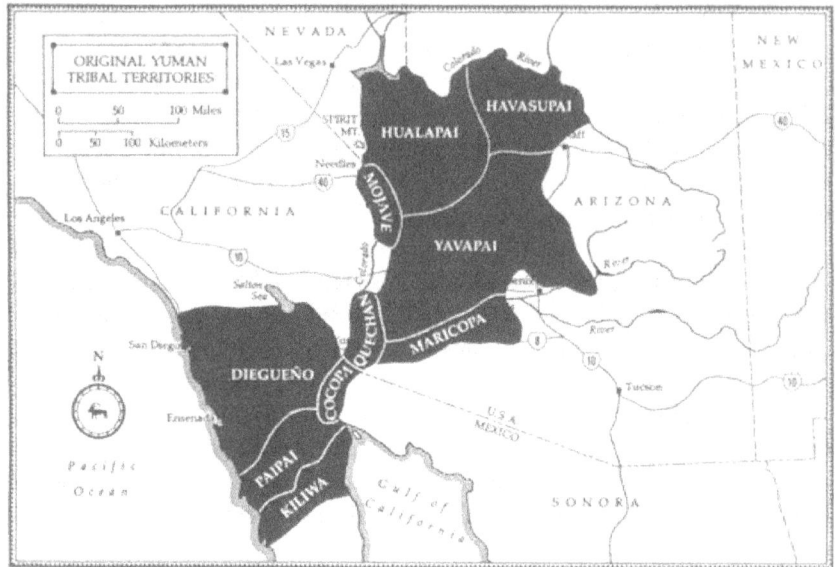

FIGURE 4.1. "Original Yuman Territories" from *Spirit Mountain: An Anthology of Yuman Story and Song* ©1984 The Arizona Board of Regents. Reprinted by permission of the University of Arizona Press.

and plants, roots, and berries. These bands also maintained local economies through light agriculture and migration around a tightly defined landscape (Hinton and Watahomigie 1984, 15).[2]

The expansion of the Spanish into this Indigenous world had minimal direct impact on the Pais, but the legacy of new technologies, animals, food, plants, and ideas was lasting. Francisco Garcés travelled along the Colorado River in the 1770s, and in 1776 people whom he called "Jaguallapais" led him to Havasupai Canyon, where he met several families. His journals indicate that he camped in territory claimed by the Truxton Canyon or Hackberry band northeast of Kingman. Garcés and his men chose to establish missions further south on the Colorado River among the Quechan nation, but local groups rose up to kill the Spanish colonists (Spicer 1962, 264; Weber 1991, 32).

Very little direct Spanish activity followed in northwestern Arizona, but trading in humans, weapons, and horses did continue to shape the region. A vast slave trade emerged in the late 1600s when Spanish communities demanded Indian labor in the borderlands. This stream of human labor flowed southward along the Colorado River through Quechan and O'odham lands and then to the Spanish markets in Sonora and Chihuahua. The demand for workers outstripped the preexisting practices of Native people as slave raiding became a goal itself rather than a byproduct of territorial disputes. This process evolved even as the destabilization of Spain's northern frontier bled into Independence and the emergence of the Republic of Mexico. As land switched hands from empire to republic in the 1820s, the borderlands competition for resources increased and Indians fell to the lowest rung of the economic ladder. The short Mexican period was also noteworthy for the conflict between the states of Sonora, Chihuahua, and Arizona, New Mexico and Texas, with the Yaqui, Apache, and Comanche nations (Braatz 2007, 16; Brooks 2002, 5; Dobyns and Euler 1976).

With the signing of the Treaty of Guadalupe Hidalgo between the United States and Mexico in 1848, the Pais faced westward-bound immigrants, military expeditions, miners, trappers, and traders interested in the resources of this new territory of the United States. U.S. Army mapping explorations led by Capt. Lorenzo Sitgreaves in 1851 foreshadowed conquest. When Sitgreaves entered Pai lands to determine their amenability to a railroad, men from the Cerbat Mountain or Hualapai Mountain band shot his guide. Miners assisted Sitgreaves and his soldiers as they killed two dozen Pais in retaliation. Ensuing explorers, such as François Xavier Aubry in 1853 and Lt. Amiel W. Whipple in 1854, exacerbated this violence. In 1857, Lt. Joseph C. Ives, an engineer for the Department of War, entered Pai country to determine if a wagon road would suffice as a train route. While scouting through the region, Ives' Mohave guide made reference to the Amat Whala Pa'a band of Pais, also known as the Hualapai Mountain people, who lived nearby. Ives misunderstood and thought Amat Whala Pa'a was the name for all Pais. When Ives submitted the *Report: Colorado River of the West* in 1861, he established the falsehood that the Anglicized term "Hualapai" applied to all Pai bands (Braatz 2002; Casebier 1980; Dobyns and Euler 1970, 1976; Goetzmann 1993).

These conflicts led to military intervention and facilitated settler colonialism, resistance to which marked the birth of Hualapai nationalism. In 1859 the Army established Fort Mohave at Beale's crossing on the Colorado River, just west of Pai lands. Fort Mohave, situated along the trading routes connecting the Southwest to the nation, was the central command for western Arizona. The onset of the Civil War stalled the buildup at the fort, but the end of the War brought changes for the Southwest because it enabled the federal government to concentrate on conquest and because ex-soldiers and civilians hoped to acquire land under the Homestead Act of 1862. Union troops established Fort Whipple outside of Prescott in 1863, and in 1864 territorial officials reached the outpost. Crews constructed a wagon road from Prescott to Fort Mohave, linking the capital with the Colorado River and the Gulf of California and the Pacific Ocean and steamboats carrying supplies traveling along the Colorado River landed at Hardyville, a port near Fort Mohave (Dobyns and Euler 1976, 31; Sheridan 1995; Wagoner 1974, 323).

During the mid-1860s, the region was quickly engulfed by racial violence, as recollected by Hualapais decades later. A member of the Whala Pa'a band, Auggie Smith was born at Walnut Creek (Tak Tadapa) in 1876. His father was Amutoo' and was related to a Pai band "chief" named Leve Leve. During an interview with the Indian Claims Commission in the 1950s, Smith narrated the conquest as told to him by his father, "When the white people first came in, they came with soldiers, and they shot down every one of them. . . . [T]his was the first time white men came. They came from the east killing from water to water until they came to this place. The white people did this."[3] Echoing Smith's story, another Hualapai recalled memories of his mother,

> The first settlers came to Big Cane Springs [in the Big Sandy region to the south]. These first settlers were friendly, they don't molest us very much. But finally other white families and white ranchers came and took over this whole valley, our gardens, our homes. We didn't give this country up voluntarily. We were just overrun by white people taking up the springs, the grass, the gardens and all of this territory. We never gave up anything: these people just overran us.[4]

In this landscape of uncertainty the military sought to concentrate northwestern Arizona Indians onto one reservation along the Colorado River. In 1864, Superintendent of Indian Affairs for the territory of Arizona, Charles Poston, met in La Paz, at the southern tip of the recently created Colorado River Indian Reservation, with hundreds of Native people from the region. Poston believed the proposal to concentrate the tribes on the single reservation was "the best both for the whites and the Indians" because the Indians would receive assistance with farming.[5] The rejection of his proposal by the Hualapais marked one of the first disagreements in the era frequently known as "the Indian Wars." Following Pais' resistance to relocation, conflict increased after the killing of a well-known Pai leader, Ana:sa. Anglos accused the Pais of retaliating for the death of Ana:sa by killing a prospector, so the population of Hardyville demanded vengeance, and the Army declared all Indians seventy miles east of the Colorado River subject to extermination. The final straw for the Pais was the murder of headman Wauba Yuma and his sons. Wauba Yuma's murder and the fears of whites about an "Indian uprising" precipitated a violent cycle: non-Indians demanded soldiers to protect them; the *Arizona Miner*, a paper in Prescott, called for the extermination of all "hostiles" in the region; and Pais and Anglos repeatedly attacked each other (Braatz 2002, 87).[6]

The result was a volley of bloodshed that lasted for half a decade. Pai leaders Schrum and Hitch Hitchi sought justice for the murder of Wauba Yuma, and Pai bands killed teamsters and miners near the Colorado River. Hardyville citizens killed two dozen Pai men and captured nineteen Pai women, and an Anglo posse joined fifty Mohaves in exterminating twenty-one Pais. During an attack on mail carriers, the Pais suffered nearly twenty casualties in a day-long fight. The anarchy brought five hundred troops from the Eighth U.S. Cavalry and Infantry in 1867, but Pai leaders continued defending their lands against settlers and the military. One such assault took place in the summer, when Schrum organized two hundred and fifty Pais and Southern Paiutes to attack the Camp Beale's Spring mail station. In the wake of the assault the commandant of Fort Mohave reported that "the most hostile band is led by Chief Chesora [Schrum], the chief of the Hualapai Tribe."[7]

The beginning of the end of warfare came with the arrival of Colonel William Redwood Price in mid-1867 when he implemented a scorched earth policy against the Pai. He penetrated Pai territory, "driving and harassing" the "degenerate" Hualapais until they were "thoroughly whipped."[8] Writing to Maj. John P. Sherburne, Price recalled how "Genl Gregg and a party had come on to a rancheria, charged it, killing four Indians, Capturing a large lot of Buckskins, Furs, and food." In letters to superiors he wrote about an excursion down Diamond Creek that resulted in killing nearly a dozen "Indians," most likely members of the Milkweed or Peach Springs band. On 8 November 1867 a lieutenant under Price "surrounded and attacked a rancheria of Hualapai Indians . . . killing nineteen Indians, and capturing Sixteen Squaws and children" while they roasted agave.[9] On 2 December he reported that a lieutenant "surprised a rancheria of Hualapais . . . killing three Indians and capturing four children and one horse, also destroying a large quantity of seed and Indian property," while another detachment "destroyed two rancherias and a large amount of property, captured one squaw, [and] killed one Indian."[10] January brought the same: an attack on a ranchería with nearly one hundred people led to the death of sixteen Pais and the capture of thirty, while another attack killed nearly twenty-five individuals. Overall, Price claimed to have killed over one hundred Pais and injured twice that many.[11]

This relentless pursuit of Pai bands revealed two competing responses that framed the parameters of an incipient indigenous nationalism: those supporting Schrum and his resistance to the military, and those supporting Leve Leve, the Peace Chief, and his program of conciliation. After a year of negotiation, in 1869 leaders of the conciliatory Pai bands under Leve Leve signed an agreement to end hostilities and discuss settlement on a reservation. The problem with this "solution" was that the military wanted them to move to the Colorado River Indian Reservation. The bands maintained their resistance until the military began rounding up families for a forced removal to La Paz on the Colorado River Indian Reservation. When the military began what Hualapais now call the Long Walk to La Paz, in 1874, band members scattered across the region as the military corralled them near Camp Beale Springs in preparation for their march (Dobyns and Euler 1976).

Recreating the removal is difficult, but memories of survivors and stories passed down by ancestors provide a window onto a traumatic experience that shaped the national consciousness of the Hualapai. Kate Crozier, a boy during removal, remembered how "all Walapai Indians we skipped off, going down into Grand Canyon [to] get out of the way. So they left Beale Spring and gone into the Grand Canyon." His group stayed there for "must have been two weeks," until Captain Byrne convinced them to return to Beale's Springs. A few days later Crozier and his family marched to La Paz.[12] Bob Schrum, son of the Pai leader Schrum, survived the march as a child. Speaking in 1944, he recalled how "the young and very old Indians [were] unable to continue the march," which ended two weeks later. Indian Honga, who was roughly seven years old when "the Indians were gathered up to go there," recounted his memories of La Paz during an interview in 1943. Honga recalled: "My family got away with the other Indians belonging to the Pine Springs group and we went to the mountains."[13] Similarly, Koara, who was related to Jim Fielding, an important leader during the early twentieth century, recalled that he and his family ran into the Hualapai Mountains, using guns taken from the military. They remained in hiding for over a year. Estimates of the number of Pais relocated range from four to six hundred, but all accounts agree that dozens died in the removal.[14]

Exodus, Space, and the Hualapai Reservation

Internment was a brutal reality that resulted in death for many, but precisely one year later Pai bands escaped and tried to return to their northern homelands and reconstitute themselves as a People. The year at La Paz allowed Anglo newcomers to take Hualapai land. Jane Huya, from the Big Sandy band, recalled her father's attempt to return to land occupied by Anglos:

> My father used to have a place down there before I was born. I saw that when I was old enough. They can't stay [at] that place without anything to eat, have to go out to mountain to hunt deer, antelope, Indian food. The white man come in and take them all away, the land—land down on the Sandy. I never heard about trading off the land to white man, or sell the land to white man. They came in themselves and took it away.[15]

Kate Crozier recalled events after La Paz: "The first settlers came to Big Cane Springs. These first settlers were friendly, they don't molest us very much," he said. By the late 1870s "other white families and white ranchers came and took over this whole valley, our gardens, our homes. We didn't give this country up voluntarily. We were just overrun by white people taking up the springs, the grass, the gardens and all of this territory. We never gave up anything: these people just overran us." Such stories were common for Hualapais in a post-La Paz era.[16]

Disputes over land and laws reflected confrontations over space as settler societies moved into Native territory, thus revealing the spatial terrain of Indigenous nations' claims to sovereignty. Most accounts of expansion focus on battles and physical struggles, but European notions of land privileged private tenure and bureaucratic definitions of space, while the science of cartography facilitated conquest. Colonial settlement redefined Indigenous lands in terms that made sense to non-Natives: latitude and longitude, township, and block replaced Hualapai names for the land (Harris 2003, 22). Lands newly classified as public domain and private property were integrated into a new field of knowledge and a matrix of laws and symbols. Politicians and surveyors redefined Pai spaces as non-Indian territories and extracted aboriginal homelands from the reach of Native peoples by new maps, new modes of power, and the growth of a system that devalued Native territories and valued capitalist economies (Fisher 2001, 472; Said 1979, 2; Todorov 1999, 4; Whatmore 2002, 3).

The Pais did not fully lose contact with or knowledge of these lands as they crossed into and tried reclaiming them in ways that reflected their traditions and cultural maps. The Pais challenged colonial boundaries by denying charges of theft and "trespassing" on private property (Carson 2002, 773). When headmen Schrum, Little Captain, and Hualapai Charley met with Lt. H.L. Haskell in 1878, they questioned ranchers such as William Grounds, who claimed that Pais killed his cattle. Little Captain retorted that white thieves or Tonto Apaches killed the stock, and several whites admitted that they could not identify the thieves. A few even praised the work of Hualapai women in their homes, who "were of more good than harm to white people."[17] The condescension aside, the comment reflected the permeability of the legal borders demarcating Native land and private property and the flexibility of racial borders between Indian and white.

As exemplified by these interactions, the cultural geography of the region had begun to change as bands of Pais competed with non-Indians for access to space in northwestern Arizona. Pai lands witnessed the emergence of towns and "settlements" that were racialized but included interactions between Indian, Mexican, Anglo, Irish, African, and "white." Non-Indians established these towns thinking that the lands were "vacant" and void of "civilization." This view required "improvements" such as roads, barns, agriculture, water wells, branded cattle, and so on (Allen 2003). The Pais lived a different existence that involved seasonal migrations to specified places, light agriculture, rancherías, and hunting. This lifestyle left a lighter footprint on the land that many non-Indians failed to perceive or respect. New property rights and capitalist resource extraction created areas of contention as the Pais tried returning to familiar locations occupied by ranchers, miners, and small towns. Thus, conquest threatened to divest the Pais of their identity, but bands negotiated new relationships with each other as they faced a common set of experiences that contributed to an emerging discourse of national identity (Crum 1994; Hall 1992, 186; Hoxie 1997, 6; Iverson 2002).

The enclosure of aboriginal territory by Anglo property lines and the related loss of the Pais' land base compelled Pai headmen to demand a reservation. This marked a turning point in Hualapai history because it signaled the preservation of a piece of their homelands, even though reservations conjured images of disease and poverty. Serious discussions about creating the reservation began in 1881 when Colonel Price, the main purveyor of violence against Pai bands, met with Pai headmen Schrum, Hualapai Charley, Soskourema, and Cowarrow. Pai leaders borrowed from their service as Indian Scouts under the command of General George Crook and Colonel Wilcox, who in the mid-1870s promised them a reservation. After relatively little debate and surprising support from William Price to Wilcox, Wilcox issued General Order no. 16, reserving land for the tribe upon approval of the President.[18]

The order was approved by President Chester A. Arthur in January 1883. Schrum, Charley, Soskourema, and Cowarrow supported the reservation on the Colorado River even though it did not seem promising for agriculture. This location contained good timber and its grazing lands and springs promised to support cattle ranching. The reservation included lands occupied by the Grass Springs, Milkweed Springs, Hackberry, Peach Springs, Pine Springs, and possibly the Cataract Canyon bands, but it excluded territories of the Red Rock, Clay Springs, Cerbat Mountain, Hualapai Mountain, Mahone Mountain, Big Sandy, and Juniper Mountain bands farther to the west and south. Finally, the executive order seemed to protect the bands' land from the railway lurching westward.[19]

The 997,000 acre Hualapai reservation affirmed Hualapais' right to a portion of their homelands and recognized the territorial and political basis for their modern sovereignty, but it left a contradictory legacy for Pai identity. The Pais traditionally consisted of thirteen bands of extended families that did not recognize a centralized leadership. They lived in rancherías and migrated throughout the year to fixed destinations and seasonal homes. They spoke a common language and shared beliefs about the world, their origins, and their cultural landscape, but their identity remained rooted in the band, not a modern tribe. This decentralization shaped reactions to the reservation. Overlaying the reservation upon a few band territories and attaching the name "Hualapai" to it acknowledged spatial and symbolic boundaries that included and excluded some bands. This bureaucratic colonization of indigenous space overshadowed Pais' use of band names and geographical monikers to describe themselves, racializing the Pais as a single group in the minds of non-Indians. Bands referred to themselves in traditional ways even as the new identity of "Hualapai," tied to a reservation, altered their self-identification—for better or worse—as a modern nation. The common experiences of internment and escape also reconceptualized the Pais from dispersed bands to a people with a similar fate. The new reality, symbolized by the reservation and the separation of identities into "white" and "Indian" across the region, caused the similarities among Pais to overshadow ambivalence about the reservation and the decentralized structure of the bands (Campbell 2001, 549; McMillen 2007, 49).

These trends highlighted the tensions among band identities, racialization and the implications of coding the reservation as a Hualapai space. As noted previously, the term *Hualapai* came into usage when non-Indians garbled the name of the Amat Whala Pa'a band of Pais. Many bands did not identify with this misplaced term, but its repeated usage and its coupling with the reservation demonstrated the power of colonization to rename peoples along racial and spatial lines. By labeling the Pais as "Hualapais," the Anglos enacted a symbolic colonization that facilitated the conquest of Indigenous peoples. Thus, the reservation revealed a double-edged sword: it served as a potential refuge within their traditional landscape, but it tied the bands to the signifier "Hualapai," itself a byproduct of racialization (Frazier, Margai, and Tettey-Fio 2003; Jett 2001, 171).

"Being Hualapai" nonetheless had a literal and symbolic utility because the Indian Office marked the reservation as a protected space within the Pai cultural landscape and because the Pais themselves changed the meaning of that same reservation. In short, the reservation became a focal point for a collective national identity, a process that revealed the complexities of settler colonialism. Hualapai-ness became part of their layered identity as members of families and bands, as well as residents on the *Hualapai* reservation, itself a new spatial dimension to their changing identity. It weakened the localized identities of the Hualapai Mountain, Juniper Mountain, Red Rock, and Big Sandy bands, but they found solace knowing that the reservation met their practical need for water and situated them near their place of origin (Whatmore 2002). Hualapai leaders who struggled to protect the reservation hoped that it would help them maintain traditions and build a tribal economy. They also saw it as compensation for serving as scouts during the campaigns against the Apaches. For many, it was a spatial representation of their past and a marker of their survival. They hoped to fill it with new memories of a nascent nation.

A Modern Indian Nation: Cultural Legitimacy and the Politics of Memory

Hualapais entered modernity as they navigated the gaze of the state and grappled with racial hierarchies, colonial citizenship, and assimilation. Tied to Hualapais' collision with modernity was an assault on the new reservation and their defense of that land with political institutions that reflected a quasi-nationalist hybridity reminiscent of anticolonial movements worldwide. Two generations after President Arthur established the reservation, a new cadre of Indigenous leadership emerged in the early twentieth century in reaction to land allotment and claims by the Santa Fe Railway that it owned a third of reservation. Several Pai political organizations incorporated the rhetoric of tradition while harnessing the modern vocabulary of human rights and self-determination. They defended the rights of all Pais through a growing reliance on a collective identity situated somewhere between the constructs of Indigenous tribalism and nationhood (Hoxie 2001, 3; McMillen 2007, 12).

The political organizations were led by a small cohort of Pai men born after the Long Walk and internment at La Paz, who witnessed the uncertainties of life on the reservation and survived the traumas of boarding school. They spoke Hualapai and English and came of age when the United States entered the world stage as an imperial power. In 1918, Fred Mahone, a key figure in these movements, returned from military service and created the "Redmen Self Dependent of America" to promote self-government, control grazing rights, and oversee boarding school education. A related organization known as the Hualapai Welfare Committee in 1919 requested control over the tribal herd. In 1921, Mahone established the "American Wallapai and Supai Indian Association" to restore Indian land rights and challenge the "rules and regulations" imposed "like slaves" upon them by the Indian Bureau. In one of his numerous letters to federal officials, Mahone argued that the Hualapais had "the right to bring any matter before the state and Federal Court to justify any wrongful causes amongst the Wallapai Indians and others." The proclamations of Mahone and the Association to protect "the Indians' right of prior occupancy of the lands and waters" covered not only the reservation but all northwestern Arizona. Following this organic leadership, in 1925 the Hualapais in Kingman created a Welfare Committee to address group rights off the reservation (McMillen 2007, 13).[20]

These bodies purportedly represented Pai bands in a centralized manner that reflected an increasingly common set of experiences that were crucial to the crafting of a national identity and history. Their political rhetoric was bolstered by the discourse and memories of older men who only spoke Hualapai and who had survived internment at La Paz. This provided the new leadership with an "authentic" foundation rooted in historical trauma and collective memory. Hybrid politics enabled these groups to attack the Bureau of Indian Affairs for mismanagement of lands and the Santa Fe Railway for its claim to one-third of the reservation.

Fred Mahone, when critiquing the BIA and renewed threats of allotment, observed, "we want freedom from the 'restrictions or wardships' under which Indians exist. We want all reservation land leases cancelled and leasees removed in our favor so that we may occupy the grazing land and use the waters upon it." Mahone then defined self-determination: "We want to be as Americans are, free to develop our resources, as a community, and to hold as community property, our reservation land for . . . future generations. No separate allotments do we desire, but urge that the Executive Order of January 4, 1883 be enforced."[21]

By the late 1920s, the Hualapais, the Santa Fe Railway, and the Indian Bureau held different views of the situation in northwestern Arizona. The railway pressed its claim to Peach Springs and odd sections of grazing land totaling 350,000 acres, and in their support, the Indian Bureau believed that the Hualapais had to assimilate and ultimately forfeit the reservation. Yet the Hualapais viewed the land claims debate as a struggle over homelands that could materially and culturally sustain them. As evidence of this, ninety-seven male members signed a letter expressing their "desire to make this tract our everlasting home for ourselves and our future generations." In 1927, tribal member Bob Schrum wrote to the Commissioner, "We are much disturbed about our land leased to cattlemen," and in reference to the Railway, he affirmed that "we want to use our reservation from now on." He concluded his letter with an insightful query: "There are Indians who wish to establish a home. But the agent objected, why?"[22]

With the onset of the Great Depression and as the conflicts over land and water accelerated, the Hualapais became increasingly nationalistic as they tried to strengthen their claims to the reservation. They grasped the foundations of the Executive Order creating their reservation and reminded officials about their service against the Apaches and in World War One. They employed discourse about citizenship and Americanism, and recalled memories of racial violence, relocation, and internment. Much of their dissent rested on the belief that their struggles gave them a "charter," or right, to redress of their grievances (Fowler 2002). Citing the relationship with the government and their aboriginal claims to the land, Hualapai leaders reminded officials that they wanted to decide their future on their terms. This confluence of history, resistance, and adaptation characterized Native leadership as communities incorporated Indigenous rights and nationalism in hybrid political responses to modernity.

The major source of Hualapai nationalism was a growing dispute over water from Peach Springs and the land claims case with the Santa

Fe Railway. Raising questions about aboriginal occupancy and the validity of federal railroad grants, the dispute tied up decisions about land use and residency because the Hualapais thought they might lose portions of the reservation. This uncertainty caused tribal members to remain off the reservation for nearly fifty years, but it facilitated Hualapai nationalism by uniting bands against a common threat. The challenge underlined their *peoplehood* by sharpening a nationalist agenda defined by "tradition" mixed with discourse on progress and a desire to maintain a reservation in their homelands (Alfred and Corntassel 2005; McMillen 2007, 92).

The hybrid leadership of young and vocal advocates backed by elder Hualapais fought a long and victorious battle against the Santa Fe Railway. They gained assistance from non-Indian attorneys Felix Cohen, Royal Marks, and Arthur Lazarus, and successfully employed oral histories and individual memories to prove that they had never relinquished reservation land to the Santa Fe. The Supreme Court ruled in favor of the tribe in 1941, citing aboriginal occupancy and chastising the government for the taking of indigenous lands (McMillen 2007, 99). The most crucial part of the case as far as this chapter is concerned is the nationalist rhetoric employed by the Hualapais during the conflict. This rhetoric marked meetings between the Hualapais and the Senate Committee on Indian Affairs during the 1930s, and drew upon memories and discourse about the past as they defended resources that were crucial to building a foundation for future generations. In one meeting, Special Commissioner H.J. Hagerman told the Hualapais that the railway would more efficiently lease grazing land on the reservation, but Bob Schrum challenged the premise of the railroad and government: "We once had this whole country to ourselves, but were put on a small reservation by the Government, and the Railroad is now after this reservation. We lived here before the white men came into this country, therefore it is ours." Kate Crozier added that "the reservation belonged to the Wallapai Indian tribe and was given to them as their own home and in recognition of their services to the government . . . under the President's order of 1883."[23]

The discourse about space and history continued through the 1930s. In 1931, Fred Mahone sent a petition signed by more than seventy-five Hualapais and members of the local American Legion to President Herbert Hoover. Mahone's letter contained provisions covering land and water issues as well as criticism of the system of leasing land to Anglo ranchers. True to form, he made grandiloquent statements in defense of his people: "All rights, privileges, and profits that have already accrued to the reservation in respect to any portion of the Colorado River, or may hereafter accrue, shall inviolably be secure to the Walapai Tribe," and he ended with a desire to "confirm and preserve the Walapai's moral right to the land" based on "the fact that their present home was a part of their ancient habitation which was guaranteed to them by the terms of the Treaty of Guadalupe Hidalgo in 1848." He defended the Hualapai tribe, not bands, using an anticolonial discourse and historical memory as his weapons.[24]

The government responded with more meetings and obfuscation. The Senate Committee on Indian Affairs convened again to discuss the land dispute with Assistant Commissioner of Indian Affairs J. Henry Scattergood and Senators Burton K. Wheeler and Carl Hayden. The committee first heard Fred Mahone, who went to the heart of the matter: "To begin with, this land belongs to the Walapai Indians in Arizona. . . . I protested against the leasing of the land or appraisal of this land because this land as our reservation itself was set aside by the United States Army officials in the early days." Wheeler asked for evidence. Mahone replied by bringing in Jim Mahone, who survived La Paz and served as a scout against the Apaches. Jim Mahone claimed that President Arthur established the reservation as a reward for the Hualapai scouts and to protect the tribe, because "there were a lot of people all over the world, just like a bunch of worms, and . . . they [were] coming to crowd out the Indians."[25]

Although non-Indians were indeed crowding out the Indians, the Hualapais were fighting the court case and moving to the reservation in unprecedented numbers. This migration to the reservation was fueled by projects sponsored by the Indian Division of the Civilian Conservation Corps, which provided jobs while they improved the range and infrastructure that enabled tribal members to live on the reservation. The convergence of a growing reservation population and the battle with the railway increased Hualapais' attention to the interrelated concerns of governance, nation building, and community identity. Leaders observed that as families followed the men working on the conservation projects, they hoped to remain on the reservation because their options in Kingman had narrowed due to the Great Depression. Anti-Indian sentiment spiked with rising unemployment rates, and members from southern bands slowly believed that moving to this space represented their best chance for survival. Additionally, they remained concerned about the conflict over land and springs, but they expressed those fears not to band leaders as they traditionally would have, but to the leaders involved with the political organizations that emerged after World War One. Their appeals to new leaders indicated a willingness to embrace new forms of political identity, but it also pointed to the high stakes of their troubling situation. Who spoke for all bands when they lacked a history of centralized leadership?[26]

In addition to "who," the "how" of the matter was crucial. How would the Hualapais make decisions about their collective leadership? Would leaders from each band vote on a council? What about the bands that had been absorbed into other bands? How would political conflicts be resolved? And finally, how would the Hualapais react to Commissioner of Indian Affairs John Collier and his proposal to overhaul Native governments and economies through the Indian Reorganization Act? The concurrent Indian New Deal programs that encouraged movement to the reservation, the lawsuit with the Railway, and questions about political leadership made the 1930s a pivotal era in the history of Hualapai nation building (Philp 1981, 1999).

Movement to the reservation and the conflict with the Santa Fe Railway precipitated a turning point in Hualapai political history that led to the creation of an Indian Reorganization Act constitution and government. The constitutions were templates practically forced on Native peoples as part of the effort to reform relations with Indian communities via John Collier's Indian New Deal. Whatever one argues about the governments, the process of voting on the constitutions was flawed because the Department of the Interior counted nonvotes as yes votes, in a move that was clearly antidemocratic. When the Hualapais "voted" on the constitution in 1937, they came out against what they believed was a foreign system imposed on them by the very same people that they had been fighting against. The Department of the Interior ignored the popular vote and counted nonvotes as yes-votes in favor of the constitution and reorganization. Thus, the Hualapai tribal council that was inaugurated in 1938–1939 lacked the support of most voting tribal members (Biolsi 1998; Deloria and Lytle 1998, 267).[27]

The origins of the new government cast doubt on its cultural legitimacy at a time when band members needed strong leadership that could cope with the changing world around them. As they moved to the reservation in greater numbers, Hualapai families and bands nonetheless crafted a new political identity as a nation. Though not everyone embraced this conceptualization of themselves, the Hualapai nation was encoded in a new constitution and government that became an important marker of collective political identity. The new government could claim victory against the Railway, but convincing tribal members of the efficacy of the new Council was something entirely different (Biolsi 1998; Dobyns and Euler 1976, 82).

With the victory against the Santa Fe behind them, Hualapai leaders worked with other Native people during the post–World War Two era to oppose a new series of policies tied to termination and relocation.

Like the organizations before it, the Hualapai tribal council proclaimed to serve all Pai bands within a greater Hualapai discourse about a common ancestry, history, and landscape. The new government attracted many of the individuals from the older organizations, but it lacked cultural legitimacy because it emerged from a dubious process marred by majority rule (and a failed example of democracy) rather than consensus building. The council faced the nearly impossible challenge of retaining legitimacy when it was so closely tied to the Bureau of Indian Affairs, long a target of anger among tribal members (Deloria and Lytle 1984; Dobyns and Euler 1976, 86; Rosier 2001).[28]

These doubts burdened the council during the 1940s, when it was tested by the policies of termination and relocation, and the associated establishment of the Indian Claims Commission. The federal government launched the Indian Claims Commission in 1946 to resolve hundreds of land claims cases that were moving through the court system. Congress hoped that after the ICC addressed these grievances it could begin a new era of Indian Affairs characterized by the liquidation of the reservations and the termination of "government to government" relations. The ICC was supposed to finalize the assimilation of Native Americans into the mainstream of society, but it unintentionally sparked a political movement in the opposite direction. The ICC enabled Native people to air their grievances, present stories of dispossession, and articulate their histories of trauma and violence. This process politicized many communities and raised their consciousness about how they had been treated in the past. Established to divest Indigenous communities of their land, the ICC fueled anticolonial sentiments against termination (Cowger 1999; Iverson and MacCannell 1999; Metcalf 2002; Philp 1999).

The Hualapais stood at the center of this historical moment because their land claims case played a pivotal role in the creation of the ICC, its decision to allow oral testimony as factual evidence, and the partnerships developed between anthropologists, lawyers, historians, and Native leaders. The Hualapais testified to the ICC about their aboriginal homelands and their claims to northwestern Arizona. The eldest tribal members revealed sacred sites, family territories, cultural landmarks, and cultural boundaries between themselves and other Native groups. They bore witness to violence, trauma, removal, internment, and the establishment of the reservation. They narrated stories of resistance and survival, fear and hopelessness (McMillen 2007).

Their stories are important for what they say about Indigenous peoples' endurance of colonialism, but they contain an implicit connection between history, memory, space, and discourse that was central to the evolution of their national identity. The transcribed interviews and testimonies contain relatively few references to discrete or separate bands, while the majority of them refer to the "Hualapai" or the "Hualapai tribe." The use of a term that had come into their lexicon fairly recently was employed by those testifying to refer to their ancestors in the past, when practically none of the latter would have embraced the notion of a collective Hualapai identity. Their use of the term might have been an expedient one based on the practicalities of speaking with non-Indians, but it raises the questions: Were the Hualapais unconsciously projecting this collective identity back onto the past and in doing so unintentionally recasting their historical memory as a unified "people?" Or, were they performing this unity because the ICC contained an antagonism toward decentralized social identities and favored hierarchical and unified forms of political organization? As the Hualapais repeatedly defended their lands and rights to non-Indians in colonial forums of judgment, they reshaped their own identities and histories in a more centralized and simplified manner (Iverson and MacCannell 1999, 117; Rosenthal 1990).

Rather than a contrived political notion of themselves, Hualapais' articulations indicate the growing importance of the Hualapai nation that supplemented band and family identities. The Hualapai nation had coalesced, if in a halting and uneven fashion, during the 1950s in the midst of another assault on indigenous lands, cultures, and ways of life. This should come as no surprise considering the imperative that the Pai bands and families had collective interests to protect, even if that required their support of a tribal council that originated in the murky colonialism of the 1930s and the Indian New Deal. In short, perhaps the most important conclusion from their testimony to the ICC is simply the ubiquity of a unified history and sense of place, rather than the reasons for that discourse. The Hualapais consciously or unconsciously projected a collective memory because they wanted to defend their land in a colonial court, and because they had increasingly come to see themselves as a unified people with a common past. It was in these contexts that the discourse of nationhood and nation building were most evident.

Conclusions: History, Memory, and the Hualapai Nation

Thirteen bands of extended families known as the Pais confronted colonialism and in the process recast themselves as a modern Indigenous nation. By the mid-twentieth century they tentatively embraced the notion of a "Hualapai Indian nation" as a politically, legally, culturally, and geographically distinct people. The Hualapai nation was a product of trauma, dislocation, historical memory, political discourse, space, and ancestry (Eley and Suny 1996, 10). Contributing to this sense of unity was a narrative of Hualapai history that sometimes dominated the stories that the bands told of themselves. Historical consciousness is an important ingredient to national identity. All nations tell stories about themselves, even if they use a language of essentialism that is less than "accurate." Sometimes they employ stories that simplify the past and deny contingency, indeterminacy, and varied perspectives. Nations use narratives to explain who they are, demarcate their boundaries, and then define who is inside or outside the history of their nation, so they can claim political legitimacy or resolve controversy (Kramer 1997, 527).

As the Hualapai nation developed over the twentieth century, its members created a "metanarrative" as both a cause and a consequence of collisions with colonialism. This narrative held the Hualapais together as a people even as it silenced the complex stories of bands and families. This general history states that the Hualapais—not bands of Pais—originated from Spirit Mountain and lived on the Colorado River until several events caused them to leave their place of origin. The Hualapais and the ancestors of the Mohaves, Navajos, Hopis, and others migrated across the region and established themselves on the Colorado Plateau. They lived amid a six million-acre landscape and exploited a diverse range of topographical features and flora and fauna. Their worlds were turned upside down as Americans brought violence in the 1850s and were responsible for the Hualapai Wars in the 1860s, followed by the Long Walk and the escape from La Paz. When the Hualapais demanded a reservation on the Colorado River in 1883, they entered the "modern" era. Although elders today remember histories of their families and bands, most Hualapais embrace this general narrative, especially when in conversation with non-Indians. It appears in official materials and exemplifies the seamlessness of many national histories. The narrative ties bands of people into a unified entity called the Hualapais, which some project into the past as if it had always existed. It explains the connections between bands, highlights their survival in the face of aggression, and ultimately places the Hualapais on their present reservation. Its conclusion in the creation of the Hualapais as a people makes it a presentist rendering that explains the connections between history and the contemporary era.

There is nothing wrong with this version of Hualapai history. It brings the Hualapais together in the tribal collective imagination and accommodates various histories that may merge into the Hualapai metanarrative. It requires important events and themes to make it comprehensible while remaining flexible enough for the Hualapais to incorporate new ideas into the storyline. Events such as the Hualapai Wars, the Long Walk to La Paz, and the escape a year later stand as foundational historical pivot points for both the Hualapai people and their notion of what history means. The pre-Hualapai War era barely qualifies as "history": that category is reserved for the period beginning in the early 1860s and going up to the creation of the reservation. The time before the Hualapai Wars is referred to as "a long time ago" or "before whites came" or simply "before La Paz." The Pai past becomes "history" at the precise moment when violence and invasion disturbed the indigenous landscape, an ironic point considering the violence done to Native people by the Western profession of history itself (Biolsi 2005, 243).

This narrative has played a powerful role in setting a basis for how the Hualapais think about who they are as a people, even though the unity expressed in the metanarrative did not always exist. Some of the most important events of their history include pre-Indian Reorganization Act leadership, which revealed differences between various leaders and bands. Off-reservation communities offered diverse responses to colonialism and strained the ability of the Hualapai leadership to present a united front to BIA officials and Arizona politicians. They challenged the narrative that tied Hualapai historical identity to the reservation. Yet their decentralized responses were common to bands that saw themselves as independent from others, even when nationalist leaders such as Fred Mahone advocated for "all Hualapais." Cultural schisms, changing gender roles, and bands that refused to move to the reservation strained the cohesive power of the metanarrative of Hualapai history.

As these historical tributaries reveal, the Hualapai past is a dialogue open to interpretation and critique. Just as it is nearly impossible to separate the metanarrative as a construct from subsidiary band and family histories, it is difficult to isolate a moment when the Hualapai became a nation. Neither the narrative reconstruction of Hualapai pasts nor the construction of a nation is a linear process. The Hualapai past includes moments of agreement and unity punctuated by dissonance and acrimony in the narrative sense and their existence as a nation in various "presents." Due to decentralized band identities, it has been difficult to draw clear borders around the Hualapai nation and illuminate one common history. I argue that the Hualapais engaged their past as they built their future and used history in complex and surprising ways in the process of self-definition and resistance. They employed it while confronting skeptical institutions such as the Indian Claims Commission, the Supreme Court, and the National Park Service. Thus, Hualapai national history has performed work that has been crucial to their land, culture, and identity.

In conclusion, Hualapai history has remained a crucial part of the cultural landscapes and indigenous geographies of the American Southwest. The Hualapais have reshaped traditional identities within a modern context and held onto a history that reflected their band identities, national adaptations, and dynamic interaction with colonial settler communities. Considering the trauma that has befallen them, the Hualapais continue to persevere. Political leaders are recalled and reelected a few years later. Their language suffered due to boarding school experiences, but students learn it in their classes, and people speak it on the reservation. Poverty persists, but the community adapts and finds new ways to survive—see the Grand Canyon Skywalk, for instance. Popular culture and the Internet compete with Hualapai ceremonials, but reggae music and basketball have enabled the youth to create social bonds, strengthen their sense of self-esteem, and find new ways of "being Hualapai." Despite myriad social and economic problems, the Hualapais seek solutions to their own problems in ways that borrow from the surrounding world and yet are tailored to the realities, histories, and needs of The People.

Notes

1. Mahone to Albert B. Fall, Secretary of the Interior, 1 July 1921, Central Classified Files, Box 447, Part 1, Folder 34163-21-175—General Service, RG 75, NARA, Laguna Niguel.

2. Suwim Fielding, interview by Fannie Woodward, 10 July 1968, Peach Springs, Arizona, 8 (Doris Duke no. 464), American Indian History Project, Supported by Doris Duke, Western History Center, University of Utah, Salt Lake; Hinton and Watahomigie, 1984, 15; based on ethnographic and historical research, as well as interviews with Hualapais, Henry Dobyns and Robert Euler (1970, 1976) propose the following names for Pai bands: WiKawhata Pa'a (Red Rock People), Ha"Emete' Pa'a (Cerbat Mountain), Amat Whala Pa'a (Walapai Mountain), Teki'aulva Pa'a (Lower Big Sandy), Ha' Kiacha Pa'a (Mahone Mountain), Whala Kijapa Pa'a, (Juniper Mountain), Tanyika Ha' Pa'a (Grass Springs), Ha Dooba Pa'a (Clay Springs), Kwagwe' Pa'a (Hackberry Springs), He'l Pa'a (Milkweed Springs), Yi Kwat Pa'a (Peach Springs), Ha' Kasa Pa'a (Pine Springs), and Havasooa Pa'a (Blue Green Water).

3. The political structure of the Pai bands was decentralized, and it lacked a single hierarchical leader. Rather, it included several leaders of different bands, as well as leaders (or chiefs) that dedicated themselves to peaceful and diplomatic

objectives while others focused on "military" necessities. Leve Leve (also spelled Levi Levi) was one of the leaders of a band, as well as a "chief" or "headman" who addressed issues of peace or diplomacy. Amatoo' was probably the brother of Leve Leve. Dobyns, *The Walapai Country,* Section 10, The Whala Pa'a Band, 90.

4. Dobyns, *The Walapai Country,* Section 10, The Whala Pa'a Band, 28 (parentheses added).

5. Extract from the Annual Report of the Commissioner of Indian Affairs, 1864, in U.S. Congress, Senate, *Walapai Papers,* 33, hereafter cited as *WP.*

6. Braatz, 2002, 87.

7. Casebier, 1980, 21; Dobyns and Euler, 1976, 36; Wagoner, 1974, 253–255; Sheridan, 1995; Report of George W. Leahy, Superintendent of Indian Affairs, Arizona Territory, 12 April 1866, La Paz, WP, 37; Report of George W. Leahy, Superintendent of Indian Affairs, to D.N. Cooley, Commissioner of Indian Affairs, Washington, D.C., in Letters Sent, vol. 3, RG 393, NARA, Washington, D.C.

8. Price to Lt. Thomas T. Wright, A.A.A.G. Dist. Arizona, 20 January 1868.

9. Price to Sherburne, 10 November 1867, Camp Willow Grove, Arizona Territory, NARA, Washington, D.C.

10. Price to Sherburne, 7 December 1867.

11. Price to Sherburne, 15 January 1868; Letter Press Books, Wright to Maj. John P. Sherburne, Assistant Adjutant General, Department of California, 20 July 1867, RG 363, NARA, Washington, D.C.

12. Kate Crozier, interview by Henry F. Dobyns, 1953, in Indian Claims Commission, The Hualapai Tribe of the Hualapai Reservation, Arizona, Petitioner v. The United States of America, Defendant, Docket no. 90.

13. Indian Honga, interview, 6 April 1943, Peach Springs, Arizona, and Felix Cohen to Judge Richard H. Hanna, 17 April 1943, Field Service, Office of Indian Affairs, Land Division, Box 48-A, Folder, "U.S. vs. Santa Fe Railway" RG 75, NARA, Washington, D.C.

14. Deposition of Indian Koara, 17 February 1900, Hackberry, Arizona, Box 486, RG 123, NARA, Washington, D.C.

15. Affidavit of Jane Huya, 19 November 1927, Central Classified Files, Box 26, Folder 31229-23, Part 2 of 3, RG 75, NARA, Washington, D.C.

16. Kate Crozier, interview, 5 April 1943, Peach Springs, Arizona, and memorandum and documents from John Collier to Judge Richard S. Hanna, Box 48a, Folder "U.S. vs. Santa Fe Railway," RG 75, NARA, Washington, D.C.

17. H.L. Haskell to the Assistant Adjutant General, Department of Arizona, 20 August 1878, WP, 119; Report of the Governor of Arizona, 1879, 123; Lt. George Wilson to Whipple Barracks, Prescott, Arizona, 18 November 1879, WP, 124–126.

18. Dobyns and Euler, 1976, 60; Brig. Gen. O.B. Willcox, to Headquarters, Department of Arizona, Whipple Barracks, Prescott, 22 November 1879, WP, 128; Price to the Secretary of the Interior, 22 July 1881; Dobyns and Euler, 1970, 89.

19. Executive Order Creating Hualapai (Walapai) Indian Reservation, Executive Mansion, 4 January 1883, signed by President Chester A. Arthur, WP; Dobyns and Euler, 1976, 62.

20. Light to the Commissioner of Indian Affairs, 29 June 1923; Fred Mahone, Jim Fielding, and "the Wallapai Indian Tribe," to the Commissioner of Indian Affairs, 23 April 1923, Records of the Bureau of Indian Affairs, Box 11, Folder 30310-23, Truxton Canyon Agency 174.1, RG 75, NARA, Washington, D.C.

21. Fred Mahone, Jim Fielding, and "the Wallapai Indian Tribe," to the Commissioner of Indian Affairs, 23 April 1923.

22. Bob Schrum, Philip Quasula, and Jim Fielding of the Walapai Tribe Committee to Hubert S. Works [sic], 17 January 1928, Central Classified Files, Box 26, Folder 31229-23, Truxton Canyon Agency 313, Part 2 of 2, RG 75, NARA, Washington, D.C.

23. Affidavits of Jim Mahone and Kate Crozier, 18 August 1930, Central Classified Files, Box 26, Folder 31229-23, Part 2 of 3, Peach Springs, RG 75, NARA, Washington, D.C.; U.S. Congress, Senate, Committee on Indian Affairs, Subcommittee, Survey of Conditions, 71st Cong., 3rd sess.; Hearings at Valentine, AZ., U.S. Senate, Subcommittee of Committee on Indian Affairs, Valentine, Ariz., Friday, 22 May 1931, WP, 240.

24. The United States of America v. The Atchison, Topeka, Santa Fe Railway Company, L-338-Prescott, 1931.

25. U.S. Congress, Senate, Committee on Indian Affairs, Subcommittee, Survey of Conditions, 71st Cong., 3rd sess.; Hearings at Valentine, AZ., U.S. Senate, Subcommittee of Committee on Indian Affairs, Valentine, Ariz., Friday, 22 May 1931, *WP*, 240.

26. *WP*, 242; Emergency Conservation Work Report, 1 November 1933, Hualapai Indian Reservation, Truxton Canyon Agency, Superintendent Guy Hobgood, and O.H. Schmocker, Camp Supervisor to Superintendent Hobgood, September 26, 1933, both in Records of the Bureau of Indian Affairs, Central Classified Files, Indian Emergency Conservation Work, Box 41, Folder 341-8, RG 75, NARA, Laguna Niguel; Collins, 1999, 256; *Indians at Work*, 1 September 1935, 48.

27. U.S. Department of the Interior, Bureau of Indian Affairs, Constitution and By-Laws, 1–3; Minutes, 1 March 1937, Hualapai Tribal Council Meeting, Peach Springs, Arizona, Records of the Bureau of Indian Affairs, Indian Service Records, Hualapai Tribal Minutes, Boxes 71–73, Row G3, RG 75, NARA, Laguna Niguel. Hereafter cited as Minutes plus the date.

28. Hualapai Tribal Council Minutes, 7 January 1939; Minutes, 2 November 1940.

References

Primary Sources

Affidavit of Jane Huya, 19 November 1927, Central Classified Files, Box 26, Folder 31229-23, Part 2 of 3, RG 75, NARA, Washington, D.C.

Affidavits of Jim Mahone and Kate Crozier, 18 August 1930, Central Classified Files, Box 26, Folder 31229-23, Part 2 of 3, Peach Springs, RG 75, NARA, Washington, D.C.; U.S. Congress, Senate, Committee on Indian Affairs, Subcommittee, Survey of Conditions, 71st Cong., 3rd sess.

Brig. Gen. O. B. Willcox, to Headquarters, Department of Arizona, Whipple Barracks, Prescott, 22 November 1879, in Walapai Papers, 128.

Kate Crozier, interview, 5 April 1943, Peach Springs, Arizona, and memorandum and documents from John Collier to Judge Richard S. Hanna, Box 48a, Folder "U.S. vs. Santa Fe Railway," RG 75, NARA, Washington, D.C.

Kate Crozier, interview by Henry F. Dobyns, 1953, in Indian Claims Commission, The Hualapai Tribe of the Hualapai Reservation, Arizona, Petitioner v. The United States of America, Defendant, Docket no. 90.

Deposition of Indian Koara, 17 February 1900, Hackberry, Arizona, Box 486, RG 123, NARA, Washington, D.C.

Emergency Conservation Work Report, 1 November 1933, Hualapai Indian Reservation, Truxton Canyon Agency, Superintendent Guy Hobgood, Records of the Bureau of Indian Affairs, Central Classified Files, Indian Emergency Conservation Work, Box 41, Folder 341-8, RG 75, NARA, Laguna Niguel.

Executive Order Creating Hualpai (Walapai) Indian Reservation, Executive Mansion, 4 January 1883, signed by President Chester A. Arthur.

H.L. Haskell to the Assistant Adjutant General, Department of Arizona, 20 August 1878, WP, 119; Report of the Governor of Arizona, 1879, 123.

Hearings at Valentine, AZ., U.S. Senate, Subcommittee of Committee on Indian Affairs, Valentine, Ariz., Friday, 22 May 1931, in Walapai Papers, 240.

Hualapai Tribal Council Minutes, 7 January 1939.

Hualapai Tribal Council Minutes, 2 November 1940.

Indian Honga, interview, 6 April 1943, Peach Springs, Arizona, and Felix Cohen to Judge Richard H. Hanna, 17 April 1943, Field Service, Office of Indian Affairs, Land Division, Box 48-A, Folder, "U.S. vs. Santa Fe Railway" RG 75, NARA, Washington, D.C.

Light to the Commissioner of Indian Affairs, 29 June 1923; Fred Mahone, Jim Fielding, and "the Wallapai Indian Tribe," to the Commissioner of Indian Affairs, 23 April 1923, Records of the Bureau of Indian Affairs, Box 11, Folder 30310-23, Truxton Canyon Agency 174.1, RG 75, NARA, Washington, D.C.

Lt. George Wilson to Whipple Barracks, Prescott, Arizona, 18 November 1879, WP, 124–126.

Mahone to Albert B. Fall, Secretary of the Interior, 1 July 1921, Central Classified Files, Box 447, Part 1, Folder 34163-21-175 General Service, RG 75, NARA, Laguna Niguel.

Price to Lt. Thomas T. Wright, A.A.A.G. Dist. Arizona, 20 January 1868.

Price to Sherburne, 10 November 1867, Camp Willow Grove, Arizona Territory, NARA, Washington, D.C.

Price to Sherburne, 15 January 1868; Letter Press Books, Wright to Maj. John P. Sherburne, Assistant Adjutant General, Department of California, 20 July 1867, RG 363, NARA, Washington, D.C.

Report of George W. Leahy, Superintendent of Indian Affairs, Arizona Territory, 12 April 1866, La Paz, in Walapai Papers: Historical Reports, Documents, and Extracts from Publications Relating to the Walapai Indians of Arizona, 37.

Report of George W. Leahy, Superintendent of Indian Affairs, to D.N. Cooley, Commissioner of Indian Affairs, Washington, D.C., in Letters Sent, vol. 3, RG 393, NARA, Washington, D.C.

Schmocker, O.H. Camp Supervisor to Superintendent Hobgood, September 26, 1933, Records of the Bureau of Indian Affairs, Central Classified Files, Indian Emergency Conservation Work, Box 41, Folder 341-8, RG 75, NARA, Laguna Niguel Indians at Work, 1 September 1935, 48.

Schrum, Bob, Philip Quasula, and Jim Fielding of the Walapai Tribe Committee to Hubert S. Works [sic], 17 January 1928, Central Classified Files, Box 26, Folder 31229-23, Truxton Canyon Agency 313, Part 2 of 2, RG 75, NARA, Washington, D.C.

Suwim Fielding, interview by Fannie Woodward, 10 July 1968, Peach Springs, Arizona, 8 (Doris Duke no. 464), American Indian History Project, Supported by Doris Duke, Western History Center, University of Utah, Salt Lake.

The United States of America v. The Atchison, Topeka, Santa Fe Railway Company, L-338—Prescott, 1931.

U.S. Congress, Senate, Committee on Indian Affairs, Subcommittee, Survey of Conditions, 71st Cong., 3rd sess.

U.S. Department of the Interior, Bureau of Indian Affairs, Constitution and By-Laws, 1–3 Minutes, 1 March 1937, Hualapai Tribal Council Meeting, Peach Springs, Arizona, Records of the Bureau of Indian Affairs, Indian Service Records, Hualapai Tribal Minutes, Boxes 71–73, Row G3, RG 75, NARA, Laguna Niguel.

Secondary Sources

Alfred, Taiaiake and Jeff Corntassel. 2005. Being Indigenous: Resurgences against Contemporary Colonialism. *Government and Opposition* 40 (September): 597–614.

Allen, John. 2003. *Lost Geographies of Power*. New York: Wiley-Blackwell.

Anderson, Benedict. 1983. *Imagined Communities: Reflections on the Origin and Spread of Nationalism*. New York: Verso.

Biolsi, Thomas. 1998. *Organizing the Lakota: The Political Economy of the New Deal on the Pine Ridge and Rosebud Reservations*. Tucson: University of Arizona Press.

———. 2005 "Imagined Geographies: Sovereignty, Indigenous Space, and American Indian Struggle." *American Ethnologist* 32(2): 239–259.

Blackhawk, Ned. 2006. *Violence over the Land: Indians and Empires in the Early American West*. Cambridge, MA: Harvard University Press.
Braatz, Timothy. 2002. *Surviving Conquest: A History of the Yavapai Peoples*. Lincoln: University of Nebraska Press.
Brooks, James. 2003. *Captives and Cousins: Slavery, Kinship, and Community in the Southwest Borderlands*. Chapel Hill: University of North Carolina Press.
Bruyneel, Kevin. 2007. *The Third Space of Sovereignty: The Postcolonial Politics of U.S.-Indigenous Relations*. Minneapolis: University of Minnesota Press.
Byrd, Jodi. 2011. *The Transit of Empire: Indigenous Critiques of Colonialism*. Minneapolis: University of Minnesota Press.
Campbell, Gregory R. 2001. The Lemhi Shoshoni: Ethnogenesis, Sociological Transformations, and the Construction of a Tribal Nation. *American Indian Quarterly* 25(4): 539-578.
Carson, James Taylor. 2002. Ethnogeography and the Native American Past. *Ethnohistory* 49(4): 769-788.
Casebier, Dennis G. 1980. *Camp Beale's Springs and the Hualapai Indians*. Norco, CA: Tales of the Mojave Road Publishing Company.
Chakrabarty, Dipesh. 1992. Postcoloniality and the Artifice of History: Who Speaks for 'Indian' Pasts? *Representations* 37 (Winter): 1-26.
Chatterjee, Partha. 1993. *The Nation and Its Fragments: Colonial and Postcolonial Histories*. Princeton, NJ: Princeton University Press.
Cherniavsky, Eva. 1996. Subaltern Studies in a U.S. Frame, *Boundary* 2 (Summer): 85-110.
Collins, William S. 1999. *The New Deal in Arizona*. Phoenix: Arizona State Parks Board.
Cowger, Thomas W. 1999. *The National Congress of American Indians: The Founding Years*. Lincoln: University of Nebraska Press.
Crum, Steven J. 1994. *Po'I Pentum Tammen Kimmappeh: The Road on Which We Came. A History of the Western Shoshone*. Salt Lake City: University of Utah Press.
Deloria, Vine, Jr., and Clifford Lytle. 1998 [1984]. *The Nations Within: The Past and Present of American Indian Sovereignty*. New York: Pantheon Books.
Deloria, Philip. 2004. Historiography. In *A Companion to American Indian History*. Philip Deloria and Neal Salisbury, eds., pp. 6-25. Malden, MA: Wiley Blackwell.
Denetdale, Jennifer. 2007. *Reclaiming Dine' History: The Legacies of Chief Manuelito and Juanita*. Tucson: University of Arizona Press.
Dobyns, Henry. F. *The Walapai Country, Section 10, The Whala Pa'a Band*. Report Submitted to Marks and Marks. Phoenix, Arizona, 24 May 1954. Box 31-A, p. 90. Mohave Museum of History and Arts, Kingman, Arizona. [Unpublished document.]
Dobyns, Henry F., and Robert C. Euler. 1970. *Wauba Yuma's People: The Comparative Socio-Political Structure of the Pai Indians of Arizona*. Prescott, AZ: Prescott College Press.

———. 1976. *The Walapai People*. Phoenix, AZ: Indian Tribal Series.
Eley, Geoff, and Ronald Grigor Suny, eds. 1996. *Becoming National: A Reader*. New York: Oxford University Press.
Fisher, Andrew H. 2001. They Mean to Be Indian Always: The Origins of Columbia River Indian Identity, 1860–1885. *Western Historical Quarterly* 32(4): 468–492.
Fowler, Loretta. 2002. *Tribal Sovereignty and the Historical Imagination: Cheyenne-Arapaho Politics*. Lincoln: University of Nebraska Press.
Frazier, John, Florence M. Margai, and Eugene Tettey-Fio, eds. 2003. *Race and Place: Equity Issues in Urban America*. Boulder: Westview Press.
Garcés, Francisco Tomas. 1900. *On the Trail of a Spanish Pioneer: The Diary and Itinerary of Francisco Garcés in His Travels through Sonora, Arizona and California, 1775–1776*. Trans. Elliot Coues. New York: Harper Collins.
Goetzmann, William. 1993. *Exploration and Empire: The Explorer and the Scientist in the Winning of the American West*. Austin: University of Texas Press.
Gooding, Susan Staiger. 1994. Place, Race and Names: Layered Identities in United States v. Oregon, Confederated Tribes of the Colville Reservation, Plaintiff-Intervenor. *Law and Society Review* 28(5): 1181–1230.
Guidotti-Hernandez, Nicole. 2011. *Unspeakable Violence: Remapping U.S. and Mexican National Imaginaries*. Durham, NC: Duke University Press.
Hall, Stuart. 1992. The West and the Rest: Discourse and Power. In *Formations of Modernity*, Stuart Hall and B. Gielben, eds., pp. 184–227. Cambridge: Polity Press and Open University.
Harris, Cole. 2003. *Making Native Space: Colonialism, Resistance and Reserves in British Columbia*. Victoria: University of British Columbia Press.
Hinton, Leanne, and Lucille Watahomigie, eds. 1984. *Spirit Mountain: An Anthology of Yuman Story and Song*. Tucson: University of Arizona Press.
Hobsbawm, Eric J. 1997. *Nations and Nationalism since 1780: Programme, Myth, Reality*. Cambridge: Cambridge University Press.
Hobsbawm, Eric J., and Terence Ranger, eds. 1983. *The Invention of Tradition*. Cambridge: Cambridge University Press.
Holm, Tom, J. Diane Pearson, and Ben Chavis. 2003. Peoplehood: A Model for the Extension of Sovereignty in American Indian Studies. *Wicazo Sa Review* 18(1): 7–24.
Hoxie, Frederick. 1997. *Parading through History: The Making of the Crow Nation in America, 1805–1935*. New York: Cambridge University Press.
———. 2001. *Talking Back to Civilization: Indian Voices from the Progressive Era*. New York: Bedford/St. Martin's.
Iverson, Peter. 2002. *Diné: A History of the Navajos*. Albuquerque: University of New Mexico Press.
Iverson, Peter, and Linda MacCannell. 1999. *Riders of the West: Portraits from Indian Rodeo*. Seattle: University of Washington Press.
Jacobson, Mathew Frye. 2001. *Barbarian Virtues: The United States Encounters Foreign Peoples at Home and Abroad, 1876–1917*. New York: Hill and Wang.

Jett, Stephen C. 2001. The Navajo Homeland. In *Homelands: A Geography of Culture and Place across America*, Richard Nostrand and Lawrence Estaville, eds., pp. 168–183. Baltimore, MD: Johns Hopkins University Press.
Kaplan, Amy. 2005. *The Anarchy of Empire in the Making of U.S. Culture*. Boston: Harvard University Press.
Kramer, Lloyd. 1997. Historical Narratives and the Meaning of Nationalism. *Journal of the History of Ideas* 58(3): 525–535.
McMillen, Christian. 2007. *Making Indian Law: The Hualapai Land Case and the Birth of Ethnohistory*. New Haven, CT: Yale University Press.
Metcalf, R. Warren. 2002. *Termination Legacy: The Discarded Indians of Utah*. Lincoln: University of Nebraska Press.
Ostler, Jeffrey. 2004. *The Plains Sioux and U.S. Colonialism from Lewis and Clark to Wounded Knee*. New York: Cambridge University Press.
Philp, Kenneth R. 1981. *John Collier's Crusade for Indian Reform, 1920–1954*. Tucson: University of Arizona Press.
———. 1999. *Termination Revisited: American Indians on the Trail to Self-Determination, 1933–1953*. Lincoln: University of Nebraska Press.
Prakash, Gyan. 1995. Subaltern Studies as Postcolonial Criticism. *American Historical Review* 99(5): 1475–1490.
Rifkin, Mark. 2009. *Manifesting America: The Imperial Construction of U.S. National Space*. New York: Oxford University Press.
Rosenthal, Harvey D. 1990. *Their Day in Court: A History of the Indian Claims Commission*. New York: Garland.
Rosier, Paul. 2001. *Rebirth of the Blackfeet Nation, 1912–1954*. Lincoln: University of Nebraska Press.
Said, Edward. 1979. *Orientalism*. New York: Vintage.
Sheridan, Thomas. 1995. *Arizona: A History*. Tucson: University of Arizona Press.
Sibley, David. 1995. *Geographies of Exclusion: Society and Difference in the West*. New York: Routledge.
Silva, Noenoe. 2004. *Aloha Betrayed: Native Hawaiian Resistance to American Colonialism*. Durham: Duke University Press.
Smith, Andrea. 2005. *Conquest: Sexual Violence and American Indian Genocide*. Cambridge: South End Press.
Smith, Linda Tuhiwai. 1999. *Decolonizing Methodologies: Research and Indigenous Peoples*. London: Zed Press.
Spicer, Edward. 1962. *Cycles of Conquest: The Impact of Spain, Mexico, and the United States on the Indians of the Southwest, 1533–1960*. Tucson: University of Arizona Press.
Stoler, Ann Laura, ed. 2006. *Haunted by Empire: Geographies of Intimacy in North American History*. Durham, NC: Duke University Press.
Todorov, Tzvetan. 1999. *The Conquest of America: The Question of the Other*. Norman: University of Oklahoma Press.
Wagoner, Jay J. 1974. *Early Arizona: From Prehistory to Civil War*. Tucson: University of Arizona Press.

Weber, David J. 1992. *The Spanish Frontier in North America*. New Haven, CT: Yale University Press.

Whatmore, Sarah. 2002. *Hybrid Geographies: Natures, Cultures, and Spaces*. London: Sage Publications.

Wolf, Eric. 1982. *Europe and the People without History*. Berkeley: University of California Press.

CHAPTER 5

Courting the Nation

Articulating Potawatomi Nationhood at the Indian Claims Commission

Christopher Wetzel

Introduction

In January 1964 Robert Bell, an attorney representing the Hannahville Indian Community and Forest County Potawatomi Community, opened nine days of testimony and oral arguments before the Indian Claims Commission (ICC) in Washington, D.C., with an evocative description of the Potawatomi Nation. He stated, "The history of the Potawatomi nation is *a continuous, flowing thing*. It was a nation. It wasn't a group of bands. And it was emphasized . . . that they declared war as a nation. They made peace as a nation."[1] Native nations' struggles before the ICC, the institution created by Congress in 1946 to address tribal nations' outstanding land claims, were intentionally complex.[2] Authorizing legislation required three steps in the claims adjudication process, each with distinct standards of proof. Further, attorneys representing the Potawatomi not only confronted lawyers from the Department of Justice but also multiple advocates for the "Eastern" and "Western" Potawatomi. Despite this antagonistic milieu, it is striking—and, I argue, telling—to witness Bell's expression of national dynamism. Framing the Potawatomi Nation as "a continuous, flowing thing" was consistent with a culturally rooted vision of the Potawatomi Nation expressed by Potawatomi people.

During the duration of the ICC's proceedings—stretching December 1946 with the Canadian Potawatomi filing of their first claim through

September 1978 when the Commission transferred unresolved cases to the federal Court of Claims—the Potawatomi bands were engaged in contentious interactions. While elsewhere I analyze Potawatomi litigation related to the 1833 Treaty of Chicago, the final major land cession in their eastern homelands (Wetzel 2015), here I want to interpret the Indian Claims Commission period in a different light. Extending Heidi Kiiwetinepinesiik Stark's (2010) scholarship on the international valences and implications of treaty-making, I argue that scholars, policymakers, and tribal citizens must see contemporary discussions of treaties, as well as the treaties themselves, as critical sites of Indigenous intranational narratives and identity formation.

The Potawatomi Nation is an important case to consider the role of treaty-related stories for contemporary Native nationhood and revitalization. Before the Indian Removal Act most Potawatomi lived in villages around the southern Great Lakes area but, as a consequence of negotiating nearly two dozen treaties and confronting the prospect of westward removal, citizens increasingly scattered across a region stretching from central Oklahoma to northern Ontario (Clifton 1977; Edmunds 1978). However, over the last three decades, members of the Citizen Potawatomi Nation (headquarters located near Shawnee, Oklahoma), the Forest County Potawatomi Community (Crandon, Wisconsin), the Hannahville Indian Community (Wilson, Michigan), the Match-e-be-nash-she-wish (Gun Lake) Band of Pottawatomi Indians (Dorr, Michigan), the Nottawaseppi Huron Band of Potawatomi Indians (Athens, Michigan), the Pokagon Band of Potawatomi Indians (Dowagiac, Michigan), the Prairie Band Potawatomi Nation (Mayetta, Kansas), Walpole Island First Nation (in Lake St. Clair north of Windsor, Ontario, Canada), and Wasauksing First Nation (Parry Island, Ontario, Canada) have participated in a range of national events, such as an annual Gathering of the Potawatomi Nation and language revitalization projects. These same communities were, in some shape or form, also engaged with ICC litigation. In many ways, the national narratives articulated and the renewal of relationships during the ICC's tenure enriched the recent national renaissance.

As a sociologist, my research has long focused on questions related to the distribution and structures of power (the field of political sociology), how groups make and perceive meanings (sociology of culture), and the multiple ways actors come together seeking to effect change (social movements). I came to work with the Potawatomi Nation at least in part because of my professional interest in nation-building projects and events they have created. Moreover, as a non-Indigenous academic, my approach to research—both in defining questions and deploying methods—is always informed by a commitment to engage in responsive and responsible conversations with communities, modeling the reciprocity that is integral to vibrant research (Alfred 2007; Smith 2012). This chapter, drawn from a larger research project on the dynamics of Potawatomi national revitalization and more than a decade of research with Potawatomi communities in the United States and Canada, is informed by numerous conversations about treaties: in interviews and informal discussions with community members, ethnography in national spaces, observation of how treaties are represented at museums developed by the Potawatomi governments, and at Native American and Indigenous Studies Association annual meetings. I returned to copies of archival documents from the Indian Claims Commission proceedings related to Potawatomi treaties, analyzing dozens of filings, depositions, and exhibits. I adopted a grounded approach to coding that requires not using preexisting categories but instead responding to themes and concepts that emerged from repeated readings and coding (Bryant and Charmaz 2007).

This chapter begins by relating both a general history of the ICC and the Potawatomi Nation's experiences therein. Next, I describe the state of the literature on Native nationalism to develop a conception of Potawatomi nationhood as rooted in social, cultural, and ceremonial solidarity. In the following section, I look across decades of archival records to analyze three recurring stories about the Potawatomi Nation as a "continuous, flowing thing": connection of places, connection of families, and connection of culture. Perceptions of the Potawatomi Nation are never completely harmonious, nor do they reflect total unanimity. Yet, these narratives, evidenced in texts produced by communities and collected by the United States government, reflect Potawatomi experiences of larger and persistent relationships. Finally, the conclusion revisits questions about contemporary Potawatomi nationhood.

Reclaiming History at the Commission

Prior to 1946, Native American tribes and individuals were required to file land-related grievances with the federal Court of Claims. The Indian Claims Commission Act, passed by Congress in 1946, was intended as a mechanism to redress long standing claims about illegal taking of Indian lands by the federal government (Rosenthal 1990).[3] At the Commission's inception, three appointed commissioners were slated to serve ten-year terms and adjudicate claims filed between 1946 and 1951.[4] Over the five years, tribes filed 370 petitions that were eventually divided into more than 600 dockets. Only 17 of the 176 known tribes did not file one or more claims. Accordingly, legislators expanded the ICC to five members and granted a series of extensions allowing it to hear claims for thirty-two years (Rosenthal 1990; U.S. Indian Claims Commission 1979).

All claimants experienced difficulties in resolving cases. Claims required approximately two decades, on average, to proceed from filing to final disposition (Lurie 1985). Dockets that went to trial faced a three-part process of adjudication, each of which had different evidentiary and procedural standards: title, to establish the exclusive territory occupied by a tribe; value-liability, to gauge fair market value at the time the land was taken; and offsets, to reduce any award for "gratuitous expenditures" made by the government to tribes (U.S. Indian Claims Commission 1979). Formal and informal rules at the Indian Claims Commission frequently precluded tribal citizens from providing expert testimony in cases related to their nations (Tanner 2007). Further, while many hoped litigation would restore control of their abrogated lands, the ICC Act allowed only for monetary damages (Deloria 1992). Land values were calculated based on costs at the time of taking, typically in the mid- to late nineteenth century, not when the claim was adjudicated. Further, tribes were precluded from seeking interest on the determined value. Although the ICC ultimately awarded tribes more than $800 million, the benefits of cash settlements were negligible (Lurie 1985; Rosenthal 1990; U.S. ICC 1979). Indeed, many tribes regarded the process as fundamentally corrupt, leading to a resurgence of extra-institutional protests such as land seizures to assert reserved treaty rights (Wetzel 2009).

During the Indian Claims Commission's existence, the Potawatomi bands filed claims about, and fought over, a number of treaties (Figure 5.1). The Canadian Potawatomi filed the first lawsuit in December 1946, followed by the Prairie Band in December 1947, Forest County and Hannahville bands in May 1948, and the Citizen Band in March 1951. Potawatomi claims were divided into fifty-one dockets: fourteen for the Citizen Band, eighteen for Forest County and Hannahville, and nineteen for the Prairie Band.

Several "hot periods" mark the history of the Potawatomi relationship with the ICC over the four decades of its existence (Schwartz 1982). While still relatively early, two important national moments occurred in May 1948, when groups came together to give depositions related to the Potawatomi Nation's history and treaties. Seventeen Potawatomi people

Treaty	Location	Citizen	Prairie	Eastern Pot.	Royce Area	Land Ceded
August 3, 1795	Greenville	338	15E	29C	11	12 million acres
July 4, 1805	Ft. Industry	307	15H	29D	53 and 54	1 million acres
November 11, 1807	Detroit	307	15G	29E	66	7.8 million acres
August 24, 1816	St. Louis	216	15L	29I	77 and 78	1.4 million acres
September 29, 1817	Miami Rapids	308	15I	29G	87 and 88	4.8 million acres
October 2, 1818; October 20, 1832	St. Mary's; Tippicanoe	306; 311	15D; 15P	29B; 29N	98; 177	2.1 million acres
August 29, 1821	Chicago	146	15M	29K	117	2.8 million acres
October 16, 1826; September 9, 1828; October 26, 1832; October 27, 1832	Mississinewa; St. Joseph; Tippicanoe (2)	128; 309; 310	15N; 15O; 15Q; 15R	29L; 29M; 29O; 29P	132 and 133; 145 and 146; 180; 181	3 million acres
July 29, 1829	Prairie du Chien	217	15K	29J	147 and 148	3.6 million acres (plus mineral deposits)
September 26–27, 1833	Chicago	71	15C	29A	187; 188, 189, 190; part of 160	5.2 million acres
1846	Council Bluffs; Osage River	71A	15J	29-J; Invervene	151 and 265; or 265 (Iowa) and 266 (Kansas)	5 million acres
1861; 1867		111	15B			

FIGURE 5.1. Potawatomi Indian Claims Commission Dockets. This table provides a synopsis of the various treaties and lands for which parts of the Potawatomi Nation filed claims.

were deposed in Topeka, Kansas, on May 17 and 18, including Eliza Clay Bear, Ernest Darling, Minnie Evans, Albert Joetah, Patrick Matchie, Curtis Pequano, David Puckee, Pean Shopteze, Ellen Vieux, John Wabnum, and Alice Wahwasuck, Sr. Offering depositions with the aid of an interpreter were Kody Jackson, Patrick Mish-no, Kittas (Josie McKenny), Vina Wezo, Mike Wamego, and Oscar Shohn. Later that same month, on May 28, Bill Daniels, Isaac George, William Keshick, Peter Johnson, Valentine Ritchie, and James Wahmexico were deposed at the Circuit Court House in Crandon, Wisconsin. The next day, Telford Adams, Frank Elie, Robert George, Henry Jackson, Alex Philemon, and Harrison Williams gave statements in Wilson, Michigan.

The years 1949 and 1950 were largely consumed with posturing between Citizen Band's attorney Howard Moses and Prairie Band's attorneys O.R. McGuire and Robert Stone as they petitioned the Commission to prevent the other from representing the entire Nation. In December 1951, May Fairchild, Autwin Blaze Pecore, and Dan Nadeau were deposed for the dockets in Oklahoma City, Oklahoma.

Starting in 1953, hearings before the Commission focused on the treaties of 1846, 1861, and 1867 that dealt with lands west of the Mississippi River. Although the "Eastern" Potawatomi—the bands in Michigan, Ontario, and Wisconsin—sought to intervene in these dockets in February 1953, the Commission moved forward by hearing testimony and oral arguments in September 1953, December 1955, and September 1956. Ultimately, the court ruled in favor of the "Western" Potawatomi—the bands in Kansas and Oklahoma—in 1961 and determined that the "Eastern" Potawatomi had no interest in these treaty lands.

By 1963 the Commission turned to the lands related to the treaties up to and including the 1833 Treaty of Chicago. These treaties, dealing with the Potawatomi's historic homelands in the southern Great Lakes area, were fraught. The "Western" Potawatomi moved to have their "Eastern" kin dismissed in April 1963, starting nearly eight years of intense legal and national debate over the status of the Potawatomi at the time of the eastern land cessions. The Potawatomi Indians of Indiana and Michigan, Inc., the community now known as the Pokagon Band of Potawatomi Indians, filed an intervening petition in July 1965.[5] In January 1968, the Commissioners ordered a new, separate proceeding to determine the Potawatomi Nation's status. Oral arguments in December 1968, January 1969, and March 1970 finally yielded a decision in March 1972. A closely divided commission ruled that the Potawatomi Nation was a single entity prior to 1833. While the "Western" Potawatomi appealed this decision, the

Commission's remaining years largely focused on resolving the remaining dockets and issuing awards before turning dockets over to the Court of Claims in 1978.

After more than thirty years, thousands of pages of petitions, hundreds of exhibits, and countless hours of testimony, the Potawatomi emerged from this lengthy process with millions of dollars of compensation from the federal government and a complex national future. Yet by carefully reading the archival records one can see recurring narratives of the Nation, expressed by Potawatomi people. Stark insists that to understand the meaning of treaties we must incorporate Native understandings of the relationship. In this way, treaties must be read as a type of Indigenous story that emphasizes respect, responsibility, and renewal. "Treaty making was about making relationships," Stark contends. "They were not mere agreements that ceded one thing in exchange for another. Treaties bound nations to one another. They carried commitments that did not end with the exchange of land for annuities. These agreements connected people. Treaties were a vision for what a multinational society could entail" (Stark 2010, 157). In fact, not only should treaties be interpreted as Native stories about appropriate relationships and histories *between* sovereign governments, but contemporary Native accounts of treaties also have a critical *intranational* dimension. That is, stories about the treaties are critical sites to see the ongoing articulation of contemporary Potawatomi and, by extension, Native nationhood.

Theorizing Native Nationalism

Many social scientists regard the nation as a contingent social construct (Calhoun 1994; Gellner 1983; Weber 1978). This line of research tends to ask how, rather than if, nations are imagined. Eclectic processes of shared learning and forgetting forge coherent national memories and unify populations (Anderson 1991; Hobsbawm 1983; Zerubavel 1996). These approaches also tend to focus on the state as the object of national aspirations; that is, the nation is a "community of sentiment which . . . normally tends to produce a state of its own" (Weber 1946, 176). While these valuable works move beyond seeing nations as natural or inevitable, they also present problems for studying Indigenous nationalisms. Colonial categories and assumptions such as a narrow focus on the state as the goal of nationalist movements limit the ability of these theories to adequately capture the "spectrum of assertions" of Indigenous nationalisms (Alfred 1995).

Western, state-centered notions of sovereignty emphasize authority, hierarchy, and territoriality while, by contrast, Indigenous nationalisms rely on equality and customs derived from the Creator (Boldt and Long 1984). Many Native peoples regard the universe as a sacred gift from the Creator that must be respected. As such, their visions of nationhood are "still informed by their own understandings of land, sacred center, autonomy of government, and culture" (Champagne 2008, 1683; Champagne 2005). Unfortunately, these differences are rarely understood by either the federal government or the American general public. These contradictory epistemologies are manifested in numerous ways, such as the weak institutionalization of Indian Reorganization Act constitutional governments among tribal nations in the continental United States (Cornell 1988).

Recognizing that the nation has come to dominate Native political imaginaries, scholars have begun to analyze the production of multiple Native nationalisms (Biolsi 2005; Deloria and Lytle 1998). Works on Blackfoot, Dene, and Seminole nationalisms, to cite a few, acknowledge the distinctive subjects and objectives of Indigenous nationalisms (Cattelino 2008; Ladner 2000; Watkins 1981). For example, scholars of literary nationalisms draw on the pioneering work of Simon J. Ortiz. Noting the "nationalistic impulse" among Indians to make use of foreign rituals, ideas, and material on their own terms throughout Indian Country, Ortiz insists this impulse is part of a larger anticolonial struggle. The creative use of oral and, more recently, written stories "substantiates life, continues it, and creates it" (Ortiz 1981, 11). Literature, in Ortiz's account, is a persistent call to Indians to liberate themselves by creating their own meanings. Heeding Ortiz's call, scholars have recently analyzed contemporary Native literatures and recovered the insights of historic Native intellectuals such as William Apess (Ortiz 1997; Warrior 2005; Weaver, Womack, and Warrior 2006; Womack 1999).[6]

My analysis builds on a burgeoning line of research that contemplates the sociocultural dynamics of Native nationalisms. In asserting themselves culturally and politically, Native societies are not attempting to connect with or mimic the values and institutions of the dominant society. Indigenous communities "have various other bases for nationhood, such as religion, kinship, or culture, which contradict the Western framework based on territorial boundaries and the normalization of key Western values" (Alfred 1995, 11). The struggle to restore the integrity of national Native communities relies on the articulation of distinctively Indigenous principles. Taiaike Alfred and Jeff Corntassel (2005) identify four elements central to the plural, diverse forms that Indigenous nationalisms take: relationship to the land, a common spiritual bond, language use, and sacred history (Corntassel 2003; Holm, Pearson, and Chavis 2003).

Consider two illustrations of the specific forms contemporary Native nationalisms can take. First, Audra Simpson analyzes the everyday conversations and debates about band membership that occur within the Kahnawake Mohawk Reserve. Nationhood here is a "cultural articulation," replete with colonial ironies that respond to the dominant context (Simpson 2000, 117). Although surrounded by government structures and the people of Canada, Kahnawake Mohawk nationalism "is a Herculean gesture away from the enframing efforts of the Canadian state, toward a place and a state of being that is our own" (Simpson 2000, 126). This is reflected in the ways that community members talk with one another, which underscores the complexity of the situation, diversity of opinions, and depth of Indigenous knowledge.

Second, Jessica Cattelino interrogates the process of cultural production for the Florida Seminole Tribe. While the wealth generated by the tribe's Hard Rock Casinos have created cultural opportunities, such as workshops and seminars at the tribal museum and renewed social gatherings, Cattelino posits that money and wealth are not antithetical to Seminole national culture. Rather, community members are finding new ways to figure relationships through innovative forms. "Values of self-reliance, hard work, . . . are being retooled . . . recast in a new language of economic power" (Cattelino 2008, 94). Generating new revenues has supported the expansion of endeavors such as a language preservation program that facilitates communicating with others, especially Elders, as well as recasting group boundaries. Even ostensibly individual consumption reinforces webs of relations, especially through matrilineal clan obligations.

Much like Simpson and Cattelino, I argue that Potawatomi nationhood emphasizes the social, cultural, and ceremonial ties that unite the communities. Nationhood here is a strategic, creative, and intentional vision of the Potawatomi people. Culture is a critical point for the Potawatomi, like other Indigenous peoples, to express and exercise sovereignty as they articulate collective meanings and community boundaries. The nation-building project being pursued by the Potawatomi does not currently aim toward consolidating gains in the form of a common governing body. Instead, Potawatomi nationalism is a struggle for self-determination that challenges colonial ways of knowing and being. In order to elaborate these general ideas, I analyze three stories of the Potawatomi Nation that were repeatedly expressed during the proceedings of the Indian Claims Commission.

Reading the Nation: Three Potawatomi Stories

Connecting Places

When talking about the social, cultural, and ceremonial ties that continue to unite the Potawatomi Nation, several elements are evident in the government archives from the Indian Claims Commission. First, narratives from this period illustrate how Potawatomi people connected seemingly disparate places. Many scholars demonstrate the importance of place for Indigenous communities and their collective identities (Basso 1996; Blackhawk 2006; Tsosie 2007). Deloria and Lytle (1998) argued that Indians have long been concerned with the preservation of "the people," a religious conception shaped by a deep connection to a sacred place given to them by the Creator and the special responsibilities that result from that relationship. James Clifford (2001) noted how land signifies the past in the future and attaches an identity to a place for Indigenous peoples. As a group, these scholars have highlighted how Native peoples succeed in conceptually and practically connecting geographically distant nodes. Through stories about treaties the Potawatomi simultaneously describe their own movements across spaces as well as historic travels across a national landscape.

In the ICC records, people often related stories of their own movements that link sites within a Potawatomi national landscape. For example, during his deposition in Topeka on May 17, 1948, David Puckee related that his father was a member of the Prairie Band, his mother was from the Citizen Band, and that he himself lived on the Prairie Band reservation in Kansas for many years. However, from November 1909 until June 1910, Puckee left Kansas to live in Wisconsin.[7] Frank Wandahsega, Sr., was born to a Potawatomi family in Canada and moved to Menominee County, Michigan, when he was young. When he was deposed in Jackson, Michigan, in April 1953, Wandahsega related that at the age of five or six his family took a trip to Topeka, Kansas, to visit his paternal aunt who lived on Prairie Band reservation. The Wandahsega family spent six months in Kansas before returning to Michigan.[8] Valentine Ritchie's family had similarly wide and deep national roots. His father, Harry, was a federal Indian agent in Wisconsin, while his great-great grandfather, Echepwias, signed the 1833 Treaty of Chicago. In the summer of 1963, Ritchie took attorneys Walter Maloney and Robert Bell, who represented the "Eastern" Potawatomi, on a trip through Wisconsin and Michigan to visit Potawatomi communities. They held meetings in Athens, Dowagiac,

Niles, and Wilson, Michigan, as well as Lake Lucerne, Wisconsin.[9] When asked whether members of the Forest County Band live away from the reservation in northern Wisconsin, Ritchie replied: "Yes. Of course, you know, people have to make a living, so we have people all over the United States, nearly, all except the South—and we have a few down there. There are a lot of Potawatomis living in Milwaukee, on account of being employed there. But they go home."[10]

These stories of connected places, linking Potawatomi sites in Kansas, Oklahoma, Ontario, Michigan, and Wisconsin, are prevalent in the archival record. Although travel was often difficult and distances long, the Potawatomi found ways to remain in touch with their relatives and "go home." Consider the close connections evidenced in the life of Curtis Pequano. An enrolled member of the Prairie Band, Pequano lived in Arpin, Wisconsin, from 1907 through 1915. Pequano's exchange with Prairie Band attorney Robert Stone highlights continuous links between Potawatomi places and people:

> Q [from Stone]: All I am trying to get at is, is there a distinction between the Prairie Pottawatomies, who lived in and around Clifford, Wisconsin, and Arpin, Wisconsin, and those Indians who are known as the Wisconsin Pottawatomies?
>
> A [by Pequano]: Yes.
>
> Q: Now, what is that distinction?
>
> A: The Prairie Pottawatomies belonged in Kansas.
>
> Q: Yes?
>
> A: We're enrolled here [in Kansas] but the Wisconsin Pottawatomies probably had their own agency and headquarters.
>
> Q: And the Prairie Pottawatomies who went back up to Wisconsin they just picked up from here and went up there because they liked the country better or something?
>
> A: Yes, and some came back, they had been going back and forth for all these years.[11]

While Pequano acknowledges the existence of a "distinction" between the Prairie and Wisconsin Potawatomi, he also unproblematically notes that the people "had been going back and forth for all these years." From David Puckee to Curtis Pequano, Potawatomi people clearly describe the ways in which they regularly moved between spaces in the nation. By mentioning specific places, people also mapped and defined explicitly the Potawatomi Nation's extent, thus giving shape to and corroborating the idea of a single national entity with recognizable sociogeographic boundaries.

Narratives articulated before the ICC also describe how deponents' relatives connected places within the Potawatomi Nation in the past. Sixty-three-year-old Henry Jackson lived his entire life on Christian Island in Canada. He recalled how his chief, "Ogemax-Waj-Won," originally led a group of Potawatomi in Wisconsin that left after he refused to sign the 1833 Treaty of Chicago. The group moved to Drummond Island in the Mackinaw Straits of upper Michigan, on to Manitoulin Island in Ontario, and finally to the town of Penetanguishene, Ontario. From there, the Potawatomi were invited by other chiefs to join Ontario-based bands at Sarnia, Walpole Island, Cape Croker, and Saugeen. Jackson said there was a fair amount of movement by Potawatomis back and forth across the international border in the old days.[12] This history parallels stories recounted by people like Dan Nadeau, then Citizen Band Chairman, who talked about Citizen Band people who remained in Kansas instead of moving to Oklahoma after signing the 1861 treaty, and Madeline Maloney, who described how members of her family lived everywhere from Canada to Wisconsin to Michigan to Kansas.[13] Dr. Nancy O. Lurie also testified about a sizeable migration from the Kansas reservation to Michigan and Wisconsin after World War One.[14]

Narratives of historic connections between places are even reflected in moments of tremendous difficulty, such as the signing of the 1833 Treaty of Chicago and the resulting removal, infamously known as the Trail of Death. A petition filed by the "Eastern" Potawatomi in February 1953 made exactly this point. They argued that the Potawatomi who resisted removal were actually the majority of the nation. Of the approximately 6,000 Potawatomi in 1833, 3,543 fled from their reservations; of this group, 1,986 were driven into Canada and 1,557 remained in Wisconsin, Michigan, and Indiana.[15] Their rationale for escaping was clear:

> The Indians were subjected to abuse and violence, both by military and civilian authorities; that the removal parties were inadequately organized and equipped for the comfort and

welfare of the Indians. . . . To avoid said violence by both the military and civil authorities many of the Indians fled from their homes and villages to remote parts of Michigan and Wisconsin, some crossing over into what is now part of the Dominion of Canada.[16]

Even when confronted with the dislocations of forced removals in the nineteenth century, Potawatomi ancestors drew on their relationships with and across a broad national landscape, "crossing over" to Canada for safety.

Although the nation was diasporized after the 1833 Treaty of Chicago and the Trail of Death, Potawatomi people continued to come together for important meetings. When testifying before the ICC in Washington, D.C., seventy-two-year-old Michael Williams of Hartford, Michigan, described one of the meetings he remembered attending as a young boy in 1887:

> Ordinarily, the people will come from the counties of Allegan, Arenao, Barry, Berrien, Branch, Calhoun, Cass, Fern, Hillsdale, Isabella, Kalamazoo, Kalkaska, Missaukee, Muskegon, Newaygo, Oceana, Ottawa, St. Joseph and Wayne, in Michigan; Elkhart and St. Joseph in Indiana, but Potawatomis would also come from other counties and other states; even from Canada. They came from where they were living when notified; or as they heard of any gathering.[17]

Even to attend regular community meetings, Potawatomi people traveled from nineteen different counties. But "when notified; or as they heard of any gathering," people would be drawn from "other counties and other states" or even across the international border in order to participate in critical national assemblies. Across great distances, and despite the cost and difficulties of travel, members of the Potawatomi Nation linked together nodes of the national landscape.

Connecting Families

During the Indian Claims Commission's proceedings, Potawatomi people also related narratives about the dense linkages between families. Such stories speak of a larger Potawatomi national entity, as well. After conducting depositions in Crandon, Wisconsin, the preceding day, on May

29, 1948, people reconvened about ninety miles to the east at the Potawatomi Community Building in Wilson, Michigan. Alex Philemon, member of Hannahville Indian Community, was the second person deposed that day. He was born in Ford River, a small town just south of Escanaba in Michigan's Upper Peninsula, and lived there until he was thirty years old. He then moved a few miles west to Hannahville. Called to share his story at the age of sixty-five, Philemon's exchange with Jay Hoag, an attorney representing the "Eastern" Potawatomi, related his deep knowledge about the family backgrounds of people living at Hannahville:

> Q [from Hoag]: Well, there were older people living around this community when you lived—when you were a boy, I take it.
>
> A [from Philemon]: Oh, yes.
>
> Q: Where did those older people come from, if you know?
>
> A: Well, the most of them from Canada.
>
> Q: Where did the others come from?
>
> A: Well, the others from Kansas, the way I heard it—the Potawatomi.
>
> Q: Some Potawatomi came up from Kansas and others came over from Canada?
>
> A: Yes.
>
> Q: All right, what did the Potawatomi that came up from Kansas say about it, if you heard any talk?
>
> A: Well, you know how the people are, your white people married to Indians—that was the same thing with the Potawatomi from Kansas, they came up here and they got married together. They must have had a big gathering in Chicago, you know, and some Potawatomi from Kansas and some Potawatomi from here, so the young people got married."[18]

Even in the late nineteenth century, when Philemon was growing up, Hannahville saw a significant mixture and intermarriage of Potawatomi people from across the nation. Not only did people travel to far northern Michigan from places like Canada and Kansas; eventually, the "young people got married" to one another. When Michael Williams testified in Washington, D.C., in September 1953, his story contained themes similar to Philemon's, together with examples from specific families. He said:

> There can be no escape from the fact that we have relations out west and the westerners have relations east of the Mississippi River. The Negonquets of Kansas are related to the Wawasuks of Michigan. Alice Mooso, daughter of Joe Mooso of the Pokagon group, is married to a member of the Prairie Band and is now living in Kansas. Nicholas Augusta, of the Pokagon group, is related to Wamego family of Kansas. . . . Thus we might go on indefinitely if we just would take the time to trace the genealogies and relationships of the western Potawatomies with those of the east.[19]

Family connections linked Potawatomi places. The Negonquets and Wawasuks, like the Augustas and Wamegos, were but some of the family connections that bound groups in southwest Michigan and Kansas. Indeed, the problem was not the lack of connections between Potawatomi in the east and west ("we might go on indefinitely if we just would take the time to trace the genealogies and relationships") but rather the time constraints imposed by the Commission's process.

While Commissioners and government attorneys were often preoccupied with establishing the legal facts of the case, the broad family relationships across the nation were readily evident to the Potawatomi. When John R. Winchester of the Potawatomi Indians of Indiana and Michigan (now known as the Pokagon Band of Potawatomi Indians) came to Washington, D.C., to testify in the late spring of 1963, the existence of these intranational family relationships was largely unproblematic.[20] Attorney Bell asked, "Do you have relatives out west in Kansas or Oklahoma, Mr. Winchester?"; to which Winchester replied, "Yes; I have an uncle, Joseph Topash, the son of my grandfather Tom Topash, in Kansas." Bell followed up:

> Q [from Bell]: Do you know whether there are a lot of other—
>
> A [by Winchester]: Yes.
>
> Q:—inter-family relationships between eastern Potawotomie and Wisconsin—"[21]

Winchester did not even need to think about the answer, let alone hear Bell's entire question. While the reality of "inter-family relationships" between Potawatomi in the east and west as well as within the east might have been an open question for non-Indians, this was simply part of the fabric of Potawatomi national life. Winchester went on to elaborate that he continued to visit his family in Kansas and people from there also came back east for visits. Although separated across four states and two countries for more than a century, Potawatomi families continued to connect the Nation.

Connecting Culture

Sociologist Ann Swidler noted that culture has both formal elements, such as rituals and ceremonies, and informal ones, such as stories, language, and daily practices. Culture is significant not by mechanically determining peoples' actions, perspectives, and tastes, but "by shaping a repertoire or 'tool kit' of habits, skills, and styles from which people construct 'strategies of action'" (Swidler 1986, 273; quotes in original). Recalling Simpson's insistence that Indigenous nationalism is a "cultural articulation" rather than a preoccupation with shared political bureaucratic structures (2000), we can see how Potawatomi narratives at the ICC emphasized a distinctive national culture shaped by shared history and common language.

One facet of the common history shared by all Potawatomi people was the colonial machinations of the American government. Howard Moses, attorney for the Citizen Band, related how the government intentionally misled the nation during treaty negotiations and intensified its efforts when its promises failed to compel the nation to cede their traditional homelands. Describing the negotiations at Chicago in 1833, Moses explained how the government promised that the lands in Iowa to which the Potawatomi would be relocated were abundant with game, that money would be spent to improve the land, and that the new land would be a permanent home for the Potawatomi. "The Potawatomi Nation was unwilling to sell its land and move west of the Mississippi River, and so informed the agents of the Defendant [the United States government] during the meeting in Chicago. In order to obtain the desired cession, the Defendant resorted to threats, duress, fraudulent misrepresentation and bribery."[22]

Not only were all Potawatomi people past and present affected by the challenges of negotiating land-related treaties with the federal government, so too did the history of forced removals inform conceptions of the nation. Michael Williams's June 1961 letter to anthropologist Sol Tax addressed "the sad event of fatal treaty making" and removal's lasting legacy. "Many of the people who did go west defected; they could not adjust their lives to the treeless terrains out there, so they came back to the scenes of their birth. Besides, there were those who during removal days took to the jungles and wilderness to hide from the caravans waiting to transport them to assigned areas west of the Mississippi River."[23] Indeed, attorney Bell noted that while the federal government sought through treaties and removals to bring all of the Potawatomi together in one location in the West, Potawatomi people resisted these efforts. Instead, they came together in their own way and on their own terms. Bell said, "What was not done by formal treaty has happened anyway by reason of the admixture of Indians, interrelationship, intermarriage, traveling, moving around, not only from the Midwest to the East but from the East to the Midwest, and in fact all over the world, since the treaty period."[24] Both accounts describe how Potawatomi people adapted to common historical circumstances not always of their own making, but did so through "interrelationship, intermarriage, traveling, moving around," which facilitated their own articulation of the nation.

A shared language, Bodewadmimwen, was also a unifying aspect of Potawatomi national culture. Proficiency in an official language is often a sign of social distinction, and language knowledge and use is particularly salient for the articulation of Indigenous collective identities (Bourdieu 1991; Kepa and Manu'atu 2006; Morgan 2009). A letter from attorney Robert Bell to the Commission specifically invoked shared language as a basis for seeing the whole of the Potawatomi Nation, insisting that the Potawatomi were "the same people by kindred, by feeling, and by language. . . ."[25]

During Valentine Ritchie's testimony before the Claims Commission in January 1969, common language was invoked to address the Potawatomi Nation's shape. Recall that Ritchie had taken attorneys for the tribe on visits to Potawatomi communities, that Ritchie's father was an Indian agent in Wisconsin, and that his great-great grandfather signed the 1833 Treaty of Chicago. The discussion of language started with this exchange between attorney Bell and Ritchie:

Q [from Bell]: Can Potawatomies from one area understand Potawatomi as spoken by Potawatomies in other areas?

A [by Ritchie]: That is right. They can understand each other.

Q: Is there any difference between language as spoken?

A: Very little. . . .

Q: Have you talked with Mike Williams?

A: Yes, I have.

Q: Where is he from?

A: Niles, Michigan.

Q: Does he speak as good Potawatomi as you do?

A: Yes, sir.

Q: Is there any different in the type of Potawatomi you talk?

A: No, no difference.[26]

Ritchie clearly explained that there was "very little" difference between how Potawatomi people in different areas speak the language such that they can readily "understand each other." When asked specifically about Michael Williams from southwest Michigan, himself a frequent and vocal participant in ICC testimony, Ritchie agreed that he and Williams were equally proficient in Bodewadmimwen. Later on, Bell posed more questions about language and connections between Potawatomi communities:

Q [from Bell]: Mr. Ritchie, are there Potawatomies who have come from Kansas living in the Forest County area?

A [by Ritchie]: Yes.

Q: Pardon?

A: Yes. There are at least 75 living there right now.

Q: Do they speak Potawatomi?

A: Oh, yes, sir, same language.

Q: Same Potawatomi language you do?

A: Same Potawatomi language. . . .

Q: You have talked to other Potawatomies [in southern Michigan], and they speak the same language?

A: Yes. Not only that—

Commissioner [John T.] Vance: Do all Potawatomies speak the same language?

[A: By Ritchie] The Witness: Yes.

Commissioner Vance: No matter where they live they speak the same language?

The Witness: Yes. May I do a little pointing?

Commissioner Vance: Please do.

The Witness [pointing at the map]: You cross Port Huron here. I have been into Canada. . . . These are all Potawatomi-talking Indians, every one of them. I even went to a Potawatomi church in Seney, Ontario, . . . where a Potawatomi man preached a sermon in his own language.[27]

Ritchie is simultaneously testifying and educating. When the commissioner broke into the questioning to probe whether or not all Potawatomi truly speak the same language, Ritchie drew on his travels and knowledge of history to elucidate the widespread use of Bodewadmimwen. From Kansas, to Wisconsin, to far northern Ontario "(t)hese are all Potawatomi-talking Indians."

Language also served as a vehicle to inject levity into lengthy proceedings. Consider the language lesson imparted by Michael Williams during his May 1963 testimony:

Q [from Bell]: What is the Potawatomi word for village?

A [by Williams]: Odan. . . .

Q: What is the Potawatomi word for tribe?

A: Ezhyawud. . . .

Q: What is the Potawatomi word for band?

A: There is no Potawatomi word for band. If you mentioned that word to a Potawatomi, the first thought that would come to him is a bunch of people tooting on shiny horns, harmonizing, mak[ing] music.[28]

Much like Ritchie, Williams illustrates how the language is one element of a unifying Potawatomi national culture. Moreover, he also explicates how the language provides a sense of national meaning. While there are words in Bodewadmimwen for "village" and "tribe," there is not a term for "band," save for "people tooting on shiny horns." His knowledge and use of the language enables Williams to explain a Potawatomi worldview. Invoking shared history and language became a mechanism for the Potawatomi to tell stories about national persistence.

Linking the Past and Present

Heeding Stark's call for interpreting treaties as ongoing stories (2010), I have illustrated that stories about treaties inform listeners about intranational relationships through a range of overlapping narratives. Recollections of treaties have been integral to the Potawatomi's recent national revitalization. Although the federal government designed the Indian Claims Commission to be an adversarial process, Potawatomi people still used it to express an on-going vision of the nation. Specifically, national articulations about treaties during these decades emphasize enduring connections. Participants in the ICC spoke about the connections between sites in the Potawatomi Nation, illustrating how people frequently traveled between communities. People also told stories about the extensive relationships between families, describing the frequency of intranational marriages. Finally, the people related information about a shared national culture, specifically focusing on how they were subjected to similar forces and also spoke a common language. Uniting people, places, and culture in stories about their treaties enabled the Potawatomi to articulate their own vision of the nation before the ICC.

More than three decades after the end of the Indian Claims Commission, talk of treaties remains a vital and vibrant element of Potawatomi national discourse. Exhibits at the Citizen Band and Forest County Band museums, for example, describe in vivid detail the actual treaty negotiations and their consequences for the nation. Treaties are invoked in conversations at annual national events such as the language revitalization conference and Gathering of the Potawatomi Nation, which are hosted by different bands at their reservations each summer. Indeed, in many ways, these contemporary national developments are inseparable from the reality of treaties. Consider this account of the Gathering written by Stewart King (2000, 1), an Elder from Wasauksing First Nation and frequent speaker at national events:

> It has been a number of years now since we have gathered together annually as the "Bodwewadmi" Nation but the love and the friendship that we all share at this time continues to grow. To fully comprehend the true impact of witnessing this event, it is necessary to take a step back in time to the Treaty of 1833 in Chicago, when the Diaspora of the Potawatomi Nation commenced in earnest. We are told that at this time, the seeds of separation had been sowed and many differences were very much in evidence for our people. . . . The friendships we established in previous years continue to grow and the spirituality that has been recognized determines who we are today. As we proceed along this good red road we must pick up those things that were left along the roadside for us by those ancient ones and use them only in a good way.

King seamlessly weaves together strands of the national past, present, and future. He points to a specific treaty that marked the beginning of the nation's diasporization. While having confronted "the seeds of separation"—particularly during periods like forced removal in the nineteenth century and the Indian Claims Commission in the twentieth century—the Potawatomi people have responded with "friendship" and "spirituality," setting out toward a stronger national future.

This analysis underscores how Potawatomi nationalism is organized around and motivated by a sense of social, cultural, and ceremonial solidarity. In telling treaty stories focused on linked places, people, and culture, the Potawatomi articulate a unique vision of their nation based on their own understanding of relationships between people and sacred places. This work, much like the research of scholars including Alfred, Champagne, Corntassel, Ladner, and Simpson, calls for taking seriously the experiences and epistemologies of Indigenous communities and then using these understandings to reconsider hegemonic theories on nations and nationalism. My analysis also honors the persistence and hard work by generations of Potawatomi to maintain relationships and reenergize shared visions of the nation.

Notes

1. National Archives and Records Administration, Record Group 279, Docket 28, Box 455, "Transcripts of Oral Arguments, January 20 and 21, 1964," page 20. Emphasis added. All subsequent references to items from this collection of public documents will be designated as NARA RG 279 and provide the item's docket number, box number, and item title or description.

2. More generally, January 1964 was a complicated time for the United States government as it contended with anti-American rallies in Panama, transformations in African nation-states, and a coup in South Vietnam. Domestically, a constitutional amendment barring poll taxes was ratified, and President Lyndon B. Johnson launched the so-called "War on Poverty."

3. Anti-Indian legislators also imagined that resolving tribal land titles would ultimately eliminate Native Americans' trust status and open new lands to settlers and development.

4. Land claim petitions filed after 1951 would again be referred to the federal Court of Claims.

5. The federal government arbitrarily prevented the Potawatomi bands in southern Michigan from establishing constitutional governments under the terms of the Indian Reorganization Act. Although people from the bands petitioned President Franklin Roosevelt and Commissioner of Indian Affairs John Collier, the officials from the Bureau of Indian Affairs decided the state of Michigan was adequately meeting the Potawatomi's needs. NARA Record Group 75, Item Number 1011: Records Concerning the Wheeler-Howard Act, Box 5, Folder 4894-1934-066. The Pokagon Band of Potawatomi Indians was recognized by Congressional Act in 1990, the Nottawaseppi Huron Band of Potawatomi was recognized by the BIA in 1994, and the Match-e-be-nash-she-wish Band of Pottawatomi Indians was recognized by the BIA in 1999.

6. Scholars will disagree on this point. David Treuer, for one, questions the metrics used to identify and categorize an authentic genre of Native literature. Noting that he writes in English for a wide audience, Treuer (2008) insists that his writing neither reflects nor can it save Ojibwe culture: "My novels are exercises in art, not cultural revitalization or anthropology" (Treuer 2006).

7. NARA RG 279, Docket 15, Box 85, "Transcripts of witness depositions, May 17 and 18, 1948."

8. NARA RG 279, Docket 29A, Box 466, "Plaintiffs' Exhibit #97: Testimony of Frank Wandahsega, Sr. in Jackson, Michigan, April 6, 1953."

9. NARA RG 279, Docket 254, Box 2345, "Transcripts of Oral Arguments."

10. NARA RG 279, Docket 254, Box 2345, "Transcripts of Oral Arguments," page 1227.

11. NARA RG 279, Docket 15, Box 85, "Transcripts of witness depositions, May 17 and 18, 1948," pages 142–143.

12. NARA RG 279, Docket 29A, Box 466, "Plaintiffs' Exhibit #93: Depositions for Petitioners."

13. For Nadeau see NARA RG 279, Docket 111, Box 1176, "Depositions of witnesses taken in the above styled cause on December 3, 1951 at Oklahoma City, Oklahoma, before Edgar E. Witt, Chairman Indian Claims Commission." For Maloney see NARA RG279, Docket 254, Box 2344, "Transcripts of Oral Arguments."

14. NARA RG 279, Docket 254, Box 2344, "Transcripts of Oral Arguments."

15. NARA RG 279, Docket 29H, Box 493, "Petition."

16. NARA RG 279, Docket 29H, Box 493, "Petition," pages 3–4.

17. NARA RG 279, Docket 29A, Box 466, "Plaintiffs' Exhibit #94: Testimony for the Indian Claims Commission, Washington, DC, September 8, 1953."

18. NARA RG 279, Docket 29A, Box 466, "Plaintiffs' Exhibit #93: Depositions for Petitioners," page 68.

19. NARA RG 279, Docket 29A, Box 466, "Plaintiffs' Exhibit #94: Testimony for the Indian Claims Commission, Washington, D.C., September 8, 1953."

20. The transcript of the oral arguments notes that Winchester brought a document given to him by his grandfather. When asked about this item, described as "House of Reps. Misc. Document #5, 43rd Congress, 2nd Session," Winchester explained: "Grandfather Topash told me that this is a document 'that you will want to save in years to come.' It referred to how the Indians were treated and how they were investigated." NARA RG 279, Docket 254, Box 2344, "Transcripts of oral arguments," page 329.

21. NARA RG 279, Docket 254, Box 2344, "Transcripts of oral arguments," page 331.

22. NARA RG 279, Docket 71, Box 844, "Petition," pages 8–9.

23. NARA RG 279, Docket 29D, Box 484, "P-128, Letter from Michael B. Williams, President of the Potawatomi of Indiana and Michigan, Inc., to Sol Tax, coordinator of the American Indian Chicago Conference, June 4, 1961," page 5.

24. NARA RG 279, Docket 28, Box 455, "Transcripts of oral arguments," page 87.

25. NARA RG 279, Docket 29L, Box 512, "Letter from Robert C. Bell to the Indian Claims Commission, July 11, 1963," page 1.

26. NARA RG 279, Docket 71, Box 846, "Transcript of oral arguments," pages 59–60.

27. NARA RG 279, Docket 71, Box 846, "Transcript of oral arguments," page 69.

28. NARA RG 279, Docket 254, Box 2344, "Transcripts of Oral Arguments," pages 810–811.

Public Documents

National Archives and Records Administration (NARA)
Record Group 75: Records of the Bureau of Indian Affairs.
Record Group 279: Records of the Indian Claims Commission, Dockets 15, 28, 29A,
29D, 29H, 29L, 71, 111, and 254.

References

Alfred, Taiaiake, and Jeff Corntassel. 2005. Being Indigenous: Resurgences Against Contemporary Colonialism. *Government and Opposition* 40(4): 597–614.
Alfred, Gerald R. 1995. *Heeding the Voices of Our Ancestors: Kahnawake Mohawk Politics and the Rise of Native Nationalism.* Toronto: Oxford University Press Canada.
———. 2007. Sovereignty. In *Sovereignty Matters: Locations of Contestation and Possibility in Indigenous Struggles for Self-Determination*, Joanne Barker, ed., pp. 33–50. Lincoln: University of Nebraska Press.
Anderson, Benedict. 1991 [1984]. *Imagined Communities: Reflections on the Origin and Spread of Nationalism.* New York: Verso.
Basso, Keith H. 1996. *Wisdom Sits in Places: Landscape and Language Among the Western Apache.* Albuquerque: University of New Mexico Press.
Biolsi, Thomas. 2005. Imagined Geographies: Sovereignty, Indigenous Space, and American Indian Struggle. *American Ethnologist* 32(2): 239–259.
Blackhawk, Ned. 2006. *Violence Over the Land: Indians and Empires in the Early American West.* Cambridge, MA: Harvard University Press.
Boldt, Menno, and J. Anthony Long. 1984. Tribal Traditions and European-Western Political Ideologies: The Dilemma of Canada's Native Indians. *Canadian Journal of Political Science* 17(3): 537–553.
Bourdieu, Pierre. 1991. *Language and Symbolic Power.* John Thompson, ed., Cambridge, MA: Harvard University Press.
Bryant, Antony, and Kathy Charmaz, eds. 2007. *The Sage Handbook of Grounded Theory.* Thousand Oaks, CA: Sage.
Calhoun, Craig. 1994. Social Theory and the Politics of Identity. In *Social Theory and the Politics of Identity*, Craig Calhoun, ed., pp. 9–36. Oxford: Blackwell.
Cattelino, Jessica R. 2008. *High Stakes: Florida Seminole Gaming and Sovereignty.* Durham, NC: Duke University Press.

Champagne, Duane. 2005. Rethinking Native Relations with Contemporary Nation-States. In *Indigenous Peoples and the Modern State*, Duane Champagne, Karen Jo Torjsen, and Susan Steiner, eds., pp. 3–23. Walnut Creek, CA: AltaMira Press.

———. 2008. From First Nations to Self-Government: A Political Legacy of Indigenous Nations in the United States. *American Behavioral Scientist* 51(12): 1672–1693.

Clifford, James. 2001. Indigenous Articulations. *The Contemporary Pacific* 13(2): 468–490.

Clifton, James A. 1977. *The Prairie People: Continuity and Change in Potawatomi Indian Culture, 1665–1965*. Lawrence: University of Kansas Press.

Cornell, Stephen. 1988. The Transformations of Tribe: Organization and Self-Concept in Native American Ethnicities. *Ethnic and Racial Studies* 11(1): 27–47.

Corntassel, Jeff. 2003. Who is Indigenous? "Peoplehood" and Ethnonationalist Approaches to Rearticulating Indigenous Identity. *Nationalism and Ethnic Politics* 9(1): 75–100.

Deloria, Jr., Vine and Clifford M. Lytle. 1998. *The Nations Within: The Past and Future of American Indian Sovereignty*. Austin: University of Texas Press.

Deloria, Jr., Vine. 1992. The Evolution of Federal Indian Policy Making. In *American Indian Policy in the Twentieth Century*, Vine Deloria, Jr., ed., pp. 239–256. Norman: University of Oklahoma Press.

Gellner, Ernest. 1983. *Nations and Nationalism*. Ithaca, NY: Cornell University Press.

Edmunds, R. David. 1978. *The Potawatomis: Keepers of the Fire*. Norman: University of Oklahoma Press.

Fishman, Joshua A. 1991. *Reversing Language Shift: Theoretical and Empirical Foundations of Assistance to Threatened Languages*. Clevedon, England: Multilingual Matters.

Hobsbawm, Eric. 1983. Inventing Traditions. In *The Invention of Tradition*, Eric Hobsbawn and Terence Ranger, eds., pp. 1–14. New York: Oxford University Press.

Holm, Tom, Diane J. Pearson, and Ben Chavis. 2003. Peoplehood: A Model for the Extension of Sovereignty in American Indian Studies. *Wicazo Sa Review* 18(1): 7–24.

Kepa, Mere, and Linta Manu'atu. 2006. Indigenous Maori and Tongan Perspectives on the Role of Tongan Language and Culture in the Community and in the University in Aotearoa-New Zealand. *American Indian Quarterly* 30(1&2): 11–27.

King, Stewart. 2000. Reflections on Gathering 2000. *Potawatomi Traveling Times* 6(4): 1.

Ladner, Kiera L. 2000. Women and Blackfoot Nationalism. *Journal of Canadian Studies* 35(2): 35–60.

Lurie, Nancy Oestrich. 1985. Epilogue. In *Irredeemable America: The Indians' Estate and Land Claims*, Imre Sutton, ed., pp. 363–382. Albuquerque: University of New Mexico Press.

Massey, Doreen. 1994. *Space, Place, and Gender*. Minneapolis: University of Minnesota Press.
Morgan, Mindy J. 2009. *The Bearer of This Letter: Language Ideologies, Literacy Practices, and the Fort Belknap Indian Community*. Lincoln: University of Nebraska Press.
National Archives and Records Administration (NARA), Record Group 75, *Records of the Bureau of Indian Affairs*. Item Number 1011: Records Concerning the Wheeler-Howard Act.
———, Record Group 279, *Records of the Indian Claims Commission*. Various dockets.
Ortiz, Simon J., ed. 1981. Towards a National Indian Literature: Cultural Authenticity in Nationalism. *MELUS* 8(2): 7–12.
———. 1997. *Speaking for the Generations: Native Writers on Writing*, Tucson: University of Arizona Press.
Parman, Donald Lee. 1994. *Indians and the American West in the Twentieth Century*. Bloomington: Indiana University Press.
Rosenthal, Harvey D. 1990. *Their Day in Court: A History of the Indian Claims Commission*. New York: Garland Publishing.
Schwartz, Barry. 1982. The Social Context of Commemoration. *Social Forces* 61(2): 374–402.
Simpson, Audra. 2000. Paths Toward a Mohawk Nation: Narratives of Citizenship and Nationhood in Kahnawake. In *Political Theory and the Rights of Indigenous Peoples*, Duncan Ivison, Paul Patton, and Will Sanders, eds., pp. 113–136. Cambridge: Cambridge University Press.
Smith, Linda Tuhiwai. 2012. *Decolonizing Methodologies: Research and Indigenous Peoples, Second Edition*. London: Zed Books.
Stark, Heidi Kiiwetinepinesiik. 2010. Respect, Responsibility, and Renewal: The Foundations of Anishinaabe Treaty Making with the United States and Canada. *American Indian Culture and Research Journal* 34(3): 145–164.
Swidler, Ann. 1986. Culture in Action: Symbols and Strategies. *American Sociological Review* 51: 273–286.
Tanner, Helen Hornbeck. 2007. In the Arena: An Expert Witness View of the Indian Claims Commission. In *Beyond Red Power: American Indian Politics and Activism since 1900*, Daniel M. Cobb and Loretta Fowler, eds., pp. 178–200. Santa Fe, NM: School for Advanced Research Press.
Treuer, David. 2006. *Native American Fiction: A User's Manual*. St. Paul: Greywolf Press.
———. 2008. If They're Lost, Who Are We?, *Washington Post*, April 4.
Tsosie, Rebecca. 2007. How the Land Was Taken: The Legacy of the Lewis and Clark Expedition for Native Nations. In *American Indian Nations: Yesterday, Today, and Tomorrow*, G. Horse Capture, D. Champagne, and C.C. Jackson, eds., pp. 240–279. Lanham, MD: AltaMira Press.
U.S. Indian Claims Commission. 1979. *Final Report, August 13, 1946–September 30, 1978*. Washington, D.C.: Government Printing Office.

Warrior, Robert. 2005. *The People and the Word: Reading Native Nonfiction*. Minneapolis: University of Minnesota Press.
Watkins, Mel. 1981. Dene Nationalism. *Canadian Review of Studies in Nationalism* 8(1): 101–113.
Weaver, Jace, Craig S. Womack, and Robert Warrior. 2006 *American Indian Literary Nationalism*. Albuquerque: University of New Mexico Press.
Weber, Max. 1946. Structures of Power. In *From Max Weber: Essays in Sociology*, H.H. Gerth and C. Wright Mills, eds., pp. 159–179. New York: Oxford University Press.
———. 1978. E*conomy and Society: An Outline of Interpretive Sociology*. Guenther Roth and Claus Wittich, eds. Berkeley: University of California Press.
Wetzel, Christopher. 2009. Theorizing Native American Land Seizure: An Analysis of Tactical Changes in the Late Twentieth Century. *Social Movement Studies* 8(1): 15–32.
———. 2015. *Gathering the Potawatomi Nation: Revitalization and Identity*, Norman: University of Oklahoma Press.
Womack, Craig S. 1999. *Red on Red: Native American Literary Separatism*. Minneapolis: University of Minnesota Press.
Zerubavel, Evitar. 1996. Social Memories: Steps to a Sociology of the Past. *Qualitative Sociology* 19(3): 283–299.

Conclusion

The Push for Change Continues

Wanda Wuttunee

I am Cree from Red Pheasant Cree Nation, Saskatchewan in Canada and will introduce you to a glimpse of the Canadian context for the push to operationalizing nationhood. This is done in the shared context set out in this work with Indigenous communities across North America. Here, I will use the phrase "Indigenous peoples" to refer to Native Americans and Aboriginal Canadians.

In Canada, a Royal Commission on Aboriginal Peoples (RCAP) concluded their work in 1996 with 440 recommendations that focused on Aboriginal nations within Canada and the relationship with the government (Government of Canada 1996). This was an arm's length body mandated by the Canadian government to conduct research and investigate the relationship between Aboriginal people, the Canadian government and, generally, Canadian society. Beyond simply an "Aboriginal problem," the Commission was called upon for solutions to the problems that have plagued these relationships for many years (Government of Canada 1996). What is interesting in this context is to see how a group of diverse commissioners concluded that the most meaningful way for Aboriginal communities in Canada to accomplish real change was through nations. The starting point for meaningful change is to recognize Aboriginal nationhood. The six volumes and numerous reports are filled with the words of the people who spoke at numerous hearings.

Traditionally, there were checks and balances that were functional and appropriate for the Anishnabek. The leaders were servants to the people and upheld the values that were inherent in the community. Accountability was not a goal or aim of the system; rather it was embedded in the very make-up of the system.

—Union of Ontario Indians,
Brief to the Commission (1993)

We cannot become the independent people we want to be and that we have a right to be without access to the resources of this very affluent country.

—Sophie Pierre, Ktunaxa/Kinbasket Tribal Council,
Cranbrook, British Columbia

We have to be allowed to make our own mistakes. We have to be allowed to fall down from time to time and pick ourselves up. That's part of the process of being able to govern yourselves as a people and as a nation.

—Gerald Morin, President, Métis National Council

The Commission concluded that Aboriginal peoples can claim their nationhood based on a history in which they were recognized as nations by the European powers through military and trade alliances and treaties that marked resource partnerships. This status can be claimed today as community ties remain coherent, distinct, and held by its members. While some communities—such as the Sechelt First Nation and West Bank First Nation of British Columbia, which both chose a legislative route—may choose other strategies for moving ahead, those Indigenous communities that want to operationalize and claim their inherent status as nations are numerous; a sample is highlighted in this volume.

The Commission went on to suggest an innovative approach in which groups of a certain size join together in new "nations," thus conceptualizing their own nationality in a way that had never been done before. Following governmental policies, many communities are quite small due to relocation and disease, among other factors, and need to be reconstructed into larger groups in order to operate more effectively as nations. In the words of the Commissioners (Government of Canada 1996),

We believe strongly that membership in Aboriginal nations should not be defined by race. Aboriginal nations are political communities, often comprising people of mixed background and heritage. Their bonds are those of culture and identity, not blood. Their unity comes from their shared history and their strong sense of themselves as peoples. The work of reconstructing their nations poses great challenges for Aboriginal people. They will need to:

- reconnect communities split apart by years of band or settlement administration;
- develop constitutions, design structures, and train personnel to make laws and administer decisions;
- negotiate new relations with the other two orders of government in Canada.

Paraphrasing the Commissioners' words, healing from the discouraging past must continue so that attitudes promoting self-government can be adopted. Community members would need to develop skills to support this community administration through an Aboriginal public service (Government of Canada 1996).

While this approach of pushing the boundaries and creating new nations did not go further than the Commission findings, I believe it is important to test the waters with possible strategies that have not been tried before. The recommendations for operationalizing nationhood stand the test of time. Our people have been challenged at all levels for hundreds of years. What has changed is the recording of these lived experiences by people who might not have any personal ties to the experiences but are touched in their hearts by the stories. They are now taking an interest in analyzing and promoting the importance of Indigenous nationhood to new, broader audiences. Change is set to happen under these new circumstances. Understanding tenacity, history, and personal perspectives can have untold impacts on these new audiences.

The exploration of how Indigenous communities of North America can thrive in today's world has been the thrust of much internal effort, political focus, and heartache for hundreds of years. As Braun notes in Chapter 1, "Sovereignty has been a point of contention for Indigenous peoples in North America for as long as political groups existed on the continent, just as it has been elsewhere. Societies merged, split, traded, built alliances, sought help, and engaged in many other relations that defined and redefined the nature of their sovereignties." Government policies combined with outside forces were at odds, and continue to be at odds on the whole, with meaningful achievement in many of our communities. That has put some Indigenous communities on their heels while others have moved forward. As Satsan Herb George has noted, many similar struggles, challenges, and victories bind Canadian Aboriginal peoples and Native Americans (see Jorgensen 2007, 321). The readings presented in this book inject academic vigor to support positive movement, intellectual discourse, and an impetus to understanding meaningful change for students, life learners, policymakers, Indigenous leaders, and community members who want stronger Indigenous nations.

The contributors of this volume creatively address many of the issues surrounding Indigenous nations and nation building. Braun's essay invites communities to "reimagin[e] realities outside of the boxes" and to work with a new system that accomplishes meaningful sovereignty and control of citizenship in a much more inclusive manner that matches the reality of diverse communities. Braun develops RCAP's conclusion that membership should not be based on race. A case is made for assimilating Americans into reservations in a creative manner that increases the funds that can then be accessed for the good of the community's push for sovereignty. It is an unusual strategy that communities might want to consider as leaders push the trying relationships that currently exist.

Our history is part of what we carry today, and it defines our future. Grey's presentation of the historical battle over traditional lands of the Aquinnah Wampanoag nation of Noëpe is gripping. The vision of the community is clear, yet the legal barriers are huge. What remains is the heart of the people for their land and for their nation.

The Mi'kmaw people have inspiring attitudes, and Poliandri successfully tackles many of the ways that change is being sought. I once asked a senior member of the Atlantic Policy Congress of First Nations Chiefs (which includes the Mi'kmaw nation) what he thought of the Indian Act, and he replied, "What Indian Act?" A perfect response. Poliandri's chapter captures the strategies of this nation to operationalize their vision within a less than ideal environment. He meticulously pulls at the threads that entwine community perspectives beginning at the reserve level and concluding with a national proclamation issued at the provincial level to allow the reader insight into a unique and continuing journey to First Nationhood.

Accounting for incredible efforts by governmental policies and colonization that have impacted greatly the Hualapai Nation, Shepherd casts a lens back that captures a nation's painful journey to maintain its identity and internal relationships in the face of forced separation. Despite the odds, common ties bind this nation together. The Potawatomi Nation has withstood incredible trials to its nationhood before the Indian Claims Commission. Often history is downplayed, and the intensity of an event's importance is lost by ignoring the words spoken by those most affected. That is not the case here, as Wetzel employs direct testimonies in a holistic approach to analyze a thirty-year legal challenge involving treaties to a Potawatomi nationhood vision. The challenge was eventually defeated, and the vision was successfully protected. Wetzel notes that "contemporary discussions of treaties, as well as the treaties themselves, [are] critical sites of Indigenous intranational narratives and identity formation."

In each chapter, the reader gains insight into community history and some of the current activities undertaken by a sample of Indigenous nations that most non-Indigenous North Americans simply do not know exist. Lack of awareness of where Indigenous peoples have been and want to go has created huge gaps between the original peoples of North America and generations of newcomers. It is very difficult to achieve the building of nations and meaningful nationhood if ignorance marks the relationship with generations of newcomers. Unnecessary roadblocks or invisible support are detrimental for difficult journeys undertaken by Indigenous communities, whereas help and support of members of the general population could strongly affect outcomes.

Traditional beliefs are part of this history and infuse the way many Indigenous communities of North America form relationships with other Indigenous and non-Indigenous communities. Often ceremony is part of the experience, with Elders councils guiding Chiefs and Councils, women taking strong leadership roles in their communities, connecting Elders and youth, listening to all opinions whether or not there is agreement, and marking the groundbreaking of new community developments with proper protocols. This volume has spirit infused in every chapter, as the spirits of these communities are honored with storytelling that reaches beyond their experience, something they could not do without the interest and care of each author. The stories require patience and reflection. Grey notes tellingly, "The narrative starts in the twilight years of the twentieth century, jumps back some three centuries, and then jettisons forward to moments of critical contemporaneity. . . . [The story] ends without finality, reflecting the ongoing, never-ending labor of tribal reaffirmation."

A question that might be asked to put a current context to the nationhood movement is: What kind of communities are we working to build? This is a question for Canadian and American governments and all Indigenous communities to give attention to today, because the answers will determine our futures. Is there space for Indigenous nations and the building of nationhood? When I ask my students about their ideal kinds of community, they readily suggest wondrous, Utopian ideas. An unjaded, thoughtful, and caring vision for tomorrow is needed. *Pimatsawin* is a Cree word that means "the good life." What exactly constitutes the good life varies by individual and community, and that is what makes it wonderful. The Indigenous nations portrayed in this volume are a portion of the many Indigenous communities across North America linking meaning to nationhood. They do not forget their past but use it to fuel their journeys in a modern world that often leaves them to their own devices to sculpt a future for their children.

As outlined in this volume, the drive to nationhood has long historical roots and has not yet been achieved to the satisfaction of many communities. The struggles narrated in the community stories presented in Jorgensen's landmark 2007 collection entitled *Rebuilding Native Nations: Strategies for Governance and Development* resonate with the history, challenges, and hope thoroughly explored by the authors of this book. The reason this work is so relevant and, at the same time, humbling can be found in the words of Oren Lyons, Faithkeeper of the Onondaga Indian Nation (in Jorgensen 2007, vii):

> The Peacemaker told us, "When you sit and you counsel for the welfare of the people, think not of yourself, nor of your family, nor even your generation." He instructed us to make our decisions on behalf of seven generations coming—those faces are looking up from the earth, each layer waiting its time, coming, coming, coming. We have a responsibility to them, to hold fast to our cultures, to hang on to our land, to follow the instructions, and to rebuild our nations.

The authors of this volume agree with a nation-rebuilding process based on long-term strategies to implement sovereignty in ways that are meaningful and hold close to the visions of Indigenous communities. Part of the renaissance that has been illustrated and discussed here is economic. The concept of "tribal economics" is used in the introduction to this volume and notes the benefits of tribal economic activities going to the tribe itself. A related concept presented by a Prince Albert Grand Council in northern Saskatchewan is "community capitalism" (Loizides and Wuttunee 2005, 2). For the twelve-member Council, stopping at the calculation of return on investment for projects was meaningless until the final step where the needs and vision of the community were taken into consideration. In this inclusive model, entrepreneurs and band-owned businesses are equally supported. True sovereignty means that different approaches, even within the same vision, can be expected. For example, Braun's concept of citizenship takes a perspective that has the power to stir the imagination and influence tribes that might have been waiting for such a push.

Much like the concepts of "community capitalism" and "tribal economics," community economic development focuses on members before profits. Fairbairn noted that, historically, "Aboriginal communities in Canada practiced many forms of shared or mutual economic activity" in the context of a discussion on social economy (2008, 8). It is clear that what is now recognized as social economy rests on values that Aboriginal people have held in the past and continue to hold today in modern contexts, as strategies of nation building continue to reflect values and visions held tightly by Indigenous communities. Fairbairn (2008, 10) noted that not all Aboriginal communities grab hold of ideas like co-ops, while others do. In line with much of the discussion offered here by Poliandri and his coauthors, sovereignty means the ability to make choices, make mistakes, and adjust by making new choices. Indigenous communities thrive when they are not slotted into categories or must meet expectations of outsiders. Generally speaking, Canadians are quite ignorant of Aboriginal history and current claims for nationhood. I was reminded of this when an educated and otherwise compassionate man said to me, "I am a Canadian and have no ties to Europe. So how can a group of people (Aboriginal) claim stronger ties to being Canadian than mine just because they were here first?" He also recommended that people accept that what worked in the past does not work anymore, so they should just move on. This conversation demonstrated several things to me. The first comment underlines our responsibility as Aboriginal people to work hard at building understanding in the general population as to who we are, what we hold important, and why. The task is tiring, taxing, and unending, but the need is great, and the cost of doing nothing is even greater. It is the general population who can sway politicians to make decisions that support our efforts. It is also the parents who can teach their children tolerance and understanding in meaningful ways that will support our efforts, and those of our youth, in the long run.

The second comment is directed at traditional pursuits notwithstanding lasting economic and personal value to people and their communities.

For some, traditional pursuits have been dropped as values have shifted to other interests or by circumstance and not by choice, such as when hunting areas are flooded by dams, as in the case of the James Bay Cree in Quebec and the Misipawistik Cree Nation in Manitoba. With land at the heart of nations and nationhood, it makes sense to examine the continuing role of traditional activities such as hunting, fishing, and trapping as well as food security initiatives that revitalize sovereignty claims over what is to be harvested for community needs.

The United Nations has upheld rights to self-determination, to political, cultural, and economic freedom, and holds that communities "may not be deprived of their own means of sustenance," as set out in Article 1 of the International Covenant on Economic, Social and Cultural Rights (United Nations Human Rights 1976). As Poliandri notes, the extra time for four countries, including Canada, to sign this declaration demonstrates the hesitancy that exists to recognize and uphold a nation-to-nation relationship with Indigenous nations. Further, the U.N. Declaration on the Rights of Indigenous Peoples spelled out clear support for the place of traditional practices:

> *Recognizing* that respect for indigenous knowledge, cultures and traditional practices contributes to sustainable and equitable development and proper management of the environment. (2007, 2; emphasis in original)

One example of an active Aboriginal organization in this regard, the Northern Saskatchewan Trappers Association Co-operative (NSTAC), demonstrates the depth of community commitment to this aspect of their nation (Pattison and Findlay 2010). NSTAC's vision is to recapture Aboriginal territory and support trapping as a viable economic activity for today and the future. In line with Nancy Turner's (2001) work on the harvesting and marketing of nontimber forest products, Pattison and Findlay have drawn attention to alternative opportunities that allow for an income that is in touch with the land and are complementary to a trapping lifestyle. They write,

> Over two hundred nontimber forest products are harvested commercially in British Columbia, including wild greens, specialty wood products, wild mushrooms, and wild medicinal plants, with an estimated value of more than $80 million. Complementary activities are key. (Pattison and Findlay 2010, 14)

Pattison and Findlay employed Turner's words (2001, ix) to illustrate this point:

> Pickers, buyers, and marketers of all of these products, under a coordinated co-operative system encompassing a range of products harvested over a broad, diversified land base, could develop complementary harvesting and marketing plans that could yield a predictable, reasonably stable income for many people.

As times change, communities are strengthened when they consider a comprehensive vision of nationhood that includes sustainable economic activities supporting culture and tradition while acknowledging contemporary, nontraditional opportunities. This trappers' co-op sees the multiplicity of benefits not only to the economy but radiating to "added value of positive cultural and socioeconomic benefits in education, employment, health, justice, and sustainability as products of the entrepreneurial activities and wisdom of trappers" (Pattison and Findlay 2010, 36). This is an effort conceived in partnership with all interested parties including communities, the private sector, and the public sector. Pattison and Findlay (2010, 36–37) concluded,

> In the global context of resource depletion, environmental degradation, growing inequality, and concerns about food security, healthy living, and sustainability, the key roles of the NSTAC in the traditional as well as the social economy need to be broadly communicated. Trapping should be understood not as a residual cultural practice, a curious legacy of the past, but as an important player representing the values of both the ongoing and revitalizing traditional economy and the social economy. The social economy is associated with alternative development models and concerned with people before profits; with community economic development and multiple bottom lines; with autonomous management, inclusion, and democratic participation; and with sustainable environments and livelihoods.

Initiatives such as these require all the energy and focus of key community members to succeed in the process of achieving nationhood on both sides of the border. This continued economic and lifestyle choice is linked to and dependent upon nationhood to survive. Dedication and commitment to what some might see as lost causes are indeed worth the effort on many levels, including the national level, as the authors of this volume illustrate. Each chapter highlights that Indigenous peoples demonstrate resilience in the face of huge obstacles and work to take control over the things that matter to them as they build their nations. Poliandri sets the stage with his comment, ". . . Native peoples are now pushing back in the ever-growing attempts to regain their rights to self-define, self-identify, and self-rule. First nationalism and nation *re*-building embody some of the strongest attempts to achieve these goals going through the second decade of the twenty-first century."

It is these efforts, where no issue related to nationhood is too minor, that deserve attention and care. Those who strive for maintaining and, at the same time, building national Indigenous identity, finding ways to grow Indigenous nations, and promoting nation building in all aspects of Indigenous community, social, and economic life will be satisfied with the journey. A common thread throughout this volume, as articulated by Shepherd, is that nations are products of powerful internal and external historical forces that can turn and twist. Further, Grey recommends in anticipation of achieving the goal of nationhood to look backward and take lessons from our Elders' wisdom in an environment that is still characterized by power and instability. Those who do not understand why these ideas are important have the opportunity to be educated through lived experience and thoughtful academic contemplation so the future of our nations can be safely passed to coming generations.

References

Fairbairn, Brett. 2008. *Imagination and Identity: The Social Economy and the State in Canada*. Saskatoon: University of Saskatchewan.

Government of Canada. Royal Commission of Aboriginal Peoples. 1996. Available at http://www.collectionscanada.gc.ca/webarchives/20071115053257/http://www.ainc-inac.gc.ca/ch/rcap/sg/sgmm_e.html (accessed September 2015).

Jorgensen, Miriam. 2007. *Rebuilding Native Nations: Strategies for Governance and Development*. Tucson: The University of Arizona Press.

Loizides, Stelios, and Wanda Wuttunee. 2005. *Creating Wealth and Employment in Aboriginal Communities*. Canada: Conference Board of Canada.

Pattison, Dwayne, and Isobel M. Findlay. 2010. *Self Determination in Action: The Entrepreneurship of the Northern Saskatchewan Trappers Association Co-operative*. Saskatoon: Centre for Co-operative Studies, University of Saskatchewan.

Turner, Nancy J. 2001. Foreword: Co-operative Arrangements in Non-Timber Forest Product Harvesting, Marketing and Regulations. In *Assessing the Feasibility of Applying the Cooperative Model to First Nations Community Based Development Initiatives: A Case Study of the Xaxl'ep and a Native Plant Nursery* by K. Chambers. British Columbia Institute for Co-operative Studies, Occasional Paper 1.

United Nations. 2007. United Nations Declaration on the Rights of Indigenous Peoples. September 13, 2007. Available at http://www.un.org/esa/socdev/unpfii/documents/DRIPS_en.pdf (accessed September 2015).

United Nations Human Rights. 1976. International Covenant on Economic, Social and Human Rights. United Nations Human Rights. January 3, 1976. Available at http://www.ohchr.org/EN/ProfessionalInterest/Pages/CESCR.aspx (accessed September 2015).

Contributors

SIMONE POLIANDRI is Assistant Professor of Anthropology at Bridgewater State University. He holds a PhD in anthropology from Brown University and he is a member of the Phi Beta Kappa Society. He has worked with the Mi'kmaw people of the Canadian Maritimes since 2000 on issues of contemporary identity dynamics. His book *First Nations, Identity, and Reserve Life: The Mi'kmaq of Nova Scotia* was published by the University of Nebraska Press in November 2011. Most recently, he has turned his attention to the study of contemporary Aboriginal nationhood and nation-building strategies. Specifically, he is investigating the development, definitions, and implementation of citizenship protocols in the Mi'kmaw communities of Nova Scotia. He has also authored an essay on Mi'kmaw Residential Schooling published in an edited collection for the University of British Columbia Press in 2016, and he is working on two manuscripts about contemporary First Nations schooling and the perceptions of risk associated with an urban First Nations reserve in the Canadian Maritimes. He is an Editorial Board Member for the series "Ethnographie Americane," published at the University "La Sapienza" of Rome, Italy. He teaches anthropology and Native American Studies courses. He lives in Massachusetts with his wife and daughter.

SEBASTIAN FELIX BRAUN is Associate Professor of anthropology and Director of American Indian Studies at Iowa State University. He took a Lic.phil.I in ethnology, history, and philosophy from Universitaet Basel before earning a PhD in anthropology from Indiana University. Among his other publications, he is the author of *Buffalo Inc. American Indians and Economic Development* (2008/13 University of Oklahoma Press) and editor of *Transforming Ethnohistories. Narrative, Meaning, and Community* (2013 University of Oklahoma Press), and has contributed the chapters on the United States for *The Indigenous World*, the yearbook of the International Work Group for Indigenous Affairs (IWGIA) since 2004. Braun's interests are the intersections of politics, culture, ecology, and economics, which recently include a focus on resource extraction and energy. Based on a fascination with kinship, language, and environments, Braun wants to explore how to achieve sustainable sovereignty and sovereign sustainability.

JACKIE GREY has lectured in the American Studies program at Tufts University in Massachusetts and at a number of universities in the New York City and Northern New Jersey areas. She earned her doctorate in sociocultural anthropology at Columbia University in 2008. She conducted her ethnographic field research among Native peoples in Southern New England, with a focus on the Wampanoag tribal nations in Massachusetts. Her research interests focus on the ways in which small tribes and nontribal regimes articulate conflicting notions of belonging, especially in Indigenous territories that have been transformed into popularized places of leisure. She also investigates the ways in which settler colonialism intersects with constructions of "race" and class, and the legal and political obstacles that prevent the renegotiation of land-use agreements between tribal governments and U.S. state and federal governments. Her essay "The Labor of Belonging" appeared in the *International Journal of Critical Indigenous Studies*. She is currently working on a book manuscript, also entitled *The Labor of Belonging*.

JEFFREY P. SHEPHERD is an Associate Professor in the History Department at the University of Texas at El Paso. His research and teaching interests focus on Indigenous peoples and interactions with colonialism in North America broadly, and along the U.S.-Mexico Border in particular. He is the author of *We Are an Indian Nation: A History of the Hualapai People* (University of Arizona Press, 2010). He is also coeditor (with Myla Vicenti Carpio) of the series *Critical Issues in Indigenous Studies* for the University of Arizona Press.

CHRISTOPHER WETZEL is Associate Professor of Sociology and Chair of the Department of Sociology and Criminology at Stonehill College in Easton, Massachusetts. He received his PhD in sociology from the University of California, Berkeley, and was a UC President's Postdoctoral Fellow in the Department of Sociology at the University of California, Los Angeles. He has been doing fieldwork with Potawatomi tribes since 2003, including interviewing elders, community members, current and former elected officials, and program directors; attending the annual language revitalization conference and gathering; and participating in community events. *Gathering the Potawatomi Nation: Revitalization and Identity*, the book emerging from this fieldwork, was published by the University of Oklahoma Press in 2015. He is grateful to the Potawatomi Nation for their ongoing support of his research. He has published articles and book chapters on the field of training and capacity building organizations that work with tribal nations, gaming legalization, land seizure activism, and the Indians of All Tribes' occupation of Alcatraz Island.

WANDA WUTTUNEE is an internationally known researcher in the field of Aboriginal Community Economic Development. She is Professor of Native Studies at the University of Manitoba, Canada, where she has played a critical role in training future Aboriginal leaders about economic issues working toward vibrant, sustainable, and healthy communities. Her non-Aboriginal students have insight and tools to be allies in shaping the future role of Aboriginal communities in Canada. For the last thirty years, she has devoted her research agenda to understanding how Aboriginal values interact with capitalist values. She considers gender issues arising from economic development as well as the role of culture and tradition by working in mainstream business, through social enterprise and co-operatives. Her work brings to the forefront the many different ways in which Aboriginal peoples are contributing to the economy. She has published two books on the topic, *Living Rhythms: Lessons in Aboriginal Economic Resilience and Vision* and *In Business for Ourselves: Northern Entrepreneurs*; written numerous articles (both in academic and popular journals); and has made countless conference and invited presentations on the topic of Aboriginal economic development.

Index

Italicized page numbers refer to tables and illustrations

Aboriginal people, use of term, 23n1
Adams, Telford, 160
agriculture, 35-38, 134-35
Alamo battle, 40
Alaska Native Claims Settlement Act (1971), 84
Albert (Mi'kmaw official), 101
Alcatraz Island occupation, 42, 69
Alcatraz Proclamation: To the Great White Father and his People (1969), 42
Alfred, Gerald R. (Taiaiake): on colonial state, 9, 86, 90n25; on Indigenous nationhood and state, 2-3, 5, 32, 95, 162-63; on peoplehood, 2-3, 126-27
allotment policies, 16, 38, 124. *See also* land
Amat Whala Pa'a band (Hualapai), 129, 136
American Indian, use of term, 23n1
American Indian Movement (AIM), 69-70
American Indian Policy Review Committee, 32, 38
American Wallapai and Supai Indian Association, 137
Ana:sa (Pai leader), 131
Anderson, Benedict, 47

Andrews, Mark, 78
Anishinabek Nation (Union of Ontario Indians), 6, 116, 184
Anna (Mi'kmaw woman), 99-100
Annapolis Valley community (Mi'kmaw), 97
Anne (Wampanoag Tribal Council president), 62, 78-79, 89n15
"Antics of Anticipation in an Odyssey of Self-Rule" (Grey), 61-92
Apache nation, 25n10, 129, 134, 136, 138, 140
Apess, William, 162
Apsáalooke, 7
Aquinnah (Massachusetts town of), 62, 63, 66-67
Aquinnah Wampanoag, 17-18, 61-90, 186; lawsuit (1974), 17-18, 67-70, 72-76, 79; settlement agreement (1983), 18, 62, 64-65, 74-87, 89n12; shellfish hatchery, 64-65, 74, 85-86
Arizona Miner (Prescott), 131
Arthur, Chester A., 135, 140
Asch, Michael, 117
Assembly of First Nations (AFN), 96, 106
Assembly of Nova Scotia Mi'kmaq Chiefs (ANSMC), 19, 111-14

assimilation: and citizenship, 48; colonial policies of, 11, 16, 98, 103, 105, 136, 142; and present-day policies, 38–42; and termination policies, 45
Atlantic Policy Congress of First Nations Chiefs, 186
Aubry, François Xavier, 129

Barcham, Manuhuia, 47
Barker, Joanne, 50
basketball, 146
Baumgartner, Leona, 71
Bear, Eliza Clay, 160
Bear River community (Mi'kmaw), 97
Bell, Robert, 155, 164, 169, 171–74
Benton, Thomas Hart, 71
Bernard, Nora, 105–6
Big Sandy Pai band, 133, 135
Biolsi, Thomas, 1–2
Blackfoot confederacy, 162
Black Panthers, 68
blood quantum rules, 46–47, 95. See also race and ethnic divisions
boarding schools, 104–6, 124, 137, 146
Bodewadmimwen, 171–74
Boff, Leonardo, 33, 43
Boldt, Menno, 9–10
"Boundaries of Indigenous Nationalism: Space, Memory, and Narrative in Hualapai Political Discourse" (Shepherd), 123–54
Bourdieu, Pierre, 87
Bowie, Jim, 40
Bragdon, Kathleen J., 62
Brando, Marlon, 68
Braun, Sebastian Felix, 15–17, 29–59, 116, 185–86, 189, 195–96
Bryce, Cheryl, 6
"Building on Native Sovereignty From Ethnic Membership to National Citizenship" (Braun), 29–59

Bureau of Indian Affairs (U.S.), 69–70, 123, 137–38, 142, 176n5
Byrd, Jodi, 126
Byrne, Thomas, 132

capitalism, 13, 25n10, 36–37, 127, 188–91. See also economic development
casinos and gaming, 11, 14–15, 34, 87, 163
Cataract Canyon Pai band, 135
Cattelino, Jessica, 163
Cerbat Mountain Pai band, 129, 135
Chabal, Patrick, 48
Chabot, Lynn, 114–15
Champagne, Alfred, 176
Champagne, Duane, 13, 162
Charley (Pai headman), 134–35
Chavez, Cesar, 68
Chavis, Ben, 10–11
Chemehuevis, 127
Cherokee nation, 6, 11, 31, 56n4
Cherokee Nations v. Georgia (1831), 11, 31
Chief and Council Nationhood Conference (Halifax, 2011), 113, 115
Chihuahua (Mexico), 129
Choctaw nation, 6, 7, 25n10
Chrétien, Jean, 118n4
Christianity, 19, 39, 64, 88n3, 94, 103–4. See also spirituality and religion
Churchill, Ward, 7
Citizen Potawatomi Nation (Shawnee, Oklahoma), 156, 166
citizenship, 12–13, 16–19, 22–23, 31, 43–49, 114–17, 186, 189. See also nation and nation building
Civilian Conservation Corps Indian Division, 140
Civil War (U.S.), 129–36
clan system, 7, 11, 163. See also kinship

Clay Springs Pai band, 135
Clifford, James, 10, 164
Cohen, Felix, 139
Collier, John, 141, 176n5
colonialism: American, 31, 35–37, 124, 126–27; decolonization, 3–4, 9, 18, 126; and Hualapai, 127–36, 144–46; and national identity, 22; and pan-Indianism, 7; postcolonialism, 6, 125–26; resistance to, ix–x; and scholarship, 2, 23n3; Spanish, 128–29
Colorado River Indian Reservation, 130, 132
Comanche nation, 129
community capitalism, 188–91. *See also* capitalism; economic development
Confederacy of Mainland Mi'kmaq, 97
Confederated Salish and Kootenai Tribes, 7
conservationism, 66, 70–71
Cook Lands (Noëpe), 74, 77
Cook-Lynn, Elizabeth, 47
Cornell, Katharine, 71
Cornell, Stephen, 12, 13–14, 65, 100
Corntassel, Jeff: on economic development, 14–15; on Indigenous nations, 2, 162–63, 176; on peoplehood, 2, 11, 126–27; on self-determination, 5–6
Coulthard, Glen S, 8–9
"Courting the Nation: Articulating Potawatomi Nationhood at the Indian Claims Commission" (Wetzel), 155–81
Cowarrow (Pai headman), 134–35
Cowboy and Indian Alliance, 29
cranberry bogs (Noëpe), 72
Crockett, Davy, 40
Crook, George, 135
Crozier, Kate, 132, 133, 139

culture: and colonial power, 9; cross-cultural alliances, 29–30; and identity, 10, 49–53, 144–46, 185; and nation building, 1, 95, 124–26; official and vernacular, 52–53; oral traditions, 10; as political sedition, 39–40; sociology of culture, 156. *See also* food systems and traditions; language

Daniels, Bill, 160
Darling, Ernest, 160
Darwinian perspectives, 11
Declaration on the Rights of Indigenous Peoples (UN), 116, 190
decolonization, 3, 9, 18, 126. *See also* colonialism
Delaware nation, 56n4
Deloria, Vine, Jr., x, 7, 10, 84, 164
DeMallie, Raymond J., 84
de-nationalization, 16, 38–40. *See also* nation and nation building
Dene nation (Canada), 162
Denetdale, Jennifer, 126
Department of Fisheries and Oceans (DFO, Canada), 101
Department of the Interior (U.S.), 141
de-territorialization, 16, 25n10, 38
domestic dependent nations concept, 11, 31. *See also* nation and nation building
Domination and the Arts of Resistance: Hidden Transcripts (Scott), 90n24
Dukakis, Michael S., 73
Duwamish people, 68

Eagleton, Terry, 39–40
Eastern Potawatomi, 155, 160–61, 164–69
economic development: capitalism, 13, 25n10, 36–37, 127, 188–91; and ethnic division, 41–42; and nationhood, 1, 7, 14–17; rural

economic development *(continued)*
  marginality, 16, 33–34, 36–37, 43; social economy, 189–91; and sovereignty, 1, 14–15, 22
Elie, Frank, 160
elites, 36, 38, 41–42, 47–48, 86
enduring people, 10, 65, 67
Enlightenment, 125. *See also* Western ideas and concepts
environment and environmentalism, 5, 29–30, 42, 48, 138, 190–91
ethnic divisions. *See* race and ethnic divisions
ethnification, 16, 39–42, 51
Evans, Minnie, 160
Executive Order Creating Hualapai (Walapai) Indian Reservation (1883), 135, 138, 139

Fairbairn, Brett, 189
Fairchild, May, 160
Fielding, Jim, 132
figured worlds, 102
Findlay, Isobel M., 190–91
First Nations, 18–19, 23n1, 93, 96, 106, *107*
First Nations? Second Thoughts (Flanagan), 96
fishing rights. *See* food systems and traditions
Flanagan, Tom, 96
Fletcher, Matthew, 31, 44–46, 55n3
food security, 190–91
food systems and traditions, 6, 190; and Aquinnah Wampanoag settlement agreement (1983), 77; and Mi'kmaw, 19, 94, 100–101; and Pacific Northwest peoples, 68, 70; and state governments, 15
Forest County Potawatomi Community (Crandon, Wisconsin), 155, 156, 158
"Forever Wild" legislation (*Nantucket Sound Islands Trust* bill), 70–72

Fort Mohave, 129–30
Fort Whipple, 130
Fowler, Loretta, 51, 53
Foxwoods casino, 11
Francis/Smith orthography, 117n1
Frederick, David C., 40–41
French Revolution (1789), 125
Friends of the Island (Martha's Vineyard), 70–71
frontier image, 93
Furani, Khaled, 87
"Future of Navajo Nationalism" (Lee), 3

Gagnon, V.P., 41–42
gaming operations. *See* casinos and gaming
Ga no was'het (Hilary Weaver), 7
Garcés, Francisco, 128
Garroutte, Eva Marie, 47
Gathering of the Potawatomi Nation, 156, 175
Gay Head (Massachusetts), 62, 67, 82
Gay Head Taxpayers Association, 62, 72–75
Gay Head Wampanoag Indian Claims Settlement Act of 1985 (S.1452), 75–76
gender roles and identity, 68, 145
George, Isaac, 160
George, Robert, 160
Gilpin, John Bernard, 98
globalization, 13
Glooscap community (Mi'kmaw), 97
Goddard, Ives, 62
Goldstein, Alyosha, 74
Googoo, Morley, 113
Gosnold, Bartholomew, 63
Grabowski, Christine, 72
Grand Canyon Skywalk (Peach Springs, Arizona), 146
Grand Council (Mi'kmaw), 99
Grass Springs Pai band, 135

Great Depression (1930s), 138, 140, 141, 143
Gregory, Dick, 68
Grey, Jackie, 17, 51, 61–92, 186, 187, 192, 196
Grossman, Zoltan, 29–30
Grounds, William, 134

Hackberry Pai band, 128, 135
Hagerman, H.J., 139
Hale and Dorr law firm (Boston), 74
Hannahville Indian Community (Wilson, Michigan), 155, 156, 158
Hard Rock Casinos (Florida Seminole Tribe), 163
Hardyville (Arizona), 130, 131
Harvard Project on American Indian Economic Development, 13
harvesting rights. See food systems and traditions
Haudenosaunee people, 7, 12–13
Hayden, Carl, 140
Henderson, James (Sákéj) Youngblood, 97, 99
Hicks, Sarah L., 65
Hitch Hitchi, 131
Hoag, Jay, 168
Hoelscher, Steven, 52
Holland, Dorothy, 102
Holm, Tom, 2, 10–11
Homestead Act (1862), 130
Honga (Hualapai man), 132
Hoover, Herbert, 139
Hopis, 127, 144
Hopson, Peregrine Thomas, 98
Hosmer, Brian, ix–x, 3
Howwaswee, Zachariah, 79
Hualapai Mountain Pai band, 129, 135
Hualapai nation, 19–21, 123–48, 146n3, 186–87
Hualapai tribal council, 141–43
Hualapai Wars (1860s), 130–32, 144, 145
Hualapai Welfare Committee, 137

Hunt, Lamar, 69
hunting rights. See food systems and traditions
Huya, Jane, 133

identity: and culture and historical consciousness, 10, 49–53, 144–46, 185; and land, 22, 136, 164; and nationhood, 1–3, 7–15; and treaty negotiations, 21–22, 156, 187
identity politics, 48–49
imagined communities, 25n10, 46, 47
Indian, use of term, 23n1
Indian Act (1876), 99, 115, 186
Indian Brook First Nation, 118n5
Indian Citizenship Act (1924), 55n2
Indian Claims Commission (ICC), 155–58; and Hualapai, 142–43, 146; and Potawatomi, 21, 155, 158–61, 159, 164–75, 187
Indian Gaming Regulatory Act (IGRA, 1988), 14–15
Indian New Deal programs, 140, 141, 143. See also Great Depression (1930s)
Indian Reorganization Act (1934), 6, 20, 141, 162, 176n5
Indian Self-Determination and Education Assistance Act (Public Law 95-698, 1975), 6
Indians of All Tribes, 42, 69
Indians of Nova Scotia (Gilpin), 98
Indian Wars era, 130. See also Hualapai Wars (1860s)
Indigenous and Northern Affairs of Canada department, 115
Indigenous articulation, 10
Indigenous peoples, 23n1, 46–47, 126, 183
individualism, 39, 124–27. See also Western ideas and concepts
International Covenant on Economic, Social and Cultural Rights (United Nations Human Rights, 1976), 190

Internet, 146
Ives, Joseph C., 129

Jackson, Henry, 160, 166
Jackson, Kody, 160
Jacobson, Matthew Frye, 124
James Bay Cree (Quebec), 190
James Group (Aquinnah Wampanoag), 77–78
Joetah, Albert, 160
John (Nova Scotia Mi'kmaw chief), 99, 102
Johnson, Lyndon B., 176n2
Johnson, Peter, 160
Jorgensen, Miriam, 188
Juniper Mountain Pai band, 135
Justice Department (U.S.), 68, 70

Kahnawake (Kahnawà:ke) Mohawk Reserve, 4, 13, 163
Kalt, Joseph, 12, 13–14, 44, 46
Kaplan, Amy, 124
Kennedy, Edward M., 70, 75
Kennedy, Robert, 69
Kernaghan, Richard, 87
Keshick, William, 160
Keystone XL pipeline, 29
King, Stewart, 175
kinship: clan system, 7, 11, 163; and nationhood, 10–11, 31, 46, 95, 162–63; and social identity, 10, 48, 53, 102
Kittas (Josie McKenny), 160
Koara (Hualapai man), 132
Kurkiala, Mikael, 50–53
Kwilmu'kw Maw-klusuaqn (KMK, Mi'kmaq Rights Initiative), 100, 113, 114

Lac-du-Flambeau Ojibwe (Wisconsin), 2, 7
Ladner, Kiera L., 176
Lakotas, 7, 70

land: allotment policies, 16, 38, 124; and Aquinnah Wampanoag lawsuit and settlement, 17–18, 72–85; and Hualapai national consciousness, 20, 123–24, 133–42; and identity, 22, 44, 164; and Mi'kmaw nation building, 18–19, 94; and nationhood, 1, 3, 7, 124, 163, 190; and Potawatomi, 158; and sovereignty, 34–37, 53; trust lands, 35, 44, 89n13. *See also* Indian Claims Commission (ICC)
language: and discrimination, 39–40; Hualapai, 146; loss and revival of, 104, 146, 156, 175; Mi'kmaw, 98, 104; and national culture and identity, 10, 22, 98, 163, 171–74; Potawatomi, 156, 171–75; Wampanoag, 88n3
Lawlor, Mary, 37
Lazarus, Arthur, 139
Lee, Lloyd, 3
Leeds, Stacy, 35
Leve Leve, 130, 132
Levitas, Gloria, 70
Lewis v. Norton (2005), 43
Little Captain (Pai headman), 134
Long, J. Anthony, 9–10
Long Walk to La Paz and escape (Hualapai), 132–33, 144–45
Lyons, Oren, 5, 188
Lyons, Scott Richard, 29
Lytle, Clifford, 7, 10, 164

Made in Nova Scotia Process, 19, 94, 111–14, 117
Mahone, Fred, 123–24, 137–40, 145
Mahone, Jim, 123, 140
Mahone Mountain Pai band, 123, 135
Maillard, Pierre, 97–98, 103
Maloney, Madeline, 166
Maloney, Walter, 164

Malonson, Donald F. and Ryan, 79
Mankiller, Wilma, 69
Manning, Helen, 88n5
Marks, Royal, 139
Marshall, Donald, Jr., 100
Marshall, John, 11, 43
Marshall case (Canada, 1999), 11, 19, 43, 94, 100–101
Martha's Vineyard (Noëpe), 17, 62, 63. *See also* Noëpe
Martha's Vineyard Commission, 72
Marxism, 33, 35
Mashpee Wampanoag, 74
Massachusetts Wetlands Protection Act (1972), 72
Match-e-be-nash-she-wish (Gun Lake) Band of Pottawatomi Indians (Dorr, Michigan), 156, 176n5
Matchie, Patrick, 160
Mathews, John Joseph, 61
McDougall, Debra, 45
McGuire, O.R., 160
Membertou First Nation (Mi'kmaw), 94, 110–11
memory: and Hualapai national consciousness, 19–20, 124, 127, 130, 132, 136–44; and Mi'kmaw national consciousness, 105–6; and national identity and culture, 22, 52, 161; and Potawatomi community preservation, 21
Mi'kma'ki, 97
Mi'kmaq History Month (Nova Scotia), 113
Mi'kmaq-Maliseet Nations News, 96
Mi'kmaq-Nova Scotia-Canada Consultation Terms of Reference (2010), 114
Mi'kmaq of Nova Scotia Nationhood Proclamation (Assembly of Nova Scotia Mi'kmaq Chiefs), 19, 112
Mi'kmaw nation, 6, 7, 13, 18–19, 70, 93–119, 117n1, 186

"Mi'kmaw Path to First Nationhood: A Roadmap, Some Strategies, and a Few Effective Shortcuts" (Poliandri), 93–122
Mi'kmaw Resource Guide (2007), 97, 98
Milkweed Springs Pai band, 131, 135
Millbrook First Nation (Mi'kmaw), 25n10, 94, 97, 108–10
Mish-no, Patrick, 160
Misipawistik Cree Nation (Manitoba), 190
Mittark (Aquinnah Wampanoag sachem), 62–65
modernity, 11, 31, 37, 48, 126, 136–38
Mohaves, 127, 131, 144
Mohawk people, 4, 12–13
Morin, Gerald, 184
Moses, Howard, 160, 170
multiculturalism, 4, 124

Nadasdy, Paul, 9
Nadeau, Dan, 160, 166
Nagel, Joane, 68
Nantucket Sound Islands Trust bill, 70–72
National Centre for First Nations Governance, 100, 110
national consciousness, 1–15, 22, 126; and discrimination, 124; ethnic genesis theories of, 30; and Hualapai, 19–21, 133–42; and land, 1, 124, 133–42; Mi'kmaw, 18–19, 100–111; Mohawk, 163; pan-Indianism, 2–3, 7, 11, 105; peoplehood, 1, 2–3, 7–15, 124, 126–27, 139, 164; scholarship on, 162–63; as UN recognized right, 116; Western concepts of, 161–63, 176
National Identity (Smith), 3
National Indian Brotherhood (NIB), 96

"Nationalism and Nation Re-building in Native North America" (Poliandri), 1–28
National Park Service, 146
nation and nation building, ix–x, 2–16, 22–23, 38–40, 45–46, 53–55, 183–86; and Aquinnah Wampanoag, 65; citizenship, 12–13, 16–19, 22–23, 31, 43–49, 114–17, 186, 189; and culture, 170–74; domestic dependent nations concept, 11, 31; and figured worlds, 102–3; and Hualapai, 20; and kinship, 167–70; and land, 18–19, 164–67, 190; and Mi'kmaw, 18–19, 111–17; and Potawatomi, 163; Western concepts of, 2, 124–26
Native, use of term, 7, 23n1
Native activism (1960s and 1970s), 68–70
Native American and Indigenous Studies Association (NAISA), 4
Native American Rights Fund, 67, 70
Native Council of Nova Scotia, 97
Native Writings in Massachusett (Goddard and Bragdon), 62
Navajos, 3, 7, 144
Nesper, Larry, ix–x, 2, 3
nested sovereignty, 4. *See also* sovereignty
New Town (Reston, Virginia), 70
new traditionalists, 32
Niezen, Ronald, 50
Nipissing First Nation of Ontario, 116
Nisqually people, 68
Noëpe, 17, 62, 63, 66–67, 88n4
"No Island is an Island" (Simon), 70
Northern Saskatchewan Trappers Association Co-operative (NSTAC), 190–91
Nottawaseppi Huron Band of Potawatomi Indians (Athens, Michigan), 156, 176n5

Oakes, John, 71

Ogemax-Waj-Won, 166
Oglala Lakotas, 70
Ojibwe, 176n6
Oliver-Smith, Anthony, 49
Onassis, Jacqueline Kennedy, 66, 82–83
O'Nell, Theresa DeLeane, 51
Ong, Aihwa, 90n24
O'odham, 129
oral traditions, 10. *See also* culture
Ordinance 59 Association v. Babbitt (1998), 43
Ortiz, Simon J., 162

Pai bands, 20–21, 127–28, 131, 133, 135–36, 146n3
Paiutes, 127, 131
Palmater, Pamela, 95
Panama anti-American rallies, 176n2
pan-Indianism, 2–3, 7, 11, 105. *See also* national consciousness
Paqtnkek (Afton) community (Mi'kmaw), 97
Passamaquoddy nation, 67–68, 76
Patrick, Deval, 87
Pattison, Dwayne, 190–91
Paul, Terry, 115
Peach Springs Pai band, 131, 135
Pearson, Diane, 10–11
Pecore, Autwin Blaze, 160
Penobscot nation, 67–68, 76
peoplehood, 1, 2–3, 7–15, 124, 126–27, 139, 164. *See also* national consciousness
Pequano, Curtis, 160, 165–66
Pequot nation, 7, 11–12, 25n10
Philemon, Alex, 160, 168
Pictou Landing community (Mi'kmaw), 97
Pierre, Sophie, 184
Pine Springs Pai band, 135
Pokagon Band of Potawatomi Indians (Potawatomi Indians of Indiana and Michigan, Inc.), 156, 160
Poliandri, Simone, 1–28, 32, 93–122, 186, 192, 195

political sociology, 156
postcolonialism, 6, 125–26. *See also* colonialism
Poston, Charles, 130
Potawatomi Indians of Indiana and Michigan, Inc. (Pokagon Band of Potawatomi Indians), 156, 160
Potawatomi nation, 21–22, 155–76, 187
Pough, Richard, 71
powwow circuit (Mi'kmaw), 19, 93–94, 101–3, 110
Prairie Band Potawatomi Nation (Mayetta, Kansas), 156, 158, 165
Price, William Redwood, 131–32, 134
Prince Albert Grand Council, 188–89
Prins, Harald, 102
Puckee, David, 160, 164
"Push for Change Continues" (Wuttunee), 183–93
Puyallup people, 68

Québec, 116
Quechan nation, 128–29

race and ethnic divisions, 29–30, 39–43, 46–48, 95, 136, 138, 185–86
railroads, 20, 123, 129, 137–41
Rebuilding Native Nations: Strategies for Governance and Development (Jorgensen), 65, 188
Redmen Self Dependent of America, 137
Red Power (1960s and 1970s), 68–70
Red Rock Pai band, 135
refusal politics, 4, 12
reggae music, 146
religion. *See* spirituality and religion
Report: Colorado River of the West (Ives), 129
Report on Reservation and Resource Development and Protection (American Indian Policy Review Committee), 32

reservation system: and Hualapai, 20, 123–27, 130–46; and nation building, 1–2, 16, 36–37, 46, 48, 52–54; and Potawatomi, 164–66
residential schools, 104–6, 124, 137, 146
Rifkin, Mark, 90n25
Ritchie, Echepwias, 164
Ritchie, Harry, 164
Ritchie, Valentine, 160, 164–65, 171–73
Roberts, John, 40–41
Roosevelt, Franklin, 176n5
Rosenblatt, Daniel, 45
Royal Commission on Aboriginal Peoples (RCAP, Canada), 183–85
rural marginality, 16, 33–34, 36–37, 43. *See also* economic development

sachems, 87n2
Sacks, Albert M., 73
Santa Clara Pueblo v. Martinez (1978), 43
Santa Fe Railway, 123, 137–41. *See also* railroads
Satsan (Herb George), 100, 186
Scalia, Antonin, 40
Scattergood, J. Henry, 140
Schmitt, Carl, 55n1
Schrum (Pai leader), 131–32, 134–35
Schrum, Bob, 132, 138, 139
Scott, James C., 90n24
Seattle Legal Services, 70
Sechelt First Nation (British Columbia), 184
Section 35 of Constitution Act (Canada, 1982), 96
Sejersen, Frank, 53
self-determination: and economic development, 5–6, 13–14, 32; and Hualapai, 137–38; and nation building, 1, 3, 7–8, 93; and Potawatomi, 21–22, 163; United Nations on, 190; and U.S. policy, 13–14

"Self-Determination, Subaltern Studies, and the Critical Remapping of U.S. Empire" (Rifkin), 90n25
self-government, 7–8, 17, 64, 100, 111, 117, 185
Seminoles, 7, 162–63
Senate Committee on Indian Affairs, 18, 139
Shelton, Brett Lee, 52
Shepherd, Jeffrey P., 19–21, 123–54, 186–87, 192, 196
Sherburne, John P., 131
Shohn, Oscar, 160
Shopteze, Pean, 160
Shubenacadie Indian Residential School, 19, 94, 104–6
Silva, Noenoe K., 124
Silverheels, Jay, 68
Silverman, David J., 63–64
Simon, Anne W., 70–71
Simon v. The Queen (1985), 112
Simpson, Audra, 3–4, 12, 87, 163, 170, 176
Sipekne'katik (Indian Brook) First Nation, 118n5, 119n22
Sitgreaves, Lorenzo, 129
slave trade, 128–29
Smith, Andrea, 87
Smith, Anthony, 3
Smith, Auggie, 130
Smith, Dean Howard, 16, 33
social economy, 189–91. *See also* economic development
Sonora, 129
Soskourema (Pai headman), 134–35
sovereignty, 1, 15, 30–34, 116–17, 185–86, 189; and citizenship, 32, 43, 116, 186; and cultural authenticity, 32; and economic control and development, 1, 22, 32–37; and land, 16, 34–37, 44, 53; nested sovereignty, 4; and termination policies, 3

"Sovereignty: An Inappropriate Concept" (Alfred), 90n25
Spicer, Edward H., 10
Spirits of Resistance and Capitalist Discipline: Factory Women in Malaysia (Ong), 90n24
spirituality and religion: Christianity, 19, 39, 64, 88n3, 94, 103–4; and Hualapai, 124, 127; and Mi'kmaw, 19, 94, 103–6; and nationhood or peoplehood, 10, 15–16, 30–33, 48, 162–64; and Potawatomi, 175
St. Anne Mission and celebration (Mi'kmaw), 19, 94, 103–4. *See also* spirituality and religion
Stark, Heidi Kiiwetinepinesiik, 107–8, 156, 161, 174
Stoler, Ann Laura, 126
Stone, Robert, 160, 165
Straight, Michael, 71
Strock estate (Noëpe), 74, 89n13
Survival of American Indians Association (SAIA), 68
Swidler, Ann, 170
Switzerland, 56n5

taxation, 14–15, 44, 54, 77–78
Taylor, Peter S., 81–84
termination policies, 3, 20, 38, 97, 141–42
terminology, 2, 18–19, 23n1, 87n1, 93, 97, 183
Theorizing Native Studies symposium (Columbia University, 2010), 87
This Is Not a Peace Pipe: Towards a Critical Indigenous Philosophy (Turner), 90n25
Thomas, Robert K., 10
Thunder Valley Community Development Corporation (Pine Ridge), 52
Ting, Helen, 102

Trade and Intercourse Act (1790), 67–68
Trail of Death (Potawatomi), 166–67
trapping rights. *See* food systems and traditions
Treanor, Paul, 8
treaties and treaty negotiations, 21–22, 156, 161, 187. *See also specific treaties*
Treaties of 1760–1761 (Treaties of Peace and Friendship, Mi'kmaw), 101
Treaty and Aboriginal Rights recognition, 96
Treaty Day (Canada), 112–13
Treaty of Chicago (1833), 156, 166–67, 170, 175
Treaty of Guadalupe Hidalgo, 129, 140
Treuer, David, 176n6
tribal capitalism, 13, 25n10. *See also* capitalism; economic development
Tribal Land Corporation (Noëpe), 75
tribal recognition: Aquinnah Wampanoag, 72, 75, 79; Mashapee Wampanoag, 74; Potawatomi, 176n5
Tribal Worlds: Critical Studies in American Indian Nation Building (series), ix
Trudeau, Pierre, 118n4
Truro Power Centre (Millbrook), 108
trust lands, 35, 44, 89n13. *See also* land
Tsosie, Rebecca, 116–17
Tureen, Tom, 67–68, 72–73
Turner, Dale, 90n25
Turner, Nancy, 190–91

Union of Nova Scotia Indians (UNSI), 97, 113
Union of Ontario Indians (Anishinabek Nation), 6, 116, 184

United Kingdom, 12
United Nations, 190
US v. Bruce (2005), 43
US v. Maggi and Mann (2010), 44

Valentine, Lisa, 107
Vance, John T., 173
Vanderhoop, Edwin D. and Tobias, 79
Victor (Mi'kmaw official), 100, 109, 111, 114, 116
Vietnam War, 68, 176n2
Vieux, Ellen, 160

Wabnum, John, 160
Wahmexico, James, 160
Wahwasuck, Alice, Sr., 160
Wallis, Wilson and Ruth S., 98
Walpole Island First Nation (Lake St. Clair, Canada), 156
Wamego, Mike, 160
Wampanoag Tribal Council of Gay Head, 17, 67, 72, 73–75
Wandahsega, Frank, Sr., 164
War on Poverty (1964), 176n2
Wasauksing First Nation (Parry Island, Canada), 156
Wauba Yuma, 131
Weaver, Hilary (Ga no was'het), 7
West Bank First Nation (British Columbia), 184
Western ideas and concepts: education of non-Indians, 189–90, 192; history profession, 145; individualism, 39, 124–27; political organization, 2, 8–13, 31–32, 86, 95, 124–26, 162
Western Potawatomi, 155, 160–61
Wetzel, Christopher, 21–22, 155–81, 187, 196–97
Wezo, Vina, 160
Wheeler, Burton K., 140
Whipple, Amiel W., 129

White Paper (Canada, 1969), 97
Wiesner, Jerome, 71
Wilcox, O.B., 135
Wilkinson, Charles, 3
Williams, Harrison, 160
Williams, Michael, 167, 169, 171, 172–74
Winchester, John R., 169
Wisconsin Potawatomi, 165, 169
Witmer, Richard C., II, 14–15

Woodard, Stephanie, 52
World War One, 123, 138
Wounded Knee siege (Pine Ridge reservation), 70
Wright, Beverly, 79, 86
Wuttunee, Wanda, 23, 183–93, 197

Yaqui nation, 129
Yavapai, 127
Yuman territories, *128*